THE FRIENDLY DICTATORSHIP

Discipline of Power (1980)
Spoils of Power (1988)
Faultlines: Struggling for a Canadian Vision (1993)
The Anxious Years (1996)
Star-Spangled Canadians: Canadians Living the American Dream (2000)

THE FRIENDLY
DICTATORSHIP

JEFFREY SIMPSON

National Library of Canada Cataloguing in Publication Data

Simpson, Jeffrey, 1949–
The friendly dictatorship

Includes bibliographical references.
ISBN 0-7710-8078-6

1. Democracy – Canada. 2. Political parties – Canada. 3. Prime ministers –
Canada. 4. Canada. Parliament – Powers and duties. 5. Canada – Politics
and government – 1993– 6. Power (Social sciences) – Canada. I. Title.

FC635.S57 2001   321.8'0971   C2001-901421-X
F1034.2.S56 2001

We acknowledge the financial support of the Government of Canada
through the Book Publishing Industry Development Program
for our publishing activities. We further acknowledge the support of the
Canada Council for the Arts and the Ontario Arts Council
for our publishing program.

Design: Ingrid Paulson
Typesetting in Bembo by M&S, Toronto
Printed and bound in Canada

McClelland & Stewart Ltd.
The Canadian Publishers
481 University Ave.
Toronto, Ontario
M5G 2E9
www.mcclelland.com

1   2   3   4   5   05   04   03   02   01

To Wendy, *sine qua non*;
Tait, Danielle, Brook,
and Eve

Contents

Introduction

The Friendly Dictatorship is admittedly a pejorative title. Some Canadians certainly would not describe the federal government as friendly, having either voted against the Liberals or been alienated for a long time from Ottawa, whichever party ruled, although even grumpy Canadians must grudgingly admit that the Liberal Party's re-election to a third majority government represented a remarkable political accomplishment. No federal party had won three consecutive majorities since the Liberals secured five of them from 1935 to 1953, and no prime minister had led his party to three consecutive majorities since Prime Minister Mackenzie King in 1935, 1940, and 1945. Whatever his contemporaries' views of Prime Minister Jean Chrétien, historians will be forced to give him full political credit for these three majority victories, since electoral victory constitutes the bottom-line measure of political success. What the victor does with that success is quite another matter.

The Liberals' three-peat, however, does raise the question: Is Canada a de facto one-party state? Has Canada become a kind of dictatorship, which is the other word in the pejorative title? In one obvious sense, the answer is no, because four parties won enough seats in the House of Commons to secure official party status. A smattering of other parties also contested the election, from the Marijuana Party to the Marxist-Leninists to the Greens. Canada is not North Korea, Syria, or Eastern Europe *circa* 1970. We have a free press, a Charter of Rights and Freedoms, a proliferation of interest groups, and many ways of expressing dissent from the government. It took only a matter of days for partisan arguing to resume after the 2000 election. No sooner did Parliament reassemble after the vote, than parliamentarians resumed their ritualistic attacks on each other.

Partisan parliamentary debate, however, should not obscure the pertinence of the question – is Canada a de facto one-party state? An effective parliamentary system presumes that at least one party is ready and capable of replacing the existing government by winning an election. Clearly, no party was ready and capable in the last election, despite the pretensions of the Canadian Alliance. Will any party be ready and capable the next time, or is Canada destined to become like Japan, where one party always exercises power and political change occurs only when that party decides, for its own internal purposes, to switch leaders?

No one can foresee the political future; there are too many imponderables for sensible predictions. There will eventually be a new Liberal leader. We do not know how the economy will be performing in three or four years. We cannot predict domestic or international crises that will test the mettle of the existing government. We do not know what changes will occur in leadership or policies in the opposition parties. We can only surmise that Quebec will hold another referendum on sovereignty-association, and a yes vote in such a referendum would set off a series of completely unpredictable events.

What we can say is that none of the opposition parties – and this observation is particularly relevant to the Official Opposition, the Canadian Alliance, and to the Progressive Conservatives – has absorbed the lessons of Canadian political history, principal among which is that the Liberals can be defeated only by coalitions whose ideological fevers are tempered by Canadians' overall preference for moderation and compromise. Ideologues of the right and left, and single-issue advocates, ignore these lessons, despite repeated defeats that ought to have instructed them that Procrustean politics fail in Canada. The country remains too diverse for the siren songs of ideology.

Whether the opposition parties will learn this lesson remains unclear, but the election results did leave the Liberals in power for the foreseeable future, a dismaying prospect for those who worry about the health of Canadian democracy. The Liberals stirred little enthusiasm for themselves during the 2000 election campaign. Plenty of Liberals would have preferred someone other than Jean Chrétien at the top, to say nothing of those who voted for other parties. His sturdy longevity and evident unwillingness to depart demonstrate another part of Canada's Friendly Dictatorship beyond de facto one-party government: the massive centralization of power in one man's control within the trappings of a parliamentary system.

Canadian parliamentary democracy, as it has evolved, places more power in the hands of the prime minister than does any other democracy, far more than the U.S. president wields, but more, too, than political leaders exercise in other parliamentary regimes. Those seeking a check or balance against this almost unbridled prime-ministerial power remain frustrated, and that frustration undoubtedly grew with Chrétien's re-election. A man who has survived and thrived for so long in Canadian politics, and who will run the government for the better part of three mandates, is the last person from whom anyone would expect an interest in reform. This is the system Jean Chrétien knows and controls, and nothing within it forces him to change. He is the Sun King of the government, and the longer any occupant of the country's highest elective office remains the pivot around which all revolves, the less likely he is to think that the country's interests might be better suited by change. After all, Chrétien would assert, the people delivered their political verdict in the election campaign: carry on.

That Canadians are increasingly discouraged by their political system can be demonstrated in a variety of ways. The most obvious is their disinclination to vote. Fewer of them exercised their franchise in 2000 than in any previous election. A democracy in which only half the total eligible population votes is not a healthy one. Another piece of evidence is the documented decline in respect for politicians of all partisan stripes. They are now held in only slightly higher esteem than used-car salesmen. Still another is the reduced interest in electoral politics in contrast to the interest people increasingly show for other forms of political engagement. Citizens are not necessarily withdrawing from all political engagement, just from organized partisan politics. Parliament itself is regarded as an institution of national ridicule, where MPs conduct themselves like kids embroiled in schoolyard fights. Ordinary MPs, reduced to partisan role-playing rather than genuine legislating, are frustrated with their lot; citizens are frustrated with them.

The 2000 election campaign only served to deepen this unhappiness. Yes, the Liberals won another majority, which undoubtedly cheered their core partisans. There was throughout the entire campaign, however, a palpable lack of enthusiasm for the winners. Canadians judged the Liberals the least offensive of a bad lot, their weaknesses eclipsed by those of the other parties. The campaign itself was especially vacuous. Chrétien hurried the election call three and a half years into the mandate, correctly believing the Liberals could win. His haste showed in the shower of government announcements before the campaign and the paucity of anything fresh to offer during it. Red Book III, successor to two previous Liberal campaign documents, was thin and banal, accurately reflecting that the Liberals had devoted little time to thinking about what they would do if re-elected – except more of the same. Red Book I in 1993, and even Red Book II in 1997, reflected some concerted, even coherent, thinking; Red Book III looked like a student essay cobbled together under the pressure of an imminent deadline. It offered all the prerequisite clichés to cover the document's vain search for something interesting to say.

The Friendly Dictatorship tries to make sense of what has been happening in three areas vital to Canadian democracy: the parliamentary system, the political parties, and the electorate. What has occurred within each of these spheres has directly influenced developments in the others, and the combined effect has left Canadian democracy in a weakened state. Democracy is arguably this country's most precious legacy. Democracy requires people to care about its institutions and to participate as citizens in them, if only to bring about change. A sullen and disengaged citizenry is no friend of democracy, because at the very least these attitudes allow governments to grow insensitive and arrogant, and to fail to steer the country in directions that maximize the well-being and solidarity of its citizens.

The Friendly Dictatorship is therefore inspired by concerns about Canadian democracy. Not all readers, of course, will agree with the analysis or prescriptions, but no harm will come from that. *The Friendly Dictatorship* is intended to provoke thought and perhaps awaken debate, maybe even to get people angry, and if it can stir up those reactions, then it will have achieved its modest objectives. The book takes the form, if you like, of four extended essays rather than an academic treatise, but offers no apologies for that. Democracy is too important to be left to experts or even practitioners, and therefore debate about its health should be presented in a form as free as possible from trappings that might intrude on the argument. Therefore, *The Friendly Dictatorship* makes no pretence to academic analysis, although it is shaped by a welter of academic studies. There are therefore no footnotes or bibliography.

I thank Doug Gibson, McClelland and Stewart's publisher, who proposed this book and suggested its title because, as an engaged citizen himself, he worried about the state of Canadian democracy. He likely will not agree with everything in these pages; he might well have written a different book if given the chance. But as so many Canadian writers know, Doug Gibson, in his pleasant, prodding way, pushes ideas into the public marketplace, where, through the alchemy of debate and the passage of time, they influence how Canadians see themselves, their society and, in this case, their government. I thank, too, Pat Kennedy for her intelligent editing.

For many years now, I have been privileged to occupy the catbird's seat of the *Globe and Mail*'s national-affairs columnist. From that perch, and previous ones, I have written five books and witnessed six prime ministers, eight federal elections and many more provincial ones, constitutional debates, economic upheaval, the creation of new parties, free trade, and a range of other changes washing over Canada. There have been changes, too, in the practice of journalism, some of them diminishing the craft's coin, but the words of the *Globe*'s first political columnist, the marvellous George Bain, still ring true: that this job is the theatre-goers' equivalent to front-row seats for the best show in town.

Ottawa and Point Comfort, Quebec, 2001

Prime-Ministerial Government

Canadians believe they live in a parliamentary democracy, and by all outward appearances they do. Every so often they vote in a national election, although in fewer numbers than before, to send 301 parliamentary representatives to Ottawa. Once there, members of Parliament take their seats in the House of Commons and party caucuses only to discover that they are participating in prime-ministerial government with the trappings of a parliamentary system.

A gentle fiction describes the parliamentary system. The governor general invites a party leader to form a government if his or her party can command the confidence of the House of Commons – that is, win a majority of votes on issues of central concern to the government. This description suggests an element of risk, even danger. Perhaps the prime minister might lose this confidence so another party will be "invited" to form a government or an election might unexpectedly have to be called. This risk of an early election does occur in minority governments such as in 1957, 1962, 1963, 1965, and 1979. Sometimes a prime minister in a minority situation asks for a dissolution of the House, believing a majority victory will follow. Joe Clark, the hapless Conservative prime minister in 1979, could easily have avoided a parliamentary defeat on his government's budget with a bit of procedural manoeuvring, but misread both the intentions of the Liberals on the night of the vote and the mood of the country. He wanted parliamentary defeat; he also got a political defeat in the subsequent campaign. Ever since the 1980 election, Canada has known only majority governments, four Liberal, two Conservative.

The possible loss of Commons confidence constitutes a gentle fiction because, once possessed of a parliamentary majority, the prime minister presides over what has been dubbed by observers of the parliamentary system as an "elected dictatorship." The constraints on prime-ministerial power are paper tigers. They appear fearsome – the need to control caucus, the risk of parliamentary defeat, raucous and insulting questions in the Commons, the threat of trouble in the Senate, the possibility of being deposed by an internal party revolt, querulous media coverage, monitoring by outside agents such as the auditor general, the information commissioner, the ethics counsellor – but in the real world of politics, the prime minister is the Sun King around whom all revolves and to whom all must pay varying forms of tribute. Political scientist Donald Savoie's term the "imperial prime-ministership" better reflects the Canadian political system than the gentle fiction about parliamentary government.

The Canadian prime minister is more powerful within this system than any democratically elected leader in other advanced industrial countries. The U.S. president governs within a checks-and-balances political system in which his proposals must be chewed over by two legislative bodies with much weaker party discipline than there is in the Canadian House of Commons. Congress must approve major presidential nominations, including his cabinet choices and Supreme Court appointments. The French prime minister serves at the behest of the president, who can replace prime ministers at will, but the French president's powers do not extend to day-to-day management of government. The Australian prime minister can be deposed at any time by his own caucus and must sometimes deal with an elected Senate controlled by parties other than his own. The German chancellor invariably presides over a coalition – in recent years Christian Democrat, Christian Social Union, and Liberal Democrat or Social

Democrat/Green – and must find ways of getting legislation approved by an upper house composed of representatives of the German *Länder*, or states. The Japanese prime minister is regularly deposed by inter-factional political warfare within the perennially governing Liberal Democratic Party. Italian prime ministers come and go with merry abandon.

Only the British prime minister possesses a similar array of powers to that of the Canadian prime minister, which is hardly surprising, since the Canadian parliamentary system was originally modelled on the British and has scarcely changed since Confederation. It could once have been fairly argued that the Canadian prime minister, unlike his British counterpart, operated within a federal system with powerful provinces. That differentiation has now been weakened by the devolution of considerable powers to a Scottish Parliament and somewhat fewer powers to a Welsh Assembly. Britain recently became a federal country, and it is too soon to tell how that will affect the Westminster parliamentary system.

The British Parliament also has slightly more than twice as many MPs as the Canadian one. There are great swaths of "safe" seats for Tory and Labour MPs, although the new party system in Canada has provided more of those for, say, Alliance candidates in Alberta and Liberals in Ontario. Nonetheless, in any given British Parliament there are dozens and dozens of MPs – and depending upon the election, maybe even several hundred – who would need to do something spectacularly stupid or untoward not to win the election. Since a British cabinet can only contain so many MPs, the yawning backbenches of the governing party are awash with MPs who know they will never be in cabinet and whose constituencies are utterly safe, two conditions that embolden at least some of them sometimes to cause trouble for the party leadership. Some of Prime Minister Margaret Thatcher's toughest questions came from behind her. When Argentina invaded the Falkland Islands or when Mrs. Thatcher imposed an unpopular poll tax, her backbenches seethed with public dissent from MPs with safe seats and abandoned ministerial ambitions. Nothing as remotely hostile threatens a Canadian prime minister.

The leader of the British Conservative Party also faces a risk unknown to a Canadian prime minister. The caucus can remove the leader, as Prime Minister Margaret Thatcher discovered to her horror. The Iron Lady had alienated many of the leading barons of the parliamentary party, and those tensions, coupled with fears of electoral defeat, produced a *coup d'état* that ended the career of post-war Britain's most formidable prime minister.

Nothing of the sort has ever happened in Canadian politics. The closest Canadian equivalent was the demise of Conservative leader John Diefenbaker, who finally yielded up the party leadership in 1967 after a prolonged and stubborn fight. Diefenbaker, however, was not the prime minister when he lost the leadership. He had been defeated in two elections, in 1963 and 1965. Although a caucus rebellion of sorts erupted after the second defeat, the pressure for his departure came from the party rank and file, organized by party president Dalton Camp. The caucus lacked the power to depose the Chief; it took the rank and file to insist (for the first time) on a party review of the leadership. This produced a convention at which, predictably, Diefenbaker lost to Nova Scotia Premier Robert Stanfield.

Leaders are selected by party members, either at delegate conventions or in one-member-one-vote elections such as those recently used by the Canadian Alliance and the Conservative Party. The Liberals still prefer a delegate convention process, as do the New Democrats, although the NDP is contemplating moving to a one-member-one-vote system. Parties have inserted into their constitutions a requirement that delegates be asked at one convention between elections whether they wish to review the leadership. This review can be politically treacherous for party leaders in opposition, as Conservative Joe Clark discovered after his party tumbled from office in 1980. When a third of the

Conservative delegates voted for a review, Clark decided he could not carry on without a renewed vote of confidence. He stepped down as party leader, ran to succeed himself, but lost the leadership convention to Brian Mulroney, who, while pledging public support for Clark, had been working assiduously but covertly to undermine Clark's leadership.

The perils of intra-party review can plague opposition party leaders, since they have not delivered the fruits of victory. But a prime minister faces no such peril, since he has delivered them. No prime minister has ever resigned because the party in convention insisted on a review or failed to give him a sufficiently large vote of confidence. Not only has the prime minister, by definition, led the party to electoral victory, he has a myriad of tools at his disposal for squelching dissent in the cabinet, in caucus, and among the rank and file.

Parties are not monoliths, of course. There will always be the frustrated and the ignored, people whose ambitions have been thwarted or who believe their re-election chances would improve with another leader. When political times were tough for the Liberals under Pierre Trudeau, clutches of Liberals pined for another leader to save them from defeat, but no serious threat ever unfolded against Trudeau's leadership. Serious dissent only emerged after he lost the 1979 election, and the lessons subsequently learned by the dissenters provided a sobering reminder of the perils of regicide.

In the interregnum between the election and the victorious Conservatives' recall of Parliament, Trudeau asked, among others, former cabinet ministers Judd Buchanan and Robert Andras to canvass the Liberal rank and file informally about whether Trudeau should stay as leader. Buchanan and Andras were themselves convinced that he should not. Perhaps in their findings the wish was the father of the thought, but they concluded that indeed the rank and file believed Trudeau should leave. They reported these findings to Trudeau just before the Conservatives' parliamentary self-immolation. Trudeau, of course, did fight and win the 1980 election. Andras did not run; Buchanan did, but paid for his *lèse-majesté* by being shut out of the cabinet.

Prime Minister Brian Mulroney led the Conservatives to two majority election victories, but the Tories were extremely unpopular for long periods of time between elections. Mulroney himself left office as one of the country's most reviled leaders, his slide in popularity beginning early in his prime-ministerial career and accelerating during his second term in power. And yet, despite months and months of dismal poll ratings, no one ever challenged his leadership. Mulroney was a political magician with his caucus. He knew how the Tory caucus, usually in opposition, had caused endless headaches for Diefenbaker, Stanfield, and Clark. He was determined not to allow its endemic crankiness to threaten him. MPs carried to office in the Tory landslide of 1984 thought they owed their seats to him. That fealty made caucus management easy, but the caucus was the largest in Canadian history, and the party did plunge in public esteem, hitting rock bottom in the winter of 1986, but Mulroney never lost control of the caucus, even in the most miserable political times between elections, and no serious threat ever emerged to his leadership. Mulroney remained unchallenged even in the second term, when the party's political fortunes again nosedived. Conservative MPs who worried about their re-election assumed Mulroney would leave anyway without trying for a third term. Had Mulroney decided to try for a third term, however, nothing could have stopped him, since no intra-party process existed to replace him once he had received a vote of confidence at the first convention after his 1988 electoral triumph.

Jean Chrétien has led the Liberal Party to three majority governments without ever quite shaking the phantom menace of Finance Minister Paul Martin, whom he defeated for the party leadership. Martin has been Canada's best post-war finance minister, eliminating the staggering federal deficit and bringing down the federal debt. Although Martin lost the leadership convention to Chrétien, prime-ministerial ambitions gnawed at him, ambitions reinforced by his evident popularity in public-opinion surveys and among the Liberal rank-and-file and backbenchers.

The Chrétien–Martin relationship has been almost without precedent in Canadian political history. At one level, it has been hugely successful for the Liberal Party. A government's most important political relationship is that between prime minister and minister of finance. Very little of policy importance in any government passes without the say-so of the finance minister, and nothing of importance passes without prime-ministerial approval. The prime minister has a range of party responsibilities and prerogatives – including that of appointing cabinet ministers – that eclipses any power exercised by the finance minister. But the finance minister plays an important role when policy is decided, most obviously in crafting budgets. His ministry's bureaucrats sit as watchdogs on inter-departmental committees. He establishes the fiscal framework for the government's spending and taxing priorities. He beats down or modifies ministerial projects from departments wanting to spend additional money. His credibility, of lack thereof, influences the confidence of financial markets in Canada and abroad. The finance minister must exercise these powers with the prime minister's blessing, which necessitates negotiations on matters large and small.

Sharp policy differences have marked the Chrétien–Martin relationship, some of which spilled into the national media. Chrétien has been more inclined to spend on what Martin considers old-style and economically discredited programs such as short-term employment schemes and physical infrastructure. Chrétien has worried less about the aggregate tax gap between Canada and the United States. Chrétien imposed the Millennium Scholarship Program for university students over Martin's objections. Despite these disputes, they have usually managed to negotiate compromises, which is another way of saying that

Martin gave way more often than not, as a finance minister must when faced with a determined prime minister. The result has been a remarkably effective tag-team, with each man's personal and political skills complementing the other's.

Chrétien has always known, however, that Martin represented a phantom menace to his leadership. Political scientists can sort through all the statistics and systems, but the political game is also an intensely human one of clashing egos and ambitions. Paul Martin has wanted – and still wants – to become prime minister, and only one man stands in his way. That cabinet ministers harbour prime-ministerial ambitions is nothing new, but rarely, if ever, has a minister been so obvious an heir apparent. Nobody in the Diefenbaker, Pearson, Trudeau, or Mulroney governments ever emerged so clearly as the obvious alternative to the prime minister. Martin's status as heir apparent is not just a creation of his own ambitions; it is almost universally acknowledged among the Liberal Party, the media, and the informed public. It is also well-known to Chrétien, and therein lies the drama.

Chrétien's biographer, Lawrence Martin, aptly subtitled his first volume *The Politics of Ambition*. Underestimated and even scorned by the party élites under Trudeau, Chrétien never wavered in his determination to lead the party. When Trudeau finally departed, experienced Liberal hands assumed that the party's tradition of alternating between French- and English-speaking leaders should prevail. So did former Liberal cabinet minister John Turner, who re-entered public life assuming more of a coronation than a contest. Chrétien, however, decided otherwise. His appeal, coupled with Turner's evident rustiness, turned the campaign into a dogfight. True to form, many of the Quebec Liberal heavyweights who had always scorned Chrétien preferred Turner. Turner eventually won the leadership in 1984, but by a much narrower margin than anyone, including himself, would have believed at the beginning. Chrétien lost the leadership, but by all accounts won the campaign, an observation cemented when, after the results were announced, convention co-chair Iona Campagnolo described him as still "first in our hearts."

Chrétien understands Martin's gnawing ambition, because he was equally consumed by unrequited ambition after losing to Turner. In and out of Parliament, Chrétien carried on a guerrilla war against Turner. He did nothing overtly to destabilize his leader; indeed, Chrétien campaigned extensively for Liberal candidates across the country in the 1988 election. But these efforts were widely and correctly seen as being as much about Chrétien's future leadership ambitions as about the success of the Liberal Party. In private conversations, Chrétien let it be known he considered Turner an incompetent leader, certainly one less capable than himself. Whenever he was forced to offer platitudes about Turner in public, Chrétien sounded as if the words were being ripped from his mouth. As Chrétien travelled across Canada, speaking to Liberal audiences or promoting his best-selling memoirs, *Straight from the Heart*, the adulatory response deepened his conviction that the party had erred grievously in 1984 and would make good its mistake. It did, when Turner stepped down after losing a second election.

Martin put up a game and expensive fight against Chrétien in the struggle to replace Turner. Their most severe disagreement came over the Meech Lake Accord, which Martin supported and Chrétien opposed, despite his subsequent insistence that he had been sympathetic to Meech Lake all along. Defeat, however, did not douse Martin's ambitions, so the Liberals have known since they formed the government in 1993 that an heir apparent existed whose ambitions burned and whose performance as finance minister reinforced his status. No prime minister since Mackenzie King, who was succeeded by Louis St. Laurent, has ever had such a clearly identifiable successor sitting beside him. It was not axiomatic that Lester Pearson would replace St. Laurent, because the Liberals never expected to lose the 1957 campaign. Six months before Pearson left, no one thought Pierre Trudeau would become

Liberal leader. As the years crept on and possible successors
departed from politics, no one emerged as Trudeau's obvious
successor. Brian Mulroney left a string of pretenders, but no
obvious replacement.

Chrétien fears Martin's ambition because it so obviously
mirrors and threatens his own. They worked out a modus operandi
as prime minister and finance minister, to mutual political
benefit, but distance and distrust marked their personal relations.
Long periods passed during which the two men rarely spoke,
communications being conducted between subalterns. Two
camps emerged in the party – Chrétienites and Martinites – that
stretched from cabinet through caucus to national executive to
constituency presidents to the rank-and-file. Nothing like this
had ever occurred inside a governing party in Canadian history.
All manner of intra-party decisions were influenced by who
stood in which camp; decisions about constituency nominations,
Senate appointments, national-executive membership, fundraisers
– to the point that the party's national president lamented privately that he spent more time sorting out factional disputes than
on the rest of his duties.

These roiling tensions within the governing party – unprece-
dented, as we said, in modern Canadian political history – have
played themselves out largely in private. They surfaced publicly
once, in the run-up to the Liberals' pre-election convention in
March 2000. Stories about what happened and why depended
upon which camp offered the explanations, for there was much
to explain afterwards. According to the Martin camp, a clutch of
Martinite MPs and supporters from outside Parliament were sum-
moned to a Toronto airport hotel to prepare for the convention.
The message, ostensibly delivered by those who later were cov-
ering their tracks, was to the effect that nothing should be done
at the convention to cause trouble for Chrétien. Any public
doubting of his leadership would embolden him to carry on.

Chrétien alone would decide the timing of his departure, and if no public expressions of discontent rippled the placid waters of party support for the leader, Chrétien might decide he could leave soon thereafter with honour.

If this indeed were the plan, it went terribly wrong, since even before the convention officially opened, a few MPs spoke about this perhaps being the right time for Chrétien to go. This sent the media scurrying to report the news and to corner others, including Martin, for their comments. It appeared that an organized and certainly potentially ominous movement to dump the Prime Minister had been hatched, something Martin and his supporters were quick to deny. To the Chrétienites, and most definitely to Chrétien himself, however, it seemed incontestable that the Martin camp had contemplated if not a putsch then at least a destabilizing campaign to weaken his leadership. And he reacted with fury, dressing down Martin and his supporters in cabinet and raging privately to friends about the perfidy of his finance minister. Whatever thoughts Chrétien might have been giving to leaving politics vanished, although the Martinites doubted he ever had any. His sense of *lèse-majesté* hardened and he determined not just to remain as leader and fight another election but to do whatever he could to prevent Paul Martin from succeeding him as prime minister. Chrétien might not be able to control the succession, but to the extent that he can, he will try to thwart Martin.

This Chrétien–Martin saga reinforces the point about a successful Prime Minister's unchallenged grip on power. If these tensions had occurred within the British Conservative Party, or one of the Australian parties, the chances are that Chrétien would already have been challenged or ousted. At least the mechanism of a caucus vote would have allowed Martin to challenge Chrétien's leadership. In the Canadian system, however, the prime minister remains in place at the behest of the party membership, and mobilizing a revolt among them against a sitting prime minister is next-to-impossible. The chance only arises once, after a winning election, which, because it has been won, leaves the party membership in fine fettle. After that chance disappears, the prime minister is incontestably secure.

The Power of Appointments

Prime Minister Jean Chrétien stunned ministers one day during his first mandate by casually informing them that Perrin Beatty would become the president of the Canadian Broadcasting Corporation. Beatty had been a Conservative MP and minister in the Mulroney government before losing in the Conservatives' 1993 election debacle. Chrétien thought Beatty had been a good Commons performer. The selection of a high-profile Conservative to lead the CBC would deflect any criticism of the appointment. Ministers, however, could scarcely believe their ears. Beatty had been an ordinary cabinet minister, hardly one of the Tory stars. He had few, if any, discernible qualifications to run a billion-dollar corporation, except for a stint as Minister of Communications. Chrétien's ministers knew *they* did not manage their departments; no minister does. So Beatty's ministerial experience hardly qualified him for such an important post. The Prime Minister, however, had not consulted them, and he did not seek their views now. He just informed them of what he had decided. Next item, please.

Perrin Beatty's appointment may have been a bit more cavalier than many, but it illustrated the prime minister's unfettered power of appointment that contributes to the "imperial prime-ministership." Once elected, the prime minister shapes his government as he sees fit without the slightest formal check on his prerogatives. For starters, the prime minister selects all ministers and sends them, upon their appointment, a "mandate" letter, outlining what he expects of them. The prime minister must balance regional, linguistic, and gender considerations in choosing his cabinet, but the ultimate choices are his alone. He selects deputy ministers in consultation with the clerk of the Privy Council, sometimes checking with his ministers, sometimes not. He appoints the governor general, the chief justice of the Supreme Court, and all the other justices, the chief of the General Staff, the clerk of the Privy Council, the auditor general, the information commissioner, the ethics counsellor, and the heads of all Crown corporations and government agencies. He signs off on Canadian ambassadors, although most of these follow recommendations from the Department of Foreign Affairs. He appoints senators, parliamentary secretaries, whips, chairmen of Commons committees. About the only post the prime minister does not fill is that of speaker of the House of Commons, a job voted upon by a secret ballot of all MPs. The speaker aside, everyone of importance in the Government of Canada directly or indirectly owes his or her post to the prime minister.

A senior official in the Prime Minister's Office advises him on appointments, of which there are hundreds at the government's disposal, everything from heads of Crown corporations to part-time board appointments. The adviser consults with party members, ministers, and MPs before forwarding recommendations that the prime minister can accept, discard, or send back for review. In theory, Cabinet makes appointments – "order-in-council appointments" as they are called. In practice, the prime minister makes the important ones, although he may follow the advice of departmental or regional ministers. It is a slow, messy, often partisan, and certainly less-than-desirable way of filling government posts. Appointments can be held up by squabbles among ministers or by prime-ministerial dithering. They can be overturned at the last minute on prime-ministerial whim. More telling still, the system is not designed in all cases to uncover the best candidate – although that sometimes happily occurs – but to find the one most acceptable to the government. The British, by contrast, advertise widely for a range of public positions, with applications adjudicated by third-party tribunals to select the best available applicants. This depoliticization of appointments has much to commend it, but in Canada it would mean nicking the prime minister's power, and that would run against the very grain of the all-powerful prime-ministerial system of government.

A proper appointments system would take power away from the prime minister at least for those positions whose occupants are not expected to reflect government policy. In corporate governance, the board selects the chief executive officer, who is then responsible to the board, or through the board to shareholders. In the federal government, with a few exceptions (the National Arts Centre being one) the government selects both the board and the CEO, so that the CEO is only nominally responsible to the board. As a result, Beatty could subtly remind CBC board members at his first meeting as president that he was ultimately responsible to the government, and not to them. Lines of authority are further muddied, as at the CBC, when the government also selects the chairman of the board. This means both the chair and the CEO are responsible to the government, not to the board, a recipe for potential conflict.

When pressed, the government defends the appointments system by arguing that it is ultimately responsible to the shareholders, namely the citizens of Canada, for the administration of public monies. This constitutes a rather hackneyed defence of prerogative, stretching theory to the breaking point to defend expediency. Ministers do answer occasional questions in the Commons about Crown corporations by replying that they will relay concerns to the head of the agency. A circular reasoning therefore applies: the government accepts theoretical responsibility, except if responsibility involves interfering in the management of the corporation.

These appointments are part of the Canadian patronage system whereby supporters of the government are rewarded for past political services. On every cabinet agenda, there is an item entitled "nominations" (usually item three). Truth to tell, patronage is much less prevalent now than decades ago when the party machine could deliver jobs now filled by the Public Service Commission. Similarly, the privatization of some Crown corporations removed plum posts on boards of directors from the government's hands. The Trudeau and Mulroney governments' patronage abuses reduced the public's tolerance for the old system that had been, in its day, an indispensable tool for building and sustaining the Liberal and Conservative parties in all regions of Canada. Still, hundreds of posts must be filled, and the prime minister signs off on all those he cares about.

Spasmodic attempts have been made to let Commons committees review senior appointments. Just what these committees were supposed to do remained unclear, since they lacked the power to overturn an appointment. No Commons committee possesses the U.S. Senate's constitutional power to "advise and consent" to presidential appointments. The governing party's majority on the committee hardly wants to embarrass their government. The Opposition parties might occasionally wish to make mischief or gain a headline by attacking an appointment, but ultimately they are powerless to stop it. The futility of the exercise finally became so apparent that committees now seldom bother.

Academics and the Canadian Bar Association have proposed new methods for appointing judges to the Supreme Court. The prime minister makes these appointments after consultation with the minister of justice, who, in turn, is supposed to consult widely with the legal profession. To be fair to both Prime Ministers Mulroney and Chrétien, their Supreme Court appointments have been of a universally high quality, but some check on prime-ministerial authority would be useful. Checks and balances are seldom needed when everything is being done right, or when the appointment is a good one, but they are required to prevent or slow down something bad. That no poor appointments have yet been made is not a guarantee that a prime minister might be tempted in the age of increasing controversy surrounding Supreme Court decisions to select someone who, if not inadequately qualified, is possessed of a decidedly fixed and controversial judicial philosophy. The Canadian Bar Association and academic experts, notably Professor Martin Friedland of the University of Toronto law school, have proposed alternative methods of appointment that would temper the prime minister's unfettered power somewhat, but these, predictably, have awakened no response in Ottawa. Judicial appointments are, after all, part of the system of prime-ministerial government.

The Senate

Given the Senate's marginal importance in Canada's political arrangements, Canadians might be amazed to learn that the Fathers of Confederation spent more time debating the Senate than any other subject. They argued over its powers, regional composition, and members' property qualifications. To the Fathers, the Senate needed to reflect the interests of property against unpredictable democratic urges, to provide a "sober second thought" against the impulses of the Commons, and to represent the interests of the constituent provinces that came together to form Canada.

The Fathers made a mistake with the Senate, one that has never been corrected, despite the felling of whole Canadian forests to produce the paper on which have been written proposals for change. Senate reform has been the *coitus interruptus* of Canadian politics. Correcting the Fathers' original error has defeated every reformer, in part because reform was fiendishly difficult, but also because successive prime ministers have never wanted reform. A docile Senate, whose members are appointed by prime ministers, did not challenge their control of the elected dictatorship that is Canadian parliamentary government.

The Fathers had at hand two models: an elected Senate and an appointed one. They knew about the House of Lords at Westminster and the elected Senate of the American Republic. They also understood the options from experience closer to home, since the colonies of British North America had had second chambers before Confederation, some appointed, some elected. One contingent of the Fathers supported election; a larger one favoured appointment. It took days and days of anguished and sometimes impassioned debate before the appointed Senate won. Critics underscored the potential weakness of both models. An elected Senate might frustrate the will of the Commons and paralyze the government. An appointed Senate might weaken the body's credibility as a voice for regional concerns.

Nominally alive to this criticism, those favouring an appointed Senate offered an olive branch. Article Fourteen of the Quebec Resolutions stipulated that the first Senate be nominated by provincial governments, and should reflect, roughly speaking, the party composition within the provincial assemblies. A kind of multi-party representation would therefore dilute the Senate's partisanship. This Marquess of Queensbury spirit did not long survive Confederation. Sir John A. Macdonald, the country's first prime minister, did replace a Liberal who died just after Confederation with a Liberal, but soon thereafter seized the obvious advantage of his unfettered power of appointment and sent only five non-Conservatives to the Senate for the rest of his prime-ministerial years.

The pattern was therefore established early on: the Senate would be a partisan institution, reflecting the needs of the governing party. Occasionally, it would arise that, upon arriving in office, a prime minister would confront a Senate majority of the other party, courtesy of his predecessor's partisan appointments. But as quickly as possible, prime ministers used their appointment powers to rebuild their own party's senatorial majority – and docility returned. Prime Minister Jean Chrétien treated the

Senate no differently from all his prime-ministerial predecessors. He wanted a Senate he could count on, so his appointments were overwhelmingly Liberal.

Senate appointments are an exclusive prime-ministerial prerogative. The prime minister can, and usually does, consult with ministers and party worthies from the province that has a Senate vacancy. He is under no obligation to heed anyone's advice but his own. It is hard to sympathize with someone wielding such unfettered power, but Senate appointments do sometimes cause headaches for the prime minister. For every nominee there are many more disappointed supplicants. That is perhaps one reason why Chrétien has appointed so many senior citizens to the Senate; their short tenures in the Senate allow him to make more appointments and thereby satisfy more people wanting to sit in the Red Chamber. The Senate has always been, and remains today, a kind of prime-ministerial slush fund for rewarding the faithful, thereby neutering the Senate's constitutional powers and diluting its role as a chamber of "sober second thought." The weaker the Senate is in practice, the more secure the prime minister in his control of Parliament.

It is possible that a government can run into heavy weather with its own senators. The Senate can delay or reject Commons legislation, although a Senate rejection can be overturned by another Commons vote. Clusters of governing senators can join forces with opposition (or independent) senators to frustrate the government. Senators are appointed until the age of seventy-five – they used to be in the Red Chamber for life – and security of tenure occasionally, but only occasionally, emboldens those from the governing party to cause trouble for their colleagues in the Commons. However, lacking legitimacy as appointees and anxious to support the party that sent them there, government senators can usually be counted upon to deliver what the prime minister desires: no trouble.

The Fathers' original error has produced many unfortunate consequences for Canadian government and federalism, but two stand out. The Senate has never become a credible voice for Canada's regions, as some of the Fathers hoped. And its docility has strengthened the prime minister's control over the elected dictatorship that is Canada's parliamentary government.

Scattered voices have insisted that the best way of correcting the Fathers' original error is to abolish the Senate. For some on the political left, everything about the Senate is so repugnant, in theory and practice, that it merits only abolition. The majority of critics, however, have lamented the lost opportunity for the Senate to become a credible vehicle for regional expression in the sprawling Canadian federation. Other federations have always believed that a second chamber is essential for expressing regional views, to provide an offsetting perspective to that of the popularly elected lower chamber. The United States has its one-state-two-senators chamber for that purpose, among others. Other federations use a variety of elected second chambers. Germany has an upper house composed of representatives of state govern-ments. Spain has an upper house of four senators per province. All around the world, federations – and some unitary states – decided on a two-chamber mode, with a lower house reflecting the national popular vote and an upper one expressing regional perspectives. This synthesis lies at the heart of most modern political systems, except those still wedded to the Westminster model of an elected lower house and an appointed upper one.

Australia, in contrast to Canada, operates its federation – and operates it successfully – with two elected chambers. Australians elect twelve senators from each of their six states and a pair from each of their territories. The senators are elected on a proportional-representation basis with a preferential ballot. Half are chosen every three years for six-year terms, unless both the Senate and the House of Representatives are simultaneously

dissolved – a "double dissolution" after deadlock between the
two chambers that has occurred only six times in Australia's
century of self-government.

Deadlock – the fear of the Canadian Fathers – can occur in the
Australian system, but it does so infrequently. Australians reckon
that having an elected Senate with legislative power and political
credibility as the voice of the states outweighs the risk of deadlock. Proportional representation, in turn, allows senators from a
variety of parties to win seats, including some from so-called
third parties. Sometimes the governing party in the House of
Representatives has a majority in the Senate, sometimes not.
Following the 1998 election, for example, Prime Minister John
Howard's Liberal–National government held thirty-six Senate
seats and the Labour Party twenty-nine, but the balance of power
was held by nine Australian Democrats. The government was
forced to haggle with Democrat senators to get legislation passed,
but the Democrats had to use their power discerningly, since they
might be blamed for a premature election call.

A federation should be organized with an effective upper
house, since a federal system, almost by definition, is designed to
bring together far-flung or ethnically diverse regions into a functioning whole. Federations therefore need to see reflected in their
central political institutions both a national expression and more
local ones. Geographically small states with ethnic homogeneity
do not necessarily need strong upper houses – but federations do.
The Canadian Senate theoretically met that regional test, but
the appointment of senators on strictly partisan lines blunted the
chamber's regional role. Senators may proudly declare themselves
Albertans or Nova Scotians or Quebeckers. But their Liberal or
Conservative partisanship overwhelms their regional identities –
perhaps not in their own minds, but in the public's.

Senators are understandably touchy about their institution's
lamentable reputation. The Senate's fate has been to be the butt

of national jokes, but that does not deter a steady stream of supplicants. Senators will insist on their regional identities and point to any odd flourish of independence and courage that they display to support their case. There are mavericks in their midst and even a handful of independent senators, the Canadian equivalent of cross-benchers in the British House of Lords. But senators are party men and women above all else, their sinecures tied to past political service.

Senators defend themselves with two reasonable arguments, although both are of a *faute de mieux* variety. Senate committees, with more time and expertise than Commons committees, do touch up and sometimes substantially improve legislation. Special Senate committees have produced landmark reports on major national issues such as Canada–U.S. free trade, the status of women, the media, fisheries, soil erosion. The Senate has given itself this role because the other, more important, ones were blocked by the appointed institution's lack of legitimacy. An elected Senate, as in other federations, would still be able to review government legislation and occasionally produce reports of lasting consequence, but it could also provide both a useful check on prime-ministerial control of the Commons and be a forum for regional views.

Had the Senate been elected – or appointed by provincial legislatures as in Germany and other countries – the dynamics of Canadian federalism would have been quite different. A senator elected on a province-wide ballot could plausibly have argued that he or she had every bit as much legitimacy as a provincial government to speak for the people of that province. An elected Senate would have diluted the voice, if not the power, of provincial governments in the federation. Thus some federal–provincial tensions and battles might have played themselves out within the federal government itself, instead of entirely between the federal and provincial governments. As it is, no senator appointed by the prime minister can possibly argue that he or she speaks for a province as does a provincial minister, let alone the premier. A weak, appointed Senate makes for stronger provinces and, of course, for a stronger prime minister.

Demands for Senate reform are as old as Canadian Confederation. In recent years, the cry went up in western Canada for a Triple-E Senate: elected, effective, and with equal representation from all ten provinces. The Reform Party forced a Triple-E Senate onto the national agenda, where, predictably, it died.

A Triple-E died for a mixture of political and intellectual reasons. Neither of the historic parties, the Liberals or Conservatives, believed in Senate reform anyway, for the obvious reason that, once in office, their prime minister would benefit from an appointed Senate. The old-line parties appreciated an institution useful for their partisan purposes and suitably docile for their governing ones. They gave lip service to the idea of Senate reform without ever seriously contemplating its realization. An elected Senate was part of the Charlottetown Accord. The defeat of that accord in a national referendum proved politically convenient to the Chrétien Liberals, who could deflect all criticisms of their subsequent inactivity by lying with a straight face that they had favoured Senate reform, whereas Reform did not, because the party had opposed the Charlottetown Accord.

Reform's idea died for another political reason. A Triple-E Senate would have given additional Senate seats to the West and to the provinces of Atlantic Canada, but at the expense of Ontario and Quebec. That was, of course, the whole idea: to provide a counterweight in Parliament to the population strength of the central Canadian provinces in the Commons. Ontario and Quebec would have 20 per cent of the seats under a Triple-E Senate, compared to almost 50 per cent in the appointed Senate. No matter how hard Reform tried to portray the Triple-E as a form of regional equity, in central Canada it was taken for a zero-sum change, in which Ontario and Quebec would lose. Triple-E, if not exactly seen as anti-Ontario or anti-Quebec, was viewed in those provinces as diluting their convenient dominance over the federal government. When Ontario Premier David Peterson magnanimously offered up some of Ontario's Senate seats as part of reaching a constitutional deal, he was roasted at home for having offered something and received nothing in return.

Quebec was especially suspicious of Senate reform. The provincial government's agenda had always been about more powers for Quebec. Senate reform seemed at best a diversion, at worst a threat. Elected senators might contest the provincial government's self-proclaimed legitimacy to speak for Quebeckers. To accept Senate reform without getting more power struck Quebec governments as a bad bargain. Senate reform also offended Quebec's inward conviction and singular conceit that, although other provinces or regions might have complaints about Canadian federalism, none were as well-founded as its own. Every Quebec commentator sniffed that a Triple-E would give equal membership to Quebec and Prince Edward Island, of all places – a simply unimaginable state of affairs for a province that wants to think of itself *égal à égal* with the rest of Canada, not as one among ten. Finally, as a permanent minority within Canada always seeking leverage for their interests, Quebec francophones could not see how reducing their numbers and influence in one federal chamber, albeit the least important one, enhanced their interests.

The hardy breed of Senate reformers offered a plethora of formulas to ease Quebec's linguistic concerns. The formulas, however worthy, pointed to the unfathomable complexity of any kind of Senate reform. Some proponents of Senate reform suggested double majorities of French- and English-speaking senators should be required for any matter affecting the French language and culture. This was fine, as far as it went. But who would decide what constituted such a matter? The government? The speaker of the Senate? A committee of senators? And, if so, who would sit on that committee? How many French-speakers? How many English-speakers? And could not the interests of French-speaking Quebeckers be tied up in legislation that went beyond, strictly speaking, matters of language and culture? Could not budgetary allocations or regional-development funds or immigration policy or you name it be stretched to include influences on language and culture? Round and round went the complexities of dealing just with Quebec's concerns, without even touching all the others. If Quebec and Ontario considered equality of the provinces too much of a stretch, what about a Senate with equal representation among regions: West, Ontario, Quebec, and Atlantic Canada? To this British Columbia retorted that it, too, was a separate region.

If federal Liberals and Conservatives would not budge on Senate reform, why would provinces not hold Senate elections of their own, as Alberta did, and dare the federal government not to appoint the people's chosen senators? Appointing senators in this fashion, replied the federal government, would be to sanction the existing division of Senate seats so unfair to the West and to create two classes of senators, elected and appointed – a pious argument that is trotted out with depressing regularity. In other words, the federal Liberals and Conservatives seemed to be saying that Senate reform should come as a complete package rather than as piecemeal arrangements, an argument whose intellectual tidiness masked its real intent – to preserve the status quo.

The status quo now seems hard to shake. In the late 1970s, before Reform put a Triple-E Senate on the national agenda, the Trudeau government had designed its own magnificently complex formula for Senate reform. It aroused predictable opposition from every provincial government. The Supreme Court was duly asked to rule whether Ottawa could unilaterally change the

Senate. By a 9–0 margin, the justices said no. Senate reform would have to be done jointly by Ottawa and the provinces.

Then came patriation of the Constitution, Trudeau's brainchild, and the federal-provincial negotiations that resulted in the Charter of Rights and Freedoms. That constitutional package contained a multi-tiered amending formula, with different combinations of required majorities, depending on which part of the constitution is to be changed. Senate reform requires the approval of seven provinces with 50 per cent of the population, a reasonable but not insurmountable barrier. But since, as Canadians know, governments can seldom agree on the day of the week, let alone constitutional changes, it is hard to imagine them agreeing on Senate reform. Constitutional changes now would seem to require a national referendum.

This straitjacket suits the Prime Minister and the governing party. For occasional political purposes, Prime Minister Chrétien will proclaim his interest in Senate reform. No one believes him, and no one should. The fair-minded observer might conclude that Chrétien has merely acknowledged that the Senate cannot be changed without a political miracle. Rather than irritating people by stating the obvious, he has engaged in the art of practised – and in this case benign – avoidance by saying one thing while believing another. That same observer might also conclude that Chrétien learned from the debacles of Meech Lake and Charlottetown that efforts for constitutional reform in Canada divide more than they unite, or at least are so fearsomely risky that they are not worth the effort. His refusal to open the file of Senate reform is part of wider refusal to open any constitutional file whatsoever, knowing that, even if Senate reform were worthwhile in and of itself, it could not be debated in isolation. Interest groups, aboriginals, and provincial governments with other priorities would insist, as they have in the past, that their priorities be tacked on to Senate reform, so that what might have started as a rather narrow debate about one proposed constitutional change would rapidly become an endless, divisive free-for-all.

Quite apart from the constitutional difficulties in achieving another kind of Senate, an unreformed Senate makes governing easier, and what prime minister objects to that, especially when he already holds all the levers of political power? The Senate will invariably do as he wishes, unless the Opposition Party commands a majority in the Other Place. That majority, appointees all from a previous government, will sometimes irritate, occasionally confront, but almost never try to stare down the elected government in the Commons. With a majority in both houses, the prime minister is all-powerful. He need not, as in Australia, negotiate with anybody in the Senate. He need not, as in Germany, remember that provincial government representatives must be accommodated in the other chamber. He need not cajole, flatter, bribe, or treat with senators, as the U.S. president must.

There is neither a check nor a balance in the Other Place, and that suits him fine. Theorists might argue that federations are better served with a different kind of second chamber, more reflective of regional concerns. Critics of our friendly elected dictatorship might insist that some countervailing power should exist to curtail that of the Commons majority, itself built on a first-past-the-post electoral system that grossly distorts votes cast and seats won. Those who worry about regional alienation might lament the lost opportunity of having inter-regional tradeoffs more transparently debated and decided, as they would likely be with an elected Senate, rather than thrashed out in the closed confines of the governing caucus, where some regions are usually underrepresented.

The Prime Minister could not care less as a political practitioner with all the power concentrated in and around himself. If he cared, there are at least small gestures available. He could agree to appoint any senators elected under provincially held senatorial elections. After all, the U.S. Senate went from being an appointed to an elected body because a few states began to insist on electing senators. He could appoint more independents, or even members of the opposition parties, although this would cause an uproar in his own ranks and might make his own political life slightly more difficult. He could speak out forcefully for a certain kind of Senate reform, using his office as a pulpit, while warning Canadians that Senate reform is a kind of constitutional Rubick's cube. But we are dreaming here, because none of these ideas would strike any prime minister, a friendly elected dictator, as being in his interest.

Public Opinion

The ultimate check on prime-ministerial power is public opinion, the bluntest of all conceivable instruments. The prime minister may be unchallenged within his party. His majority cannot be upended in the Commons. The Senate will likely remain docile. But out there in the country, the beast of public opinion lurks, its temper unpredictable.

Arguably the prime minister's most important decision flows from his discretionary power to call an election. Prime Minister Louis St. Laurent quickly and Prime Ministers John Diefenbaker and Joe Clark slowly yielded their leaderships after losing elections. Mulroney and Trudeau (in 1984) retired, knowing they could not have won again. Trudeau had already announced his departure after losing the 1979 election, but returned when the Clark government was unexpectedly defeated in the Commons. Pearson quit having failed twice to win a majority. Actual or incipient defeat – the only effective check Canadians have on prime-ministerial power – costs prime ministers their jobs. But the chance to exercise that check comes around only every three-to-five years, depending upon political circumstances.

As long as the prime minister controls the election date, he possesses a huge advantage over the other parties, since he will choose the time most propitious for his party. Jean Chrétien did just that in the fall of 2000, calling an election long before one was needed, because he knew he could win another majority, even if not every senior Liberal shared his determination to go early to the people. Not for Canada the Australian or Swedish requirement for fixed election dates, assuming the government has not previously been defeated in a confidence vote. Both of these countries have parliamentary, not presidential, systems. But in Canada's all-powerful prime-ministerial system, the discretion to call an election when it suits the prime minister is arguably the most precious political advantage of all. No incumbent would dream of yielding such an advantage.

Knowing when to use the advantage, of course, is the supreme political test. Pearson flunked it in 1965, calling an early election but failing to win his anticipated majority. Clark willingly accepted parliamentary defeat in 1979, wrongly believing the country would not turn again to the Trudeau Liberals. Trudeau spurned his advisers' counsel to go early to the polls in 1977, only to find that his political fortunes slid throughout 1978 and 1979. John Turner foolishly hastened to the polls in 1984, rather than wait another six months, and paid a terrible political price. Kim Campbell did likewise in 1993, and suffered an even worse fate than Turner, her party crashing to only two parliamentary seats.

These prime-ministerial errors bear witness to the risks that accompany this precious political advantage. Parties in modern Canadian politics accord little mercy to prime ministers who err. Sir John A. Macdonald and Mackenzie King both lost elections, but stayed around to win again. Not since Mackenzie King in 1926 has a defeated prime minister returned to power, except for the fluky circumstances that allowed Pierre Trudeau to rescind his resignation and return in 1980. Defeat means resignation or forcible exit.

These all-or-nothing stakes require prime ministers to keep a finger in the wind of public opinion at all times, and modern tools enhance his or her ability to ascertain which way those winds are blowing. Party polls and focus groups are the most obvious of these, and they have changed the way governments operate in quite profound ways. They have also changed the dynamics of power within government, augmenting the already formidable powers of the prime minister.

Scientific polling entered Canadian politics in the 1960s, when the Liberals imported pollsters from the United States, so there is nothing especially new about polls in politics. What has changed over the years is polling's sophistication and frequency. A welter of polling firms now pours results into the ears of private clients and the press. Without ever commissioning a poll, the governing party can have a rough sense of its political stand-ing by studying the public polls. But these are never enough for the governing party (opposition parties poll too, of course), which is seldom short of cash, courtesy of the bee-to-honey attraction of money to power. Prime ministers prefer not to admit they study polls, let alone pay them any heed. It seems to offend their *amour-propre* to be thought of as bending decisions to the whims of public opinion. They prefer the gullible to believe that polls are beneath them. The reality is somewhat different. Pierre Trudeau's advisers could get the party's pollster, Martin Goldfarb, to whip up a poll in a day or two if they thought it might influence the Prime Minister. Brian Mulroney, while saying the opposite for public consumption, was fixated on polls. Jean Chrétien is mindful of them too, willing to recount privately to even casual acquaintances just how well he and the Liberals are doing compared to their political adversaries.

Years ago, prime ministers relied for an assessment of public opinion on the press, correspondence, their own soundings, and, critically, the views of backbenchers and key ministers. If the minister from Saskatchewan or New Brunswick said the winds were blowing this or that way in his province, then the prime minister had few sources to contradict him. No so in the age of polling, when the prime minister can consult a plethora of public and party polls to know with some precision how the winds are blowing in every region of Canada. He might ask one of his ministers for information as a courtesy, but he doesn't need it. He has his own information, or can get it.

Focus groups have been added in recent years to issue-specific or general political polls. Governments have become addicted to focus groups, because they seem to provide a more nuanced reading of how people react to political information. It is hard for the general public to understand how ubiquitous these focus groups have become in government, since they are conducted in private and the results are not announced unless a media organization pries loose the results months later with an access-to-information request. Very few major government policies are not tested in advance through focus groups, and very few, once announced, are not tested by focus groups for reaction. To single out the Finance Department under Paul Martin is probably unfair, since so many other departments use focus groups, but Martin's department is notorious for focus-group testing before all major policy announcements, and this information is routinely shared with the nerve centre of government, the Prime Minister's Office.

Jean Chrétien has been a particularly risk-adverse prime minister, seldom straying too far from the broad currents of public opinion. Canadians saw just how fast he can alter course in the face of adverse public reaction when, within three days of the announcement, he jettisoned proposals to assist Canadian professional hockey teams. He did not need a poll, although these were available beforehand, to underscore that idea's instant unpopularity. What took him aback was not the unpopularity per se, but the ferociousness of the reaction, including more calls to his own constituency office than on any other issue. But for something important, such as his government's Clarity Bill, delineating the terms and conditions for Ottawa's response to a potential Quebec secession, the government commissioned the largest public-opinion survey ever in Quebec. The government correctly understood from this massive sample that Quebeckers would not rise in fury against the bill's provisions. Their equanimity shocked the Parti Québécois; it did not surprise the federal government, poll in hand. Similarly, such measures as the federal-provincial health accord, gun control, young-offenders legislation, the brouhaha over Human Resource Development grants, budgetary measures, and just about everything else of importance had been extensively polled and subjected to focus-group testing as integral inputs into final decisions. And, of course, anything significant proposed by the opposition parties, such as a flat income tax, is quickly monitored so that the government can measure its appeal and decide how to attack it or, if necessary, steal it.

This monitoring of public opinion goes on every day in government, mostly through analysis of the press, judgment of interest-group comments, assessment of the performance of opposition parties, and a certain awareness of the reactions of backbenchers and ministers to feed into decisions. The governing-party caucus, despite its limited power, does serve as a political sounding board for the prime minister and cabinet. Only brave souls will stand up and tell the prime minister he is dead wrong, but MPs will recount stories from their ridings as evidence that maybe the government is heading for trouble. Increasingly, the full cabinet acts like a mini-caucus, a smaller sounding board, bereft of all but titular power, yet capable of providing general feedback for the prime minister. Most of cabinet's serious work is done in committees. The full cabinet seldom overturns a committee decision; indeed Chrétien by all accounts does not like such decisions rehashed in full cabinet. Instead, the cabinet chews over general policy directions, seldom winding up anywhere the prime minister does not wish to go, since he controls the agenda, is briefed beforehand by the Privy Council on where every minister stands, and has usually figured out what decision he wants cabinet to approve. As a mini-sounding board that meets the day before caucus, the cabinet can provide the prime minister with a preview of what he can expect from the backbenchers. Again, the dynamics of prime-ministerial government apply: information and impressions are funnelled upwards to the prime minister; decisions come back down to ministers and caucus.

The Prime Minister's Office

Sifting through that information is the Prime Minister's Office, the nexus of government. If the Canadian prime minister resembles a kind of Sun King, then his senior advisers are his most trusted courtiers. They see and talk to him more often than anyone else. They meet with him every morning he is in town and often travel with him. The Privy Council briefs the prime minister on policy and administration; his advisers do that, too, but also provide political intelligence and advice. They are the prime minister's best set of eyes and ears, apart from his own. Sometimes, as in the case of Pierre Trudeau, advisers such as Jim Coutts and Keith Davey were better raw political operators than Trudeau, and he knew it. That has not been the case for the political animals, Brian Mulroney and Jean Chrétien. The longevity of Chrétien's two principal advisers, Jean Pelletier and Eddie Goldenberg, has been extraordinary. Trudeau and Mulroney burned through chiefs of staff and senior advisers. These jobs are terrifically demanding and, when things are going poorly, it is politically easier to appease the discontented by changing advisers than leaders. The advisers never attend caucus – it being only for MPs and senators – as if to signal that they are less important than politicians, but no one believes that fiction.

Goldenberg and Pelletier had been Chrétien's top two advisers since he took office, Goldenberg having served Chrétien since his early political days. "Check it with Eddie" is a byword in the Chrétien government. Given the strained relationship between Chrétien and Martin, Goldenberg became the Prime Minister's go-between with the Finance Minister and his staff. Pelletier, for his part, deliberately chose a lower public profile, but no one in Ottawa doubted his influence with a prime minister almost everyone in the government called simply the "Boss." A former Mayor of Quebec City, Pelletier touched every Quebec file. The duo's influence eclipsed their predecessors' under Trudeau and Mulroney, in part because of their sheer longevity and in part because of their personal connection to the prime minister. Trudeau and Mulroney had lifelong friends as senior advisers – Marc Lalonde with Trudeau and Bernard Roy with Mulroney – but others were simply people those prime ministers trusted. None of them stayed nearly as long as Goldenberg or as Pelletier, who resigned as chief of staff in May 2001 to become chairman of Canadian National.

In the sharply hierarchical Canadian prime-ministerial system, in which the prime minister is not *primus inter pares* but just plain *primus*, his advisers will axiomatically be more influential than any cabinet minister. Not wishing to bruise ministerial egos, the prime minister's advisers will sharply reject any such assertion, but the ministers themselves know the truth. They are beholden to the prime minister for their portfolios. When cabinet shuffles occur, ministers are informed after the prime minister and his advisers have filled in the blanks. Ministers are rarely consulted about final portfolio decisions; senior advisers always are. Since only the prime minister can play on any file, his advisers can range over the entire ambit of government, ensuring that his bidding is done and his interests are protected. That means working with departments, individual ministers or clusters of them, backbenchers, the extra-parliamentary party, interest groups, the media, pollsters. They can troubleshoot or engage in long-range planning. They can be policy wonks one day, partisan creatures the next. They influence all aspects of the government's communications strategies. What they must have is the prime minister's utter confidence, and to him they must deliver unswerving loyalty. "Protect the prime minister" is the unwritten golden rule of any government, and the prime minister's advisers are his principal protectors. As critical conduits of information to the prime minister, they are always searching out the political winds, trying to keep them fair, since in this prime-ministerial system of government only the foul winds of public opinion can threaten his supremacy.

The Prime Minister and Parliament

To paraphrase von Clausewitz's famous dictum that war is the continuation of diplomacy by other means, Question Period is the continuation of the election campaign by other means. Elections are the supreme political test; Question Periods are a series of skirmishes flowing from and leading to those tests. Question Period is the best platform for the opposition parties to highlight issues, embarrass the government, and influence public opinion. Opposition parties theoretically have the advantage, since they can select the subject and the minister who must answer. The government, again theoretically, is on the defensive, called to account for its conduct of the nation's business. At Westminster, the British prime minister has a much easier task than the Canadian prime minister. The British prime minister attends what is called Question Time once or twice a week and for only fifteen minutes. True, he does not know precisely what questions will arise, but then neither does his Canadian counterpart, although both can make educated guesses based on the morning papers and the general drift of political debate. The Canadian prime minister, however, is expected to attend Question

Period every day he is not otherwise plausibly engaged, and to remain in his place for all forty-five minutes. He is therefore the principal target of the opposition parties, but for a variety of reasons he is seldom damaged.

Question Period is a bit of a misnomer and, as such, confuses Canadians. The name would suggest the posing of questions and the solicitation of answers. Instead, as anyone who has watched Question Period can attest, the questions are usually an interrogation mark affixed to a short political speech, while the answers are an exclamation mark joined to another short political speech. There are, to be fair, questions that genuinely seek specific information and replies that actually provide it, but these are as roses among the thorns. Question Period is political theatre played out under the media's bright glare. By contrast, Parliament's other business operates in the shadow of near-obscurity. Canadians naturally form their impression of Parliament from Question Period, because the theatrics there intrigue the media. That the impression is necessarily distorted cannot be blamed on citizens, since they receive from their media a selective rendering of what actually happens in the parliamentary process. And that rendering, based on Question Period, suggests that otherwise normal people, upon becoming politicians, shout and holler and otherwise make such fools of themselves that they should be kept away from meetings of the PTA, Rotary Club, or any other place where civilized people gather.

Question Period as political theatre demands that actors know their lines. Parliamentary convention once held that members could not read their questions; indeed, they were not even supposed to refer to notes, although some did. But that convention yielded to the age of television, which allowed MPs to see themselves on the screen and, more important, for the electors to witness them, too. Now opposition MPs arrive with accusatory questions scripted and typed, including the supplementaries, or follow-up questions on the same subject, so that, even in the unlikely event that a minister does provide a straightforward reply, the questioner, having plausibly if wrongly anticipated the usual obfuscation, is obliged to plough on to the next accusation. The best opposition performers are those with a knack for feigned outrage. In recent memory these would include Ian Deans of the NDP, Michel Gauthier and Yvon Lubier of the Bloc Québécois, John Crosbie of the Conservatives, and George Baker of the Liberals. Baker, a Newfoundlander, was arguably the best and certainly the most entertaining of the bunch, an MP who rehearsed his lines and delivery in front of a mirror before delivering them in Question Period. The bottlers of feigned outrage seem in a perpetual state of amazement at the behaviour of the miscreants on the government benches, and are much prized by the media for their outrage.

The key to tactical success in Question Period lies in remembering that the audience does not sit in the chamber. Opposition leaders and government ministers need to do well in Question Period to buck up their troops, but their real objective is to pass messages to the public through the media. Early every morning, therefore, teams of opposition MPs and staffers begin preparing for the afternoon performance, scouring the papers and scanning summaries of newscasts from the night before for possible material. The same preparation begins in ministers' offices and the PMO as the government prepares for what the opposition might raise. In the fifteen minutes or so before Question Period, the prime minister summons ministers to his third-floor office just above the Commons to review strategy. For the opposition parties, the daily theatre can have various scripts, but only one objective: to maximize the chance of getting a sound bite on television or radio or a headline in the newspapers. Figuring out what will play in the media is the essence of opposition strategy. The best-laid line of questions that brings a yawn to the media will be judged a failure. The subject might be important and the questions well crafted and delivered, but if the media does not bite, the day has been wasted.

Television, by its visual, kinetic nature, demands conflict. Nuance and subtlety are television's sworn enemies. Question Period provides institutionalized verbal combat in short, sharp bursts of rhetoric. Better still for television, Question Period offers occasionally genuine but usually rehearsed and packaged emotion. Television treats indifferently the motivation for emotion; it just wants people to show emotion, and the more of it the better. Knowing this, opposition parties place a premium on emoting, anger being for television the most visual and therefore most appealing emotion. So questions must not only be prepared according to what will catch the media's eye and ear, they must be asked in the most emotional style possible to maximize the chance of coverage. Whether the substance behind the question makes good sense is almost beside the point, since rarely do the media inquire deeply into what the opposition would do if magically transported into government. The classic example of irresponsible-but-irresistible opposition emoting was provided from 1984 to 1988 by the Liberals' "Rat Pack," a quartet of leather-lunged MPs who harangued the Mulroney government daily. They offered nothing constructive by way of alternatives, but they made great theatre. Three of them – Brian Tobin, Sheila Copps, and Don Boudria – later became ministers in the Chrétien government. The fourth, John Nunziata, subsequently bucked the Liberal line in government and was booted from the caucus to sit as an independent MP.

Once in a while, the opposition parties can genuinely place the government on the sustained defensive. This usually occurs when some well-publicized screwup has been widely reported and the opposition can amplify what is already known, as when the auditor general reported extraordinarily lax behaviour in the Human Resources Development Department's administration of grants. More rarely still, the opposition can score if the sniff of scandal lies in the air, because nothing sends the media into heat faster than scandal, real or imagined. The Pearson government, an immensely creative ministry that gave Canadians their own flag and nation-defining social programs, seemed always under seige for one mishap or another, each magnified by thunderously malevolent attacks from Opposition Leader John Diefenbaker. The Mulroney government likewise offered a string of ministers who were brought down by their personal or political misdeeds, including Michel Côté, André Bissonnette, and Sinclair Stevens. Jean Chrétien himself has been repeatedly accused of using his prime-ministerial influence to secure money for projects in his riding, including one in which it was alleged he had a pecuniary interest.

The media immediately labelled as "Shawinigate" the allegations surrounding Chrétien's involvement in securing a loan from the Business Development Bank for a hotel adjacent to a golf course in which he had had a pecuniary interest. The allegations began long before the 2000 election, but consumed Parliament in early 2001 as the opposition parties attempted to pin a conflict of interest on Chrétien. Critics cried that an ordinary MP could never have leaned on the bank's president for a loan; only the prime minister could do that, and therefore he had abused his power in seeking preferential treatment for his riding. Worse, they claimed, the success of the golf course depended upon the financial viability of the adjacent hotel, and therefore the conflict of interest was doubly obvious. The Prime Minister replied that he had sold his golf-course shares before becoming prime minister, although he did not receive payment until years later. He could not therefore be in a conflict of interest, and the lobbying done for the adjacent hotel had just been part of his ongoing work as an MP. Moreover, he insisted, the ethics counsellor had studied the entire file, advised him on how to proceed, and testified before a parliamentary committee that no conflict existed.

The manifold complications of "Shawinigate" (the media, post-Watergate, now ridiculously affixes "gate" to anything remotely sniffing of impropriety) left Canadians largely unmoved, a classic example of Peace Tower politics in which elected officials work themselves into a lather about matters far removed from the bread-and-butter concerns of ordinary people. The Liberals did not suffer in the polls, despite relentless opposition pounding. There was a good deal less to the Prime Minister's alleged misdeeds than the opposition made out, but there were sufficient unanswered questions and strange coincidences in the sequence of events to have merited some sort of objective review. That review might well have exonerated the Prime Minister's conduct, but no such review occurred, nor was one possible, given the nature of prime-ministerial power and parliamentary government. Indeed, the parliamentary performances around "Shawinigate" further underscored the nature of prime-ministerial government.

The Liberals had excoriated the Mulroney Conservatives for lax ethics, and in their 1993 Red Book they promised, among other changes, an ethics counsellor or commissioner responsible to Parliament. Chrétien, however, insisted that, as prime minister, he was ultimately responsible for ethical standards in the government – including his own conduct, of course – so that he should appoint the ethics counsellor. That meant that the ethics counsellor, rather than submitting judgments to Parliament, sent them only to the person who appointed him, the prime minister. This arrangement allowed the prime minister to be judge and jury, and left the ethics counsellor looking like a prime-ministerial poodle. During "Shawinigate," no one could prove that Howard Wilson, the ethics counsellor, had deliberately doctored reports to exonerate the man who had appointed him, but the reporting path from counsellor to prime minister suggested to critics that Wilson had at the very least chosen to interpret the evidence in a way favourable to the prime minister. Wilson would no longer have held his job had he differed publicly with the prime minister's interpretation of events. Similarly, any Liberal MP who expressed the slightest dissent on something as central to the government as the prime minister's ethical conduct would have been forever doomed, or perhaps thrown out of caucus. Backbenchers and ministers alike, their survival instincts aroused, behaved like a cheering chorus for the prime minister. The need to protect the king, the most atavistic of all political reactions, clicked in for the Liberals. Opposition MPs' attempts to secure approval for inquiries by parliamentary committees were rebuffed by Liberal majorities.

The result was, of course, that "Shawinigate" deteriorated into parliamentary mudslinging. An independent ethics commission could not investigate, since none existed. The government blocked any attempt to create an independent inquiry, such as the one into allegations against former Conservative minister Sinclair Stevens. The Liberal majority frustrated any inquiries by a parliamentary committee. In other words, no check or balance against prime-ministerial power existed, except the blunt, noisy, but usually ineffectual one of Question Period.

The opposition does not wield power, although it does have certain established parliamentary prerogatives, including the right to ask questions in Question Period. It does have influence, but that influence is almost entirely negative, such as pouncing on government errors, large or trivial, real or imagined. The opposition parties routinely insist they wish to provide "constructive criticism" of the government, as they sometimes do. But they are prized by the media by how effectively they criticize. How many opposition leaders have lamented that their Commons speeches proposing alternative policies received but a fraction of the media coverage of their Question Period assaults? Liberal leader John Turner once observed that he had delivered six major speeches on government bills that received absolutely no television coverage, whereas his daily theatrics in Question Period invariably made the news. In early 2001, Conservative leader Joe Clark was quoted as saying that he spent most of his entire day preparing for his two questions in Question Period on "Shawinigate." This parliamentary climate contributes to the pervasive one in government, in which the avoidance of publicly exposed error is an hourly preoccupation. It is fine for public-service managers to encourage their employees to take risks, but if one of these risks turns sour and becomes publicly known, there might be hell to pay for it in an unforgiving Parliament and media. That is why risk avoidance permeates Ottawa.

For all the theatrics, or perhaps because of them, Question Period is more bark than bite. The opposition's self-appointed job in any Parliament is to assist in the self-destruction of the government. The opposition cannot do the job by itself; the government has to create the conditions for its own political undoing. Governments fundamentally defeat themselves. If the government is making what strikes the largest number of people as sensible choices, given the circumstances of the moment and the opposition alternatives, no amount of barracking in Question Period will seriously damage the government. Successful prime ministers learn how to avoid Question Period traps by skirting and dodging, and, when pressed, turning the tables by going on the political attack. If they do not wish to answer, they can turn to a minister; if they do wish to answer, it is because they are well-primed, since they have the entire apparatus of government to provide them with answers, to say nothing of their own political skills. There is, too, the growing sense that Question Period's theatrics wear thin on the public, most of whom do not follow daily developments in Ottawa. Citizens hear snippets of the parliamentary exchanges in the media, but those snippets usually lack context and are out-of-mind tomorrow. The snippets are as background noise that seldom comes into sharp, politically motivating focus. What seems of earthshaking daily importance to players of "Peace Tower politics" has lost most of its resonance by the time it floats more than a few miles away.

Parliamentary debate, crystallized in Question Period, is, in the words of British author Timothy Garton Ash, a "form of limited adversarial mendacity," in which partial truths or selective interpretations are falsely elevated to wisdom. Citizens are therefore often sceptical, outraged, or rendered indifferent by the daily attempts to make whole cloth from ill-fitting bits and pieces. Citizens know they make mistakes in their own lives, as do the institutions for which they work; they recoil from the unwillingness of those in political life to admit error.

That said, there have been a few instances in recent memory when sustained opposition attacks have over time either damaged a government or caused it to pause. Opposition Leader Joe Clark definitely contributed to slowing down the Trudeau government's planned unilateral patriation of the Constitution after the 1980 election. Day after day, week after week, he led the Conservatives in an assault on unilateral action that, when joined with the premiers' own complaints, planted seeds of public doubt about the wisdom of the government's intentions. The Tories' attack in that Parliament against practices at Revenue Canada, the Turner Liberals' pounding criticisms of Canada–U.S. free trade, the Reform Party's insistent demands for tax cuts – these attacks in Question Period (and in other forums, of course) did eventually register with the public. But the key to the impact lay in sustaining these attacks. Sustaining anything in a multi-partied Parliament, however, is more difficult than in a Parliament of three parties, Liberal, Conservative, NDP. Ever since the three-party system became a five-party one, the time given opposition parties has been distributed among four of them. This has contributed to scatter-gun attacks, since seldom do all four agree on the issue of the day – and even when they agree on the subject, they differ in the line of attack. That, in turn, makes matters easier for the government and for the prime minister. In theory, the opposition should be the government-in-waiting, but in today's fractured

Canadian party system, there is no government-in-waiting, despite the dreams and pretensions of the Canadian Alliance and the Conservatives. There is only the Liberal Party, the "natural" governing party.

Backbenchers: The Prime Minister's Chorus

Edmund Burke is the patron saint of frustrated backbenchers. The English philosopher also served in Parliament, and in one celebrated message to his electors in Bristol, while campaigning in 1774, Burke explained how he saw his political role and his obligations to voters. Said Burke:

> Parliament is not a congress of ambassadors from different and hostile interests; which interests each must maintain, as agent and advocate, against other agents and advocates; but Parliament is a deliberative assembly of one nation, with one interest, that of the whole; where, not local purposes, not local prejudices ought to guide, but the general good, resulting from the general reason of the whole. You choose a member indeed; but when you have chosen him, he is not a member of Bristol, but is a member of Parliament.

Today's MPs who draw inspiration from Burke's spirit of independence might remember that he served in a Parliament with a restricted franchise, a loose party structure, and rotten boroughs where ministries were stitched together and backbenchers' loyalties secured by ministerial dispensation of patronage. Sir John A. Macdonald, governing Canada in the late nineteenth century, worried about occasional "loose fish" in Parliament; the eighteenth-century British Parliament was a sea full of them. Burke, it might be recalled, withdrew from standing as a candidate in Bristol in 1780, knowing he faced certain defeat.

Burke's reasoning holds an honoured place in parliamentary theory, but almost none in contemporary parliamentary practice. Parliament is not, as Burke said, full of "ambassadors from different and hostile interests," but rather of MPs from different and hostile political parties. Canadian parliamentary parties, especially the governing ones, are like military formations: sharply hierarchical, with a top-down command structure led by the prime minister, with all rewards demanding loyalty and all penalties taxing dissent. Prime Minister Pierre Trudeau once dismissed MPs as "nobodies" when they left Parliament Hill. He erred – within the friendly dictatorship of the parliamentary system they are also nobodies. Ask lobbyists whom they need to contact to get things moving in Ottawa. Backbenchers are at the bottom of their list. Ask the media whom they search out for clips and quotes, and government backbenchers are the last they seek. Ask the senior civil service from whom they take marching orders, and backbenchers will be last in line. The only exception comes in caucus. There, backbenchers are allowed to express views that might differ from government policy, but even in those closed confines, more than episodic dissent leads to an MP developing a reputation as a troublemaker, somehow unreliable, not quite the kind of "team player" the leadership values.

Backbenchers who misread how they got elected to Parliament fall victim to a Burkean notion of their role. It would comfort any of them to believe that they arrive in Ottawa because of their individual virtues, whereas everything we know about politics suggests they become MPs as party men and women first and foremost. The party label in an election campaign counts for more than their reputations, personalities, strengths, or weaknesses. The majority of Canadians do not know their members of Parliament; they even struggle to identify cabinet ministers. In the 1988 National Election Survey, 53 per cent of voters said they decided on the basis of party identification, compared with 27 per cent for the local candidate and 20 per cent for the party leader. Subsequent surveys have produced similar results: that the local candidate is far less consequential in voters' decisions than party identification.

Obvious exceptions exist to this general rule. A long-serving MP might enjoy a high recognition factor. A rural riding with little demographic mobility and a smaller population might allow an MP to become better known than an MP in a large suburban riding where residents are moving in and out all the time. The Canadian electoral map makes this theoretically possible, because urban ridings contain far more voters than rural ones.

Some MPs more assiduously cultivate local favour than others. Paul Martin, Sr., was legendary for his filing cabinets bursting with information about individual constituents in Windsor. He prided himself, and was appreciated in return by citizens of Windsor, for knowing so many people by name. But even Martin senior could forget. During the 1968 Liberal leadership race, he met a Windsor resident while circling a room. Alerted to the Windsor connection, Martin asked about the health of the man's mother. She died, replied the man, evincing sorrow from Martin. Somewhat later, having shaken dozens of other hands, Martin again grasped the Windsor man's hand. "And how is your mother?" he asked. "Still dead," the man replied. On another occasion much earlier in his career, Martin had been attending a United Nations meeting as Canada's foreign minister. Martin's participation had been much in the news, but when he stepped off the plane in Windsor from New York, he brushed aside reporters' questions about the U.N. meeting and inquired about the new post office in Windsor. Tip O'Neill, the legendary speaker of the U.S. House of Representatives, who insisted that "all politics is local," would have approved.

All politics is not local in Canada; indeed, very little of it is local. National party affiliation rather than local-candidate identification drives voting intentions. Backbenchers dispose of limited political discretion by funnelling federal money into constituencies. The days are long gone when MPs sorted out who got local federal jobs and which contractors received government work. These matters are now administered by bureaucrats who operate within guidelines, regulations, laws, established practices, requests for proposals, sealed bids. There remain, however, a few discretionary spending programs where an MP's recommendation can be influential, even decisive. These especially arise in programs designed for economically disadvantaged ridings, where federal spending programs are prevalent. The Transitional Jobs Fund of the Chrétien government or the wharf-improvement program of the Mulroney government invited MPs to steer local projects. Both Chrétien and Mulroney came from and represented Quebec ridings with high unemployment. They understood the local traditional political culture in those areas where MPs were expected to bring home the federal bacon. As leaders, they knew that a little largesse distributed by the MP helped politically at home and kept him or her quiescent in caucus. These programs, with their heavy emphasis on make-work employment, have diminished in importance, as government spending shrank and critics attacked them as wasteful. With the diminution went some of the MPs' local power.

Obviously, MPs are always lobbying ministers and ministries to look favourably on local projects, and if a project is approved, the announcement will usually include both the departmental minister's name and that of the local MP. A minister alone will announce a project in an opposition MP's riding, since the government is loathe to give credit or even mention the opposition. Listing federal contributions to local projects is a staple of MPs' quarterly mailings to constituents and campaign literature, an apparent signal that the MP is doing his or her job in Ottawa.

Those MPs who arrive in Ottawa as party men and women, knowing that electors sent them to Parliament as representatives of a certain party and leader, might reasonably be expected to defend that party's policies and leader. They are not being sent to Ottawa as independents to vote as they see fit, Edmund Burke notwithstanding. They presumably told the electorate that they supported a particular party platform, believed their party leader would make the best prime minister, and stood behind the principles of the party, such as they might be. For them to say all this, then turn around in Parliament and act as free souls, bucking the party line, decrying the leader, and voting as their consciences dictate, would not be true either to what they had said in the campaign or to the parliamentary system they asked to join. Therefore, the rallying cry for "free votes" in the House of Commons needs to be tempered by the reality of party politics.

Even if, however, an MP honestly disagrees with his party, the penalties for dissent can be high, because scant latitude is given for honest, public disagreement. Stephen Owen, a Vancouver Liberal MP elected in 2000, faced that dilemma soon after arriving in Ottawa. Owen had been B.C. provincial ombudsman and a former deputy minister of justice. He had been involved in judging matters of political ethics in British Columbia and had expressed public support for an independent ethics commissioner, rather than one appointed by the prime minister or premier. During the debate over Prime Minister Chrétien's involvement in government help for the Auberge Grand-Mère, the Canadian Alliance moved a motion calling for an independent ethics commissioner. Owen was on public record favouring one, but he voted with the government to defeat the motion. His swallowing of a previously held position was widely condemned in British Columbia, but Owen had legitimate ministerial ambitions. He had been named Liberal candidate at Chrétien's behest, so he owed the leader something beyond mere party loyalty. Owen also rationalized that he could influence government policy better from within cabinet and caucus, and feared developing an immediate reputation as a wild card or maverick, thereby dooming his cabinet aspirations and curbing his influence in government.

The promise of future reward, including a cabinet post, and the fear of political retribution are a prime minister's two most powerful weapons in squelching public dissent within party ranks. If the prime minister has won a majority government, he comes to believe, and not without reason, that MPs owe their seats more to him than to themselves. This turns parliamentary theory on its head, of course, since a leader takes his place as prime minister only because enough of his party's candidates won individually contested ridings, but how they won – on the party name and leader's reputation – usually suggests to the leader that his contribution eclipsed theirs. The prime minister also dispenses positions within caucus and Parliament that can bring higher salaries and increased responsibilities. The prime minister appoints parliamentary secretaries, who assist ministers in minor matters, answer for them in Question Period when ministers are absent, and receive additional salary for their efforts. Chrétien rotates parliamentary secretaries to spread the perks around. Then there are committee chairmanships, foreign trips, invitations to state dinners, internal party assignments, and other examples of prime-ministerial favour, either granted directly by him or by whips or the House leader he appoints.

Against all these pressures and blandishments, the Burkean ideal of MPs independent of "hostile interests" never had a chance within disciplined political parties. The party leader must sign the candidates' nomination papers. Once elected, MPs' ambitions within the party and the parliamentary system are at the mercy of the prime minister. The MPs themselves are largely elected on their party labels. The notion of MPs as Burke's disciples, arriving in Ottawa as quasi-independent agents, free to speak their minds "for the general good," owing their allegiance primarily to their own consciences and good judgment, finds scant place in parliamentary practice. Occasionally, the government will allow the classic "free vote," as on matters of deep personal conscience, such as capital punishment or abortion, but these votes come along very rarely. Even the Canadian Alliance, which has always demanded more parliamentary "free votes," talks a better game than it played, since the Reform Party and Alliance have seldom allowed its own members a "free vote." They have voted in as disciplined a manner as the Liberals. Whenever a Reform/Alliance MP has stepped out of line in extra-parliamentary comments, he or she is disciplined by the party leadership that wanted, as Prime Minister Brian Mulroney once said in reference to his Conservatives, "everyone singing from the same hymnbook."

These arrangements, however, are not what Canadians want. When asked by pollsters, Canadian consistently reply that they would like their MPs to vote more freely. It obviously strikes Canadians as slightly odd that the men and women they elect must act within the straitjacket of party discipline, since this system implies that MPs cannot think for themselves and will vote as they are instructed, regardless of what constituents might want. Canadians are not fools. They know that complex issues can cut across party lines, and that not everyone in a caucus sees every issue the same way. It strikes them that the balance between necessary compromise that must occur within a caucus to achieve a common position and independence of thought and action has tilted too strongly towards discipline, which renders MPs little more than cheerleaders for the party line crafted by and dictated from the top.

Under these trying circumstances, it is little wonder that MPs are held in such low regard by Canadians, since the very system within which they work accords them such limited scope for initiative and independent judgment. MPs do not even listen much to each other, since they all know that there is no room to persuade people of another political party. Parliamentary debates illustrate the futility of dialogue. The chamber is nearly vacant when MPs speak. Those who attend are required to be present, because each MP has a list of "duty days" in the Commons. The department whose bill is being debated, or the caucus research staff, will have distributed "speaking notes" for the government MPs. Anyone who has waded through Hansard will detect a striking similarity in the arguments presented by speaker after speaker from the same party, courtesy of these "speaking notes."

The media, too, has abandoned coverage of parliamentary debates. As soon as Question Period ends, the press gallery empties, as MPs resume debate on legislation or a motion presented by an opposition party. Some years ago, the Canadian Press at least kept one reporter in the Commons to file a dispatch on that day's debate, but that practice has been abandoned, so that, unless Canadians watch the parliamentary television channel, which only a handful do, they cannot possibly know what has occurred in their Parliament, apart from the theatrics of Question Period.

Canadians complain that MPs, once elected, do not listen to them. MPs do receive letters and e-mail from their constituents. They hear from voters while making their constituency rounds. They send quarterly "householders," or pamphlets to constituents, and these sometimes generate a scattered response. Some of them hold town-hall meetings at which constituents can speak their minds. MPs do, in fact, try to listen to what their electors are saying, because in small part their political survival depends upon attentiveness. Within the national or regional caucuses, they do inform each other and cabinet ministers what the folks back home are saying. But the electors cannot see any of this feedback, because, once the MPs are in Ottawa, the rigidities of party discipline require backbenchers to express dissent silently and to report back to constituents only what has been approved as the "message." This skewed form of communication – private dissent, public support – leads to the frequently levelled charge that, for example, so-and-so is not British Columbia's person in Ottawa but Ottawa's person in British Columbia.

The first-past-the-post electoral system compounds these problems. Many MPs do not receive even half the votes on election day. They represent a constituency all right, because that is the nature of the electoral system, but quite often a majority of the constituents did not vote for them. Therefore, when an MP claims that "the people of my riding" think this or that, he or she is usually guessing, engaging in a polite fiction, or imputing a consensus that does not exist. A voting system that did in fact guarantee that an MP had won at least a majority of the votes would lend greater credence to these claims and make the MP a somewhat more reliable reflection of local opinion.

The Control of Information: The Prime Minister as Gatekeeper

Information is democracy's lifeblood. Dictatorships treat information as propaganda, ensuring by every available means that people receive only information vetted by the government. Democratically elected Canadian governments cannot treat information as do dictatorships, but they still display an abiding nervousness about information. They provide extensive information about things they want Canadians to know; they hide to the greatest extent possible what they do not want Canadians to know.

The Janus-like, or two-faced, approach to information shapes the daily work of government. The federal government, to its credit, sped into the Internet world determined to put information on-line about government programs. Accountants can file citizens' tax returns on-line and rebates will be speedily returned. Firms wanting information about procurement, students wishing to enter their names for summer-job competitions, citizens wishing raw data from government agencies such as Statistics Canada, can all become better informed – and faster – than at any time. The House of Commons about twenty years ago allowed television cameras to record daily proceedings, and television now records Commons committees.

Anyone who works in Ottawa, especially a journalist, confronts a daily Niagara of press releases, issues of Hansard, annual reports of government departments and agencies, ministerial speeches, opposition-party commentaries. A check of any government department reveals legions of bureaucrats responsible for "communications." Every minister and party leader has a press secretary, who acts as gatekeeper for access to their boss and as "spin doctor," massaging the press, trying to figure out, even on an hourly basis, how to create the most favourable coverage for their boss and, by extension, the government. A mini-industry within the government exists to present the governing party in the best possible light. Every morning, long before politicians or senior civil servants arrive at their offices, summaries of the previous evening's newscasts and morning newspapers have been prepared by ministerial staffs or hired news-monitoring services. These summaries are designed to inform the government about what has been reported and, more important, to alert its members to what might become the issue of the day in Parliament or the media. "Damage control" is the abiding preoccupation of ministerial offices and especially, of course, of the Prime Minister's Office. The most accomplished practitioners of this craft are not just those who shape responses to what is already in the public domain, but those who anticipate potential problems.

Civil servants who inadvertently or otherwise say things that contradict, or even cast the slightest doubt on, the wisdom of the government's policy are severely reprimanded. There is no incentive to candour, if candour means presenting information that could lead a reasonable person to conclude that perhaps, just perhaps, the government's policy does not epitomize the last word on the subject. Backbench members of Parliament who buck the party line find that the best committee assignments dry up, their chances for advancement to the cabinet are curtailed, their reputations are sullied where it counts for their political futures – at the top of the party. In extreme cases, they are drummed completely out of the party. Dissidents, of course, are popular with the press, which is always searching for a good story about controversy within the governing party, but this press coverage stands in inverse relationship to these MPs' real influence in Ottawa. The golden rule of backbenchers' influence within the governing party runs as follows: the more they dissent from the government line, the less their influence. A dissenting quotation in the newspaper may be good for their morale or self-esteem; it may even be appreciated by their constituents. But it diminishes their career prospects within the governing party.

The cabinet has a committee on "communications," whose job consists of co-ordinating government announcements, ensuring that government spokespeople sing from the same page in the hymnbook and anticipate potentially adverse publicity. The committee also oversees how to spend the millions and millions of dollars Ottawa forks out on advertising, contracts for which inevitably are funnelled to firms with links to the governing party. Whenever a new party takes power, one of its first tasks consists of shifting the government's advertising budget to individuals and firms favourable to itself, including those firms that have crafted the party's electoral advertising.

A special eye is always kept on information sent to Quebec. For three decades, the federal government has been at political daggers drawn with the secessionists in that province, who, when in power, have never shied from using the provincial government's publicity apparatus to promote their cause and denigrate the federal system. The federalist propaganda machine extends to media advertising, sponsoring everything from hot-air-balloon competitions to cultural events, sending Canadian flags to just about any group willing to fly one, and insisting that signage and publicity acknowledge federal spending. Sporting events are also among the special targets for federal publicity, since they attract crowds. Spectators at Montreal's Olympic Stadium cannot gaze in any direction without seeing some form of federal advertising from Canada Post to VIA Rail to the federal government itself. The Molson Centre is likewise plastered with Canadian publicity. During the public debate over government assistance for Canadian professional hockey teams, western Canadians widely noted that Ottawa was pumping advertising money into arenas in Montreal and Ottawa (where the principal owner is a prominent Liberal, and where no discernible threats exist to national unity), without spending a nickel for those in Edmonton, Calgary, or Vancouver.

Nor surprisingly, spending on federal government publicity often reflects the electoral cycle. The closer the election, the more likely advertising budgets will rise. In June 2000, for example, with Prime Minister Jean Chrétien beginning to contemplate an election, Treasury Board received an additional $90 million for communications and advertising of federal government activities. The new money, spread over three years, was added to the existing $45-million advertising budget and controlled by the Cabinet committee on communications, presided over by then-Public Works Minister Alfonso Gagliano. Some of the new money was given to the Canada Information Office, established after federalism's near-defeat in the 1995 referendum to counter secessionist propaganda. But in Quebec, as elsewhere, the government's advertising serves a dual purpose. It raises the profile of the federal government all right, but contributes to enhancing the electoral prospects of the Liberal Party. The governing party never acknowledges this second objective – indeed howls of predictable government outrage greet the mere suggestion of this objective – but it is not far from the minds of the ministers who control the budget.

This massaging of information, as with everything else in Ottawa, is watched over by the Prime Minister's Office, whose occupants stand guard over all major communications. In addition to trying to make the prime minister look good, the PMO is the nexus of government information efforts in shaping overall messages and, quite often, in deciding what must not be made public. This issue of deciding what not to release has special relevance for the PMO and for the Privy Council Office that works closely with it. Some of the broad exemptions for the release of information under the Access to Information Act are those directly tied to PMO/PCO, and include national security, cabinet confidences, federal–provincial relations, and foreign policy. Anything potentially damaging to the government that might be released under an access request is flagged to PMO/PCO, just as the government receives advance copies of reports from independent agencies such as the Auditor General's Office, so that the government can prepare and co-ordinate its response.

The Access to Information Act arrived under the government of Prime Minister Pierre Trudeau, but only after years of nagging by opposition MPs (and a few Liberals), led by Conservative Gerald Baldwin. Its laudable aim, broadly speaking, was to make the widest amount of government information available to the citizens, who, after all, pay for its gathering, collation, and analysis. Philosophically, the act aimed at creating within the closed shop of government the heretical idea that the public had a right to know, but that idea often ran afoul of the government's legitimate right to debate matters in private (especially in the Cabinet) and to protect the national interest in dealings with foreign governments and provinces. The act also frightened governments, which quickly came to regard it as a Trojan Horse, presented as a defence of the public's right to know but essentially designed to allow actual or potential foes such as journalists, interest groups, or opposition parties to gain access to information that might make the government squirm.

Constant struggles have marked relations between the information commissioner and the government, struggles that have been played out in endless negotiations between commissioner and government representatives, in court rulings (often favourable to the commissioner), and, ultimately, in the court of public opinion. A parade of ministers has pledged and a series of Commons committees have recommended changes to the act to strengthen its provisions, but these have crashed against the government's ingrained suspicion of anything that might make its political lives more difficult.

A yearly theatrical performance – we might even call it a charade – accompanies the release of the Information Commission's annual report. Filled with laments about the government's dilatory response to information requests – to say nothing of its outright denials – the report becomes the opposition's plaything of the moment. Opposition MPs quote passages of the report in Question Period. Ministers do their best with feigned concern to assure Parliament that they are indeed taking the commissioner's suggestions seriously, all the while knowing that this fury of denunciation from across the aisle will pass like a summer storm. Life will then go on as before.

Commissioners have certainly done their bit to arouse the public and budge the government. They have spared few rhetorical devices in their annual reports to shame the government and alert the citizenry. In Commissioner John Grace's final report in 1998, he observed tartly that,

> if some of its architect's fine hopes were unrealistic and unrealized, the fault lies not in the stars, not in the law: It must be placed at the feet of governments and public servants who have chosen to whine about the rigors of access rather than embrace its goals; chosen not to trust the public with information which taxes have paid for. The insult is equal only to the intellectual arrogance of it all. The commitment, by word and deed, to the principle of accountability through transparency has been too often faltering and weak-kneed.

Faltering and week-kneed. Strong words from John Grace, a gentle man, who had been a journalist and privacy commissioner. The words were as nothing, however, compared to the rhetorical lashings administered by his successor, John Reid. As if warming to his task, Mr. Reid warned that he would adopt a policy of "zero tolerance" for late responses to access requests, expect a "pro-openness approach to the act, and use the full weight of his investigative powers." But by 2000, after two years in the job, the former Liberal MP (and briefly minister) castigated the government for its reaction to his vigorous pursuit of the act's aims.

"A full counterattack [is] in progress against the office of the Information Commission," he told Parliament. Reid described at length "the stubborn persistence of a culture of secrecy in Ottawa" that "distorts the thinking of the citizenry, giving rise to unfounded conspiracy theories and an unnecessarily high level of mistrust of governments." This "love of secrecy is so deeply entrenched that extraordinary steps are taken by public servants to maintain it even in the face of a legislated right of access." He described how the act had changed the way the government operates: "The attitude has truly become: 'Why write it when you can speak it? Why speak it when you can nod? Why nod when you can wink?'"

The opposition parties played their assigned role to perfection upon release of Reid's report, as did the government. The opposition, especially the Canadian Alliance, harangued the government in the Commons, lambasted it through the media, complained during the subsequent election campaign: to no discernible effect. The issue of the government's handling of information never caught on with the public. It was seen as just another manifestation of how governments always operate – after all, the Mulroney Conservatives had treated information no differently from the Trudeau or Chrétien Liberals – and seemed an issue of pressing interest only to those within sight of the Peace Tower. Sensing this, the government offered ritualistic promises of reform mixed with declarations that it was the most open government in the history of Canada.

A succession of Liberal ministers of justice has pledged to strengthen the act. After all, the Liberal Party promised in its 1993 Red Book, "Open government will be the watchword of the Liberal program." But the case for strengthening collides with three of Ottawa's entrenched cultural habits. The first is the public service's reluctance to take initiatives within a steeply hierarchical system presided over by the Prime Minister's Office. The second is the government's own determination to control information. The third is to promote at all costs and in all places, and to the greatest extent possible, the governing party's political standing.

The government's Janus-like attitude to information – eager to release what it wishes; hostile to everything else – produces two consequences. It can enhance the political prospects of the governing party, since the party can maximize control over how and what the public knows about the activities of government. Controlling the message by packaging information in the most favourable light, spending public money on advertising, ensuring a constancy of presentation, and never admitting error are the governing party's communications priorities. At least the government must think these advantages exist, or else so much time, effort, and money would not be spent on communications. But the same two-faced mentality also encourages public cynicism about government, since citizens sense they are not getting the full story about what government does. Assaulted daily by advertising's seductive implausibilities, citizens necessarily build up layers of psychological protection, including a cynical attitude toward the people who are peddling these implausibilities. The observable unwillingness of governments to admit error, except under the most exceptional circumstances, and their determination to massage information, augments the public cynicism.

The Imperial Prime Minister

Critics scoff at the thesis of the imperial prime minister. They sniff that the prime minister is hugely consequential, but what else is new? Prime ministers have always dominated the government, and those with a parliamentary majority have had their way with the House of Commons. They have always appointed senators and senior officials. Cabinet ministers have always been beholden to them. After all, did not Prime Minister Mackenzie King keep ministerial letters of resignation in his drawer, just in case he needed them? Nobody ever doubted who was "boss" when Sir John A. Macdonald ran the government, even when sympathetic newspapers euphemistically described him as "indisposed," that is, hungover or drunk. In 1896, when Sir Wilfrid Laurier attracted a star-studded cast of provincial premiers and other prominent Liberals to what became popularly known as the "ministry of all the talents," everyone knew that he still had the last word. A smattering of ministers may get their names engraved posthumously on a public building, but statues are built, lakes and airports are named, and currency is graced by former prime ministers. The parliamentary system, unlike the U.S. system of checks and balances, is designed to get things done with centralized power within a parliamentary majority. The Canadians took their conception of liberty from the British, not the Americans. The Crown was the friend of liberty, not its potential foe. Through elected ministers, the Crown would uphold liberty within the conventions of parliamentary democracy and the common law, and if ministers failed to discharge their duties, then the people could turf the rascals out. Here was the ultimate check on abuse of power or political wrong-headedness by the "elected dictatorship" of the prime minister.

The critics are right, up to a point. Power has always been largely centralized in the hands of the prime minister, but that a state of affairs has always prevailed does not by definition make it appropriate for contemporary realities. Moreover, prime-ministerial power is now more centralized than ever, and the centralization is increasingly out-of-step with the operating practices of other major institutions, the needs of modern government, and the expectations of citizens.

The prime-ministerial system is sharply hierarchical. Cabinet government presupposes collective decision-making and responsibility, a collection of equals, with some inevitably being more equal than others because of the importance of their portfolios. No one ever doubted that the prime minister – the title itself reveals the conclusion – was first among equals. But in the modern age, with the media focused on him and the entire apparatus of a sprawling government at his disposal, he is more powerful than ever. The institutional checks on his power within the parliamentary system are extremely weak. So are those within the governing party. The only checks that do exist are more nebulous ones: the shifting sands of public opinion, the possibility of adverse media coverage, and potential conflict with provincial premiers, although a clever prime minister can turn those conflicts to his political advantage. The prime minister has it both ways. He is not only *primus* within the governing party, where he exercises dominant power, but the Canadian political system provides no effective check or balance to the exercise of that power. The first-past-the-post electoral system magnifies his victories and thereby augments his power; neither the Commons nor Senate effectively check that power.

The nature of television accentuates the attention focused on the prime minister. Television struggles unsuccessfully to report issues, especially complicated ones: it prefers to tell stories through personalities. And it prefers black-and-white clashes among the fewest number of personalities possible. Therefore, the nature of television leads it to focus on the prime minister, whose every public utterance is covered as a consequence. During an election campaign, for example, parties may send ministers around the country, but their campaigning receives a fraction of coverage given to the prime minister. In the United States, there may be debates between vice-presidential candidates in addition to those between the presidential ones, but only party leaders debate in Canada. During and between campaigns, therefore, the prime minister is the only national spokesman for the party that the media consistently covers.

The full cabinet, as we have said, is not a decision-making body but rather a mini-sounding-board, a slimmed-down caucus. Memoirs of cabinet ministers and academic studies of the workings of government all attest to the prime minister's sway over cabinet. Rare indeed are the occasions when the prime minister does not get his way. Ministers seldom stand up to him. Regional ministers of bygone eras were somebodies in Ottawa and back home; only a handful of them could be so described in recent years: John Crosbie, Allan MacEachen, Lloyd Axworthy. Public-opinion surveys reveal that, when asked to identify cabinet ministers, Canadians score well for the prime minister, maybe another minister or two, then draw near-blanks.

Hierarchical systems are increasingly out-of-favour elsewhere in modern society. Private corporations now preach the gospel of flattening management structures, "inclusive" decision-making, creating incentives at lower management levels. Command-and-control management systems, it would seem, cannot maximize performance in large companies, because they do not create sufficient positive incentives for employees to excel. Flexibility is today's byword in private corporations, because communications are so swift and competition so fierce. Command-and-control systems are the antithesis of flexibility, since by the time the top echelon has absorbed the necessary information, sifted it, made decisions, then passed them back down the chain of command, the competitive world may have changed. Universities, albeit quite special institutions, are highly collective in their decision-making, sometimes to a fault, with faculty councils, senates, boards of governors, and unions. They work best, as do other public institutions, such as hospitals and schools, when professionals providing the core services (professors, doctors, nurses, teachers) feel they are part of the institutions' governance, with their views considered, their talents recognized.

Canadians live and work in a society increasingly sceptical of hierarchy. This scepticism has been widely analyzed by pollsters, academics, and thoughtful journalists as part of an overall "decline of deference" towards authority figures and established institutions. Political scientist Neil Nevitte calls these trends "turbulence in authority relations" marked in part by "declining confidence in hierarchical institutions." Yet Canada's prime-ministerial system of government remains just that. Peter Hennessy, Britain's leading student of that country's recent prime-ministerial history, ends his 686-page study by urging resistance "to a command model of central government presided over by a single (or chief) executive in the person of an unashamedly dominant Prime Minister, with an administrative back-up to match." The same might be said of the Canadian system.

*Our Friendly
Dictators*

Napoleon would not have won the battle of Austerlitz nor would Confederate General Robert E. Lee have kept the Union armies from Richmond without the blunders of their military foes. Brilliant generals both, Napoleon could not have asked for weaker opposing strategists until he met Kutuzov and Wellington, while Lee exploited the timidity and tactical errors of all the Union generals until Ulysses S. Grant assumed command of the Army of the Potomac.

In politics, as in war, leaders and parties must know their foes and capitalize upon their mistakes. Canada's Liberals, clever political strategists to be sure, have nonetheless been blessed by their opponents' folly. The Liberals' victories have been as much due to the blunders of their opponents as to their own inherent skills. All the Liberals needed to do was to avoid underestimating political adversaries, as they did with Conservative leaders John Diefenbaker and Joe Clark. Jean Chrétien knows that pitfall well, since he has made a career of being underestimated himself. Chrétien likes to compare himself to former U.S. President Harry Truman, who snatched victory from the Republicans in the 1948 election against widespread predictions of his political demise.

The Liberals were Canada's dominant party in the twentieth century. They ruled for about sixty-nine and a half years; the Conservatives for thirty-one and a half. The Liberals governed for more than two-thirds of the century, only three times briefly with a minority. The Liberals were arguably the most successful political party among twentieth-century democracies. Having won three consecutive majorities – in the elections of 1993, 1997, and 2000 – they will govern for some years yet. If their political adversaries continue to misread Canadian history and contemporary Canada, the Liberals may go on ruling for a very long time, and Canada will continue to be a country of de facto one-party governance.

The Liberals cannot be blamed for exploiting their adversaries' mistakes. The Liberals are not at fault if their opponents refuse to understand that Canadians are a fundamentally moderate people and that ideology is the enemy of political success in national politics. All those years in power created an almost atavistic Liberal sense of political self-preservation. Occasionally, the Liberals turned inwards and fired on themselves, as during John Turner's leadership, but more often they have displayed a purposeful resolve to stay united, or at least not to permit internal tensions to divert attention from remaining ahead of the opposition parties. The Liberals have been dismissed as a party without ideology, invariably by frustrated ideologues of the left or right who sit on the opposition benches. The Liberals' ideology – defined as ideas that form a theory or system – is the pursuit of power. In that narrowly defined sense, in fact, the Liberals are Canada's strongest ideologues. The Liberals do have ideas, but these need not fit into a tidy intellectual framework. The Liberals' ideology is not an intellectual system of ideas per se, but the use of ideas to pursue the narrower one of power.

This distinction between the ideology of ideas and the ideology of power has rendered the Liberals intellectually elastic and sometimes politically cynical. If an idea does not suit their ideology, which is pursuit of power, they will abandon it. If another party has an idea that threatens the Liberals pursuit of power, they will steal it. Critics sneer that the Liberals are cynical; Liberals would describe themselves as pragmatic. Either way, they have been successful, which is another way of saying that they have understood the complexities of Canada better than their opponents.

The complexity they certainly understood better was the historic one of relations between French- and English-speaking Canadians. Sir John A. Macdonald, a unilingual Upper Canadian Tory, once remarked that any Canadian government needed to be "Frenchified." Macdonald governed with that lesson in mind, but after he died it was the Liberals that practised "Frenchification" more often than Sir John's party. The Liberals did not always win Quebec, although most of the time they did, but the French fact in Canada remained central to their political calculations.

The Liberals counted on political strength elsewhere in Canada, too. They always boasted a base in the Maritimes and, after 1949, in Newfoundland. It seems hard to remember these days, but they were often the dominant party in western Canada until Conservative leader John Diefenbaker turned the Prairies Tory blue. The Liberals, heirs to the pre-Confederation Grits, always enjoyed support across Ontario. Even when Ontario's largest city was known as "Tory Toronto," the Liberals had their newspapers and supporters there; outside the provincial capital the Liberals enjoyed wide swaths of predictable support. They were competitive in the old Grit heartland of southwestern Ontario, strong throughout the North, and dominant in all ridings with French-speaking voters.

Western European immigrants who flocked to Toronto and other urban areas after the Second World War arrived under Liberal governments, and returned the favour by voting Liberal election after election. The Liberals assiduously courted these immigrant voters and proved adept at integrating them and their descendants into the party. Some of these groups were so unswervingly Liberal that Prime Minister Brian Mulroney once remarked, after his Conservatives had scored the largest victory in Canadian political history in 1984, that of all the demographic groups in Canada only "Mediterranean Catholics" had remained faithful to the Liberals. Inspired by Liberal successes, the Mulroney government raised immigration levels far beyond those of the

Trudeau years, hoping for subsequent political appreciation, although these higher immigration levels produced few gains for the Tories.

Liberal strength sprawling across Canada sensitized the party to regional complexities. The Liberals became the classic "brokerage" party, absorbing (sometimes belatedly) the concerns of every region, negotiating compromises in the prisms of Cabinet and caucus, spreading patronage through ministers and MPs, and refraining wherever possible from alienating voters in any particular region, especially Quebec – although during and since the Trudeau years, the Liberals have managed to alienate much of western Canada. Prior to Trudeau, when protest parties sprang up in the West, the Liberals simply tried to smother them by adopting policies to appeal to the disaffected. Progressives on the Prairies were just "Liberals in a hurry," observed Prime Minister Mackenzie King, who went about dousing the protest and enfolding Progressives into the Liberal ranks. Worried about the upsurge in support for the Co-operative Commonwealth Federation in the 1945 election, the Liberals hustled to introduce post-war social policies. The CCF dropped from 28 seats in 1945 to 13 in 1949; the Liberals rose from 122 to 191.

Booted from office by Conservative Prime Minister John Diefenbaker's victories in 1957 and 1958, the Liberals entered a period of effective parliamentary opposition and, more important, internal reflection. It seemed they would face a long spell in opposition, since Diefenbaker had amassed the largest parliamentary majority to that point in Canadian politics. But opposition proved a creative period for the Liberals. Their "thinkers" conference in Kingston focused on policies, particularly in the social area, and this served the party well when Diefenbaker exhausted his political capital, fell into a minority government in 1962, and turned power over to the Liberals in a minority government in 1963.

The Pearson years were full of parliamentary turmoil, but also nation-building policies. The flag, new cultural policies, Medicare, pensions, social welfare – these all emerged from that remarkably fertile period. The economy had recovered from the recession of 1961–62; the government's books remained balanced; revenues seemed sufficiently buoyant to support new programs. These were pan-Canadian policies, although the social policies were negotiated with provinces – including Quebec, whose government demanded new powers, either for itself alone or for all provinces. Pearson, a diplomat by training, tried to balance or broker the new regional forces through "co-operative federalism." A mixture of traditional brokerage politics and pan-Canadian approaches characterized the Pearson government.

Pierre Trudeau, after sixteen years as Liberal leader, narrowed but deepened the Liberal coalition. He drove western Canada almost completely away from the party and made the Liberals the decidedly second choice in large swaths of Ontario. He managed to barely survive with a minority government in 1972 because he swept Quebec, the province that remained for all his years in office the anchor of his coalition. Among multicultural Canadians, however, Trudeau's personal popularity knew few limits. He scorned Pearson's approach to Quebec nationalism that consisted of trying to mollify it through concessions, arrangements, deals, and negotiations. Instead, Trudeau attacked Quebec nationalism remorselessly and instead set about adopting pan-Canadian policies as an alternative for Quebeckers: official bilingualism, equalization, support for official-language minority groups, appointments of French-speakers to important national positions, the Charter of Rights and Freedoms. High-minded about what he defined as the important issues of state, Trudeau learned how to be a political operator. Directly, or through trusted lieutenants, he greased the Liberal Party machine, doling out patronage, assuming that his ministers would steer government contracts to Liberal friends, funnelling government spending disproportionately into Liberal ridings. At one level, then, Trudeau governed as a pan-Canadian leader with arresting ideas and a compelling vision of how to protect personal liberty and secure Canadian unity; at another, he followed the path of previous Liberal prime ministers in using political power for blatantly partisan purposes.

Doctrinaire and determined about a few core issues, Trudeau could be ruthlessly pragmatic, even cynical, about others. His economic leadership, for example, was erratic. It ranged from warning about the perils of excessive expectations for government to creating new expectations, from worrying about federal deficits to presiding over a huge buildup of them, from criticizing wage and price controls as an antidote to inflation to imposing them. Trudeau could even be pragmatic in the constitutional field, although this is usually forgotten. He floored the provincial premiers with whom he had been battling when suddenly, at a 1978 conference, he offered them fourteen points that collectively amounted to the largest package of federal concessions ever presented the provinces. Greedy and short-sighted, however, the premiers wanted more and believed they would get it from the soon-to-be elected Conservative prime minister, Joe Clark. Little did the premiers realize that Clark's government would self-destruct so rapidly, allowing Trudeau to return to power, determined this time to force through constitutional changes. Trudeau had offered concessions to Quebec premier Robert Bourassa; now he even offered some to Parti Québécois premier René Lévesque. Trudeau accepted constitutional protection for provincial control of natural resources. He curried aboriginals' favour by going way beyond what provincial premiers wanted in enshrining aboriginal rights in the constitution. Trudeau had his bottom lines, and to these he stubbornly clung, but he could be remarkably pragmatic to achieve them. Though confrontational in argument, combative by nature, confident in his intellectual prowess, Trudeau could, if politically threatened or blocked, show astonishing flexibility, explaining away inconsistencies and contradictions as insouciantly as he took his sports car for a spin. His style certainly differed from that of his grey Liberal predecessors; his willingness to shift with circumstances did not.

The Education of Jean Chrétien

Jean Chrétien could barely speak English when he arrived in Ottawa in 1963. He had a law degree, a middling practice in an unprepossessing Quebec city, a Liberal family pedigree, a sunny public disposition, and a disguised but burning ambition. Tumult greeted the rookie MP. The Liberal government of Prime Minister Pearson was beset by scandals fanned by the embittered leader of the Opposition and former prime minister John Diefenbaker. The Pearson government also struggled to cope with Quebec's Quiet Revolution. The French-speaking ministers from Quebec experienced hellish pressures after the 1963 election. They seemed to be disproportionately targeted for attacks by the wounded Tories; Quebec nationalists accused them of being sellouts. Chrétien, who was too young to be targeted by either firing line, nonetheless watched the crossfire. He learned early on that a federal politician from Quebec was subject to pressures unknown to those from other parts of Canada. Debates elsewhere were not about a politician's patriotism or personal identity – but they were in Quebec and, as such, could be nasty. A Quebec federalist in Ottawa needed a thicker skin than other politicians.

Although a graduate of a classical college and Laval law school, Chrétien never considered himself – and was certainly never considered by others – an intellectual. He could not carry himself in the grand style of a Louis St. Laurent, a Jean Lesage, or a Jacques Parizeau; he could not conduct an argument with the

fierce logic and rhetorical flair of Pierre Trudeau. He was instead
a verbal brawler, his French sometimes fractured, his sense of politics something akin to a street fight in which the weak ultimately
yield to the strong. In street fights, little room exists for middle
positions. In the existential battle for the hearts, minds, and ultimately the votes of Quebeckers, Chrétien was never tempted by
the convoluted compromises of semi-secessionists or hemi-demi
federalists seeking a way-station between outright separation
and Canadian federalism. He offered an unalloyed federalism and
settled into its corner in the never-ending bout with separatists.
From this position his political stock soared outside Quebec, but
he was left the object of scorn, ridicule, and even hatred among
Quebec nationalists. Viewing politics as a street fight, however,
provided him with instructions in the virtues of absolute loyalty,
since the other side could exploit weak links or dissidents.

Having chosen his corner, Chrétien needed to learn the complexities of success, which is another way of saying he needed a
lifelong course in the complexities of Canada. His first ministerial assignment, Minister of Aboriginal Affairs, provided an excellent introduction, and not just because he learned something
about aboriginals. That portfolio took him to corners of Canada
he would never otherwise have visited. It also provided an early
lesson in the perils of an excessively cerebral approach to politics.

Prime Minister Pierre Trudeau conceived of rights as inherent in an individual. Collective rights struck him an intellectually
dangerous, since the collectivity, in pursuing what the majority
considered its rights, could trample on those of the individual.
This was nationalism's dark side, and he wished as prime minister to wean French-speaking Quebeckers from their defensive,
collective, nationalist instincts towards fuller participation as
individuals in Canadian life. He applied the same logic to aboriginals, and so in a White Paper that Chrétien had to defend, the
federal government proposed abolishing the Indian Act and
bringing aboriginals as individual rights-holders into the Canadian

mainstream. The aboriginal leadership reacted swiftly and fiercely. Of course, they chafed at the dependence that flowed from the act, but it recognized special Crown obligations to their communities, or "nations," as they were beginning to be called in the late 1960s. So implacably did the aboriginals oppose the White Paper that Trudeau and Chrétien withdrew it. The lesson for Chrétien? Don't push people where they do not wish to go.

Subsequent portfolios, including Treasury Board and Finance, taught him about the inner workings of government and also about the arts of political camouflage. Chrétien later boasted that, at Treasury Board, he had earned the nickname of "Doctor No," because he turned down so many spending requests. He quite likely gave himself that nickname, because government spending roared ahead while he presided over the Treasury Board, and it also leapt while he was finance minister. The nickname suited his purposes, however, because he could appear simultaneously as a fiscal conservative and a big-spending liberal, thereby allowing people to read into him whatever they chose. Not burdened by ideology or weighed down by intellect, Chrétien could shift positions as political opportunism demanded – beyond certain bedrock convictions such as a passionate belief in Canadian federalism, bilingualism, and the Charter of Rights and Freedoms. He could oppose the Meech Lake constitutional accord while suggesting that, behind-the-scenes, he had tried to save it. In Opposition, he could criticize Canada–U.S. free trade as dangerous to Canadian sovereignty, then embrace it as prime minister. He could pooh-pooh the severity of the nation's deficit problem, as he did throughout his leadership campaigns, then act resolutely to eliminate the deficit in government. He could pose as "Doctor No," while presiding over large spending increases. He could come across as just a regular guy, "*le petit gars de Shawinigan*," while swanning around with the Desmarais clan of the Power Corporation, into which one of his daughters married. He could publish a largely ghost-written autobiography entitled *Straight from the Heart*, in which his portrayal of himself as a creature of emotion masked a steely ambition.

Chrétien was fully formed upon becoming prime minister, as his predecessors were not. Trudeau, for example, was fully formed intellectually but not politically. He needed to learn many of the arts of political management and public administration. Mulroney had never been in government before becoming prime minister, and had been only briefly leader of the Opposition. John Turner had served an apprenticeship in government, but his political skills rusted during his time in the private sector. Kim Campbell had been a minister, but for nowhere near as long as Chrétien. Joe Clark had served only in opposition when he became prime minister, and it showed. Chrétien had grown up, survived, and ultimately thrived within a political system that he knew and had mastered. He did not bring an outsider's scepticism to government; he had not spent very long on the Opposition benches chafing at the indignities of an MP's life; he had not been alienated by government, just disappointed when he was out of office.

Chrétien told friends before he became prime minister that he would have three overriding objectives in office: to prevent Quebec from seceding, to stop Canada from falling too closely into the embrace of the United States, and to ensure Canada did not require help from the International Monetary Fund. These were all perfectly laudable objectives of the kind any would-be prime minister might espouse. But they were all essentially defensive ambitions, meant to prevent worse things from happening. In this sense, Chrétien was the classic conservative, determined to avoid the worst outcomes, a cautious pragmatist aware of potential troubles. Chrétien was also an institutional conservative, having thrived within the existing system. He changed the cabinet committee structure, as almost all prime ministers do, but left the rest of government essentially unchanged. A veteran of constitutional wars while he was Trudeau's minister of justice, and an observer-cum-participant in Brian Mulroney's constitutional adventures, he refused to reopen the constitutional file. He did not even like holding First Ministers' meetings, and those he convened were private affairs rather than prolonged public palavers of the kind that dotted the Trudeau and Mulroney years. Such conferences invited premiers to attack Ottawa, and Chrétien recoiled from handing them this opportunity.

Within the Liberal Party, Chrétien had always played the loyal soldier, carrying out orders, expressing divergent opinions privately, cheering up Liberal supporters in and out of Parliament with partisan attacks and patriotic speeches. He expected from his backbenchers and ministers the same absolute loyalty he had always displayed when he was in their shoes. Political success, Chrétien's experience instructed him, required minimizing opportunities for trouble from whatever sources. He therefore never admitted error or gave critics an inch. Critics complained that Chrétien did not work very hard – he did like plenty of golf – but they misread his use of time. He gave mandates and instructions, and expected them to be obeyed. He learned whom he could trust, and counted on them to deliver. He kept himself in excellent physical condition. He had little time for abstract arguments or theories or sweeping structural reforms; he did not like open-ended debates. He especially disliked debates he could not control, as occurred in federal–provincial relations, constitutional reforms, Royal Commissions, free votes in the House of Commons. He was a practitioner in politics, not a pedagogue, because nothing in his intellectual makeup led him to be interested in ideas for their own sake and everything in his political experience suggested that an aroused, engaged citizenry might cause trouble for the government and, given Canada's divisions, might split the country on regional, ethnic, or linguistic lines.

He was smart with journalists, never letting them know when they got under his skin, because that would betray a sign of weakness – except in the case of *National Post* owner Conrad Black, whose ambitions he squashed for a seat in the British House of Lords. Chrétien's personal mannerisms revealed someone always on the lookout for trouble. His restless eyes roamed the room looking for the next person he would greet. Conversations swirled around his own comments, jokes, or recollections, since these he could control. He possessed an excellent sense of humour, which he used to good effect to extricate himself from tricky political situations and to convey the impression that he was just a regular guy. He definitely lacked U.S. President Franklin Roosevelt's oratorical skill and he was certainly not to the manor born, but Oliver Wendell Holmes's quip about Roosevelt might suit Chrétien: a second-class intellect but a first-class temperament. When crossed, though, Chrétien had a nasty streak, as all successful street fighters do. No one lasted long if he considered them other than loyal.

Until Chrétien became Liberal leader, he had displayed the sure-footedness of a football halfback. He executed plays designed by others, displaying a nifty mixture of straightforward determination and an ability to dodge tackles. Best of all, he did not fumble and never questioned those who designed the team's strategy. Pierre Trudeau and the Quebec intellectual ministers he trusted, such as Gerard Pelletier and Marc Lalonde, displayed a certain contempt for his analytical capacities but a grudging respect for his ability to carry out orders. Most of the Trudeau heavyweights from Quebec supported John Turner against Chrétien in the 1984 leadership race, reckoning both that the party needed an English-speaking leader after the Trudeau years and that Chrétien did not have what it took to be prime minister.

Legitimate questions circled around Chrétien as a prospective leader. Could a successful political halfback, required to execute the strategy of others and run only one play at a time, switch to being a quarterback, who needed to think several plays ahead, take the temperature of the game, and inspire not just himself but the entire team? Did someone whom the press labelled "yesterday's man" possess the vision to lead? Chrétien answered those questions affirmatively, perhaps because he understood Canada better than his adversaries, and knew that his particular mixture of intuition and skills matched the tenor of the times.

Chrétien boasted – the boast formed part of the public image he crafted for himself – that he liked to leave his office with a clean desk. Aides kept their briefing notes short; he was indeed notorious as a minister for not reading long policy papers or cabinet documents. One problem at a time, that's how he wanted to govern. Visions, even if he could articulate them, might raise expectations, and high expectations could seldom be met. Visions required some kind of philosophical framework or overarching set of ideas, and Chrétien lacked both – indeed he was suspicious of both. High-minded oratory that someone else wrote, he could read, but the words seemed flat. He spoke neither official language clearly. His mangled English syntax and errors in French grammar made sophisticated listeners wince and sometimes forced journalists to compare notes to figure out what he had meant. After almost four decades in politics, he had said nothing anyone could ever remember as memorable, except his favourite boilerplate, "Canada Is Number One."

The avoidance of trouble, Chrétien's political leitmotif, meant never engaging Canadians in serious debates about the future. He did think ahead in a problem-solving sort of way, but he preferred that Canadians did not. Thinking ahead might require admitting problems, and the admission of a problem could lead to troublesome debates that he might not control. It was safer, he thought, just to go about business rather than worrying people about tomorrow. If challenges did indeed lie ahead, it was too politically dangerous to mobilize the population to debate them. Whether this approach satisfied his critics, it, too, seemed to fit the tenor of the times.

The Canadian body politic had been pummelled for almost twenty years before Chrétien became prime minister. Canadians

ached from the battles launched and fought by Prime Ministers
Trudeau and Mulroney. There seemed no respite from them;
once one battle ended, another began, and sometimes two or
three major battles were being fought at once. Each time, these
prime ministers warned Canadians that, if they did not do this or
that, terrible consequences might follow. They were told that, as
a people, Canadians had to pull up their socks, or else. Wage-and-
price controls, Canadians were warned, had become necessary,
because without them inflation would eat the Canadian economy alive. Government spending had to be cut or the deficit
would become so unbearable that the International Monetary
Fund might intervene. Domestic energy prices had to be controlled or the Arab sheiks would hold Canada to ransom. The
National Energy Policy had to be imposed or else producing
provinces would get too rich at the expense of consuming ones.
A constitutional deal must be found or Quebec would leave
Canada. Supporters cried that free trade with the United States
was required or Canada's standard of living would decline; opponents warned that free trade would be the end of Canadian
sovereignty. Future generations would never forgive defeat of the
Charlottetown constitutional accord, cried Mulroney, while lit-
erally tearing up the accord before the television cameras. High
interest rates, soaring deficits, rising national indebtedness, constitutional psychodramas, Quebec referendums, Western alienation,
federal–provincial energy fights, Canada–U.S. free trade, the
Goods and Services Tax, patriation of the constitution, aboriginal demands, mini-scandals, the CF-18 decision . . . the whole
Canadian political world seemed a tornado of problems. By the
end of his time, Canadians wanted no more of Trudeau; long
before the end of his second government, Canadians wanted
nothing more of Mulroney.

Trudeau and Mulroney, in their different ways, were Canadian
patriots, but to get Canadians to do what they wanted, these

prime ministers constantly told Canadians, directly or implicitly, that they had to change, or else. They were warning Canadians, pushing and cajoling them, driving ambitious agendas forward, inspiring or angering the population, but leaving few Canadians unmoved. The temperature of the body politic ranged from simmering to white hot, and some of the debates left lacerating scars. Clashing visions, vaulting ambitions, exhortatory rhetoric, exhausting conferences, intense election campaigns, a national referendum – Canadians experienced them all. They were ready for a rest.

Along came Chrétien, the anti-visionary, who told them what a lot of Canadians wanted to hear: that "Canada Is Number One," that, sure, Canada had problems, but it was still the best country in the world. No sacrifices would be demanded, no existential debates launched, no bold agendas unveiled. He would solve problems because, well, they had to be tackled, but not as part of some ambitious scheme to change Canada. Canadians were a damn fine people just as they were, which is what they wanted desperately to hear, and he would ask nothing more of them and to govern as the ultimate pragmatist.

Of course, his political opponents chafed at this apparently humdrum approach to politics, because they wanted major changes – separation for the Bloc Québécois; institutional political reform, decentralization, tax reductions, and massive spending cuts for the Reform Party – and mobilized the alienated and disaffected to support them politically. But they eventually proved to be no match for Chrétien's Liberals, who enveloped chunks of the Mulroney agenda, borrowed some ideas from Reform, added a few initiatives of their own, tried hard to avoid stirring dangerous passions, and found themselves blessed by a divided opposition. Once again, the Liberals were the country's natural governing party employing a system of prime-ministerial government that, quite naturally, Jean Chrétien saw no reason to change.

The Disappearing NDP

Procrustean politics do not win elections in Canada. Parties will lose if they try to shape the country to their message rather than shaping their message to the country – the whole country, not just regional or ideological elements of it. This is not merely the lesson of the past. It resonates today, as can be seen in the Liberals' three majority governments, the collapse of the Conservatives, the repeated failure of the Reform and Alliance parties to defeat the Liberals, and the marginalization of the New Democratic Party.

The saddest failure belongs to the NDP. Once a party with influence but no power, the NDP now finds itself without either. For this sorry state of affairs, the NDP can blame only itself. To the Liberals' delight, these are the worst of times for the federal NDP. A weakened NDP allows the Liberals to worry less about their so-called left flank and to pile up additional parliamentary seats, especially in urban Ontario and parts of Northern Ontario where the NDP used to be competitive. The raw voting numbers tell the story of the federal NDP's decline. The NDP won between 14 and 20 per cent of the popular vote in every election from 1963 to 1988. In that quarter-century, the NDP captured 20 per cent of the national popular vote three times, 19 per cent once, 18 per cent three times, and 17 per cent once. It reached a high-water mark of forty-three seats in 1988, having built up parliamentary strength from seventeen seats in 1963. Since 1988, the bottom has fallen out of the NDP under its federal leaders Audrey McLaughlin and Alexa McDonough. The NDP tumbled from the 14-to-20-per-cent range to 7 per cent of the national popular vote in the 1993 election, 11 per cent in 1997, and 8 per cent in 2000. The NDP lost therefore in these three elections about half the share of the national vote it had captured in the 1963 to 1985 period.

The NDP might take some comfort from its improvement in Nova Scotia and other provinces of Atlantic Canada in the 1997 election, an improvement partly due to McDonough's profile as

a former NDP leader in Nova Scotia. It also remained competitive in the NDP heartland of Saskatchewan and the North End
of Winnipeg. But almost unrelieved gloom darkened the picture
elsewhere. The party failed to capture an Ontario riding in the
1993 and 1997 elections, and won only one Ontario seat in 2000.
That federal decline mirrored the fallen fortunes of the Ontario
provincial NDP. It used to win about a quarter of the popular vote
in the 1970s, but dropped to about half of that share in the 1990s
(except for Premier Bob Rae's fluky victory in 1990). In British
Columbia, the party could count on seven to nineteen federal
seats between 1963 and 1988; since then, the NDP has been
reduced to two or three in Vancouver. In the 1963–1988 period,
the NDP was either highly competitive or dominant across great
swaths of Vancouver Island, the mainland coast, and the northern Interior. These constituencies have now all been lost to the
Reform/Canadian Alliance. As in Ontario, the B.C. decline of
the federal NDP mirrored the reduced fortunes of the provincial
NDP, which suffered a shellacking defeat in the provincial election of 2001. For other parties, a provincial decline does not
necessarily mean trouble for the federal party, but the federal NDP
has always been structured as a kind of federation of provincial
parties. NDP organizers routinely work in both federal and provincial campaigns; the federal party relies on provincial organizations
for money and workers. Core NDP voters support the party at
both electoral levels. If the provincial New Democratic Parties
are weak, that weakness usually wounds the federal party.

The NDP remained off the map, of course, in federal elections
in Alberta and Quebec. The NDP's Quebec showing remained
derisory – 1 per cent of the popular vote in the 1993 election,
2 per cent in 1997, and 1.8 per cent in 2000. In the country's four
most populous provinces – Ontario, British Columbia, Alberta,
and Quebec – the NDP slid backwards or remained almost invisible. The failure of the NDP to be competitive in these four
provinces bodes ill for the party, since all except Quebec will

grow in population – and therefore parliamentary seats – in the decades ahead. A party rooted in provinces with stagnant or declining populations is doomed to increasing marginality.

The NDP remained largely in denial during this slide towards marginality. The British Labour Party roared into office in 1997, then won thumping re-election in 2001, but rather than learning anything from these triumphs, most of the federal NDP scorned Prime Minister Tony Blair for selling out the cause of social democracy. Nor did the federal party seem inspired by the moderate approach of the German Social Democrats under Chancellor Gerhard Schroeder. In Saskatchewan, the provincial NDP continued to be the dominant party (although it lost ground in the 2000 election), but that party's hallmark combination of fiscal prudence and progressive social policies did not impress the federal NDP. At the NDP leadership convention that chose McDonough, federal New Democrats and national trade-union leaders privately expressed palpable scepticism and even contempt for the Saskatchewan NDP, an attitude that hurt the leadership chances of Lorne Nystrom, a veteran Saskatchewan NDP MP. Compromises that the governing Saskatchewan NDP had made, of necessity, after inheriting a fiscal mess from the provincial Conservatives, only underscored for federal New Democrats what they considered their provincial cousins' milquetoast commitment to progressive reform.

An aborted process of internal party reflection occurred after the 1997 election. Wise New Democrats appreciated that the party's slight national improvement over the 1993 election result flowed from McDonough's personal popularity in Nova Scotia and from temporary regional unhappiness with Liberal changes to unemployment insurance. These cool heads understood the party's more fundamental predicament, painfully revealed in the massive National Election Study of the 1997 election that was prepared by four leading political scientists. That study ought to have punctured many of the party's self-sustaining myths. For example, Canadians employed in "manual occupations" – the classic "working" or "ordinary" Canadians targeted by the NDP – were no more likely to support the NDP than they were other parties. Public-sector unionized employees – supposedly integral to the NDP's core constituency – preferred Reform to the NDP by 23 to 18 per cent. Only 17 per cent of voters in the bottom fifth of income-earners supported the NDP. The Reform Party – to say nothing of the Liberals – won more votes among union households than did the NDP.

The NDP trumpeted its progressive attitudes towards women, but more women voted Reform than NDP, and many more women supported the Liberals than they did Reform. The core NDP vote – that is, people who identified themselves as New Democrats – had shrivelled since the 1980s. The study revealed that 53 per cent of the electorate thought the NDP "out of touch with the times," including a fifth of the NDP's own supporters. The study concluded:

> It is not simply the fact that New Democrats are located so far from the median Canadian voters that should give the party strategists pause. Even more worrying for the party is the relatively small number of voters who form its ideological constituency. [There is] a lukewarm commitment of even its own supporters to some of the party's traditional social democratic prescriptions. It is hard to escape the conclusion that these principles are simply not very relevant in the minds of Canadian voters. . . . The price of ideological purity may be continued marginalization.

Less than two years after the dispiriting 1997 election, New Democrats gathered for what was heralded as a major policy conference. Those who favoured a modernization of the NDP – that is, bringing the party closer to "median Canadian voters" – believed they had a chance to swing the party towards more electorally attractive positions. The pragmatists had organized trips for McDonough to Europe to meet British Labour Party officials and social democrats in continental European countries who had long experience in the compromises of governing. NDP caucus members took a cross-country train ride, and the pragmatists hoped that the journey's soul-searching had laid the groundwork for a rethinking of party doctrine.

McDonough, it turned out, had not learned anything in Europe. Her trips had been a complete waste of time. She confirmed her critics' worst fears: that she was an intellectual child of earlier times, incapable of understanding the economic and social shifts that made old-style socialists and 1960s-vintage social democracy irrelevant at worst, marginally relevant at best. McDonough was not prepared for a confrontation with party ideologues or trade-union leaders, who considered the NDP an extension of their own union-management battles against "corporate domination" of the Canadian economy. As a result, the convention was dominated by the union leaders, such as Buzz Hargrove of the Canadian Autoworkers' Union and those atop the Canadian Union of Public Employees, plus more radical NDP MPs such as British Columbia's Svend Robinson. McDonough was caught like the proverbial deer in the headlights. Liberal observers at the convention could not contain their glee that the NDP, having moved away from "median Canadian voters" and paid a fierce electoral price for that movement, had decided to remain there.

The chance for modernization was lost, disappointing pragmatic NDP MPs, such as Chris Axworthy of Saskatchewan and Nelson Riis of British Columbia. Instead of presenting a sober-minded, pragmatic, moderately left-of-centre approach that had brought social-democratic parties electoral success elsewhere, the NDP fell back on its old nostrums, the most comfortable of which was that the party remained the sole defender of Canada's social programs. Not surprisingly, when Chrétien called the 2000 election, this nostrum was just about all the NDP could pull down from the cupboard. It made the defence of health care the defining issue of its campaign, and paid a predictable price, since Canadians had long ceased seeing the NDP as it saw itself – as the best guarantor of the country's social programs. The party fell back to 8.5 per cent of the popular vote and thirteen seats, barely securing official party status in the Commons, and down from 11 per cent of the popular vote and twenty-one seats in 1997. The party's Atlantic Canadian enclave shrunk from eight seats to four; its share of the popular vote in Nova Scotia and New Brunswick dropped six points. The NDP remained irrelevant in Quebec and Alberta, marginal in Ontario and British Columbia.

The 2000 election punctured the party's self-serving myths even more, although these myths died hard. Nine major trade-union organizations, including the Canadian Labour Congress, commissioned a private poll to analyze the results. The poll, by Vector Research, a firm that works extensively for unions, made even more disquieting reading than the National Election Survey of the 1997 national vote. The NDP won 8.5 per cent of the votes in 2000, but among trade-union voters, supposedly the core of the NDP's constituency, the NDP took only 12 per cent, compared to 41 per cent for the Liberals and 27 per cent for the Canadian Alliance. The Alliance therefore won more than twice as many votes as the NDP among all union voters. Among private-sector unionists, the Alliance thrashed the NDP 37 per cent to 13, or by almost three-to-one. Among voters earning less than $20,000 a year, another supposedly core part of the NDP constituency, the NDP received 12 per cent, the Bloc Québécois 13 per cent; the Liberals and Alliance got 30 per cent each. What about the voters aged eighteen to twenty-four? Again, the NDP came fourth. The younger the voter, the greater the likelihood that he or she did not appreciate the NDP. Some 29 per cent of voters in the eighteen-to-thirty-four age category disliked both the party leader and NDP policies, compared to only 13 per cent of those over sixty-five years of age. Vector further underscored the futility of the NDP's single-minded campaign about health care. Voters who believed health care to be the most important issue facing Canada favoured the Liberals over the NDP 50 to 13 per cent. Vector described the failed NDP strategy as being "like a shoe store with one size."

It would be too easy for New Democrats to blame their fate on inadequate leadership, although Alexa McDonough lacked the intellectual heft and political standing of Ed Broadbent, who had led the NDP from 1975 to 1989. McDonough did not understand the need to modernize NDP thinking, but she was at least a reasonable communicator. Vector found, for example, that only 4 per cent of voters cited leadership as a reason for not voting NDP. Vector reported, "McDonough turns out in the poll to have been an asset for the NDP."

"Off the radar screen." The authors of the National Election Study of the 1997 campaign so described the NDP, and that description also applied in 2000. Preliminary analysis of the 2000 vote led the National Election Study team to conclude: "We see NDP loyalists as a stranded and dwindling band whose party failed to adjust its sails to the shifting ideological winds." Only 13 per cent of Canadians, the study team discovered, considered themselves on the left side of the political spectrum, but of these only 38 per cent voted NDP. Left-wingers over fifty years of age were "much more likely" to vote NDP than left-wingers under fifty. In other words, the core NDP vote was shrinking and getting older. Slice the electorate by income, gender, age, occupation, union membership, the NDP was not competitive with the Liberals and, even worse for the NDP's self-image, with the Canadian Alliance. The NDP could not plausibly claim to speak for a majority of any group within the Canadian electorate, even a majority of those who considered themselves left-wingers.

That the NDP disappeared from national political relevance suited the Liberals perfectly. Critics had always sniffed that

Liberals ran election campaigns from the left, then governed from the right. With the NDP "off the radar screen," the Liberals did not even have to run from the left. They could offer Red Book promises of new programs, such as Pharmacare and home care, without having to deliver politically. They could preside over widening income gaps without worrying about the NDP galvanizing public concern. As long as the federal NDP failed to learn from the more updated approach to progressive governing shown by European centre-left parties or by the Saskatchewan NDP, Canadians in increasing numbers simply wrote off the NDP as a serious party – to the Liberals' considerable delight.

The NDP found itself caught in an intellectual time warp. The party's approach to liberalized trade was a shambles. The federal NDP kept saying it favoured free trade, meaning narrowly a reduction of tariff barriers, but the party lined up instinctively with every protectionist element in the country, railed against new liberalizing trade agreements, and even dispatched MPs to link arms with street protestors at the Summit of the Americas in Quebec City. When pressed, the NDP would insist it favoured "fair trade," a euphemism for managed trade, in which governments injected themselves into all elements of trade. Tony Blair, speaking to the Canadian House of Commons, preached the advantages of free trade for industrial and Third World countries alike. Predictably, the NDP denounced him. Nobody, therefore, believed that the NDP really supported trade liberalization, although every public-opinion survey showed that most Canadians had come to accept the reality of free trade.

Canadians had also come to almost a complete national consensus on the need for balanced budgets after the string of deficits from 1975 to 1995 piled up a huge national debt, a fiscal deterioration that eventually and necessarily brought spending reductions and tax increases. The federal NDP nominally said it favoured balanced budgets, but the party always shaded that statement by adding "over the business cycle," a phrase that revealed the commitment's elasticity. The federal NDP had always struggled with the perception that it could not be trusted to manage the economy; fudging on the issue of balanced budgets deepened that perception. In Britain, Prime Minister Blair had broken with Labour Party dogma by guaranteeing the independence of the Bank of England and insisting on the necessity of balanced budgets. Blair even insisted that the progressive governments of the twenty-first century were those of fiscal prudence. The successful Saskatchewan NDP, like the CCF before it, made balanced budgets a political virtue. None of this – not sound policy nor the political success of other social-democratic parties – impressed the federal NDP.

Nor could the NDP come to terms with Canada's aggregate tax load. In the late 1970s, taxes as a share of Canada's gross domestic product stood three points higher than the corresponding share of the U.S. economy. By the late 1990s, that gap had widened to nine points. Taxes by the mid-1990s in Canada had been rising faster for fifteen years as a share of gross domestic product than those in any G7 country. The NDP, however, continued to propose completely unrealistic tax policies, and these hurt the party's credibility. Preliminary results from the 2000 National Election Study found that taxes, more than any other issue, drove even left-wingers from the NDP. Almost four-fifths of those who described themselves as left-wingers but refused to vote NDP did so because they viewed tax cuts as important, whereas the NDP did not. Autoworkers in Oshawa, forestry workers in British Columbia, teachers in Saskatchewan – taxpayers such as these, especially in two-income families – were being hit with Canada's highest marginal tax rates. They were hardly the "rich" so prominent in NDP rhetoric, and yet they saw little concern over their tax loads from the federal NDP. The NDP remained wedded to taxing the "rich," failing to note that such taxes would only produce substantial additional revenues if taxpayers clearly in the middle class were defined as "rich." The party proposed slashing the Goods and Services Tax without demonstrating credibly how to replace the lost revenue. The muddled approach to tax loads deepened the perception that the federal NDP could not run a candy store, let alone a country. As the authors of the 2000 National Election Study noted mildly, "On the tax issue, the NDP might have done better by moving toward the centre."

The NDP seemed helpless in the face of its losses, not just to the Liberals but to the Canadian Alliance. Broadbent's old seat of Oshawa illustrated the erosion. Home to major automobile-manufacturing plants, Oshawa had always been a union stronghold. Once Broadbent left politics, however, the Liberals captured the riding; the Reform/Alliance candidate came second, relegating the NDP to third. Oshawa had also become a commuter suburb for Metropolitan Toronto, and the NDP was woefully weak in suburbs across Canada. In Northern Ontario, the Liberals took all the seats the NDP had periodically won. The Reform/Alliance became the dominant party throughout what had been NDP country in British Columbia. There, the backlash against aboriginal assertiveness undoubtedly helped the Reform/Alliance and hurt the NDP. The NDP also suffered in highly unionized towns and cities, where the Reform/Alliance campaign against high taxes found a receptive audience. The Reform/Alliance replaced the NDP as the voice of British Columbians angry at Ottawa, the East, and the apparent dominance of Quebec on the national agenda. Reform/Alliance proposals for electoral and parliamentary reform, if not necessarily understood in detail, nonetheless attracted British Columbians who felt "the system isn't working." Reform/Alliance and not the NDP captured the political market for changes to Canadian democracy. Indeed, the NDP seemed uninterested in the whole subject of democratic reform, except for when issuing fitful calls for proportional representation. Western Canadians who felt the political system excluded or marginalized them could recognize their grievances in Reform/Alliance proposals, but not in anything the NDP offered.

More Canadians now own shares in the stock market – directly or through pension funds – than carry union cards. Most of the employment growth in the Canadian economy, according to Statistics Canada, came in small businesses that were not unionized, or in part-time work or self-employment. Also, more Canadians than ever were accepting less dependence on government, more "self-actualization," greater acceptance of global economic forces, but the NDP seemed either unaware of these changes or chafed against them. The NDP had nothing to say to people in the burgeoning high-technology sector. The party also continued to display a certain knee-jerk chippiness towards the United States – McDonough declined invitations to meet the U.S. ambassador to Canada from 1997 to 2000 – at the very moment when anti-Americanism had never been weaker in Canada. The NDP's failure to modernize produced intellectual ossification and political deterioration. The discourse of "opportunity" and "responsibility" that Blair injected into the British Labour Party bothered the NDP, because it diluted the party's preferred discourse on entitlements, rights, and redistribution of income.

Canadians still value their social programs, such as Medicare and pensions. Knowing this, the NDP portrayed itself as the last political line of defence for these programs, convinced that Canadians would remember the party's past fights. Instead, as Canadians showed in the 2000 campaign, those fights occurred long ago and did not count in the minds of today's voters. The NDP had little to offer about how to reform Medicare – beyond spending more money. Since every party defined itself as a blind supporter of Medicare, the NDP could not effectively draw a line between itself and the others. As we have seen, those who considered health care the country's most important issue preferred the Liberals by 50 to 13 per cent over the NDP. The more the campaign turned on health care, the more it helped the Liberals.

The federal NDP has always contained both pragmatists and ideologues; or, to put matters differently, people who are engaged in politics to move the party, however slowly, towards power, and those for whom the pursuit of power is less important than expressing a certain world view. The difference between the words "party" and "movement" perhaps overstates the inherent conflict, but it does reflect at least a difference in emphasis. Those who pour their hopes into the NDP-as-party must accept the primacy of the pursuit of power and make compromises to achieve it.

As the general secretary of the British Labour Party has explained, the first thing the Blairites decided upon taking over the party was to listen to the British people rather than demanding the British people listen to the party. Listening, coupled with the lessons of repeated political failure, modernized the Labour Party and rendered it electable. Those, however, who see the NDP as an educational vehicle for changing societal attitudes first, believing those changes will eventually manifest themselves in voting behaviour, are less inclined to make compromises. For them, the inherent unfairness of the free-market system must be exposed and explained, so that the people will be won over to social democracy. Those who hold this world view demand that the party be linked organizationally and intellectually with all groups contesting the power of capital, patriarchy, and, even in extreme cases, duly constituted authority. Unions and interest groups are therefore the NDP's natural constituencies, articulating and defending the interests of "working Canadians."

This vision of the NDP gained ascendancy in the wake of the 2000 electoral debacle. Union leaders and even many NDP MPs agreed that the party needed to become more "radical," in the words of Canadian Autoworkers' Union president Buzz Hargrove. In so doing, the NDP would more clearly set themselves apart from the Liberals, rekindle support within the NDP's historic constituencies, put the party on the political map by enhancing its visibility, and generally give the governing Liberals hell. The Liberals again smiled at the folly of their adversaries.

The "radical" vision of the NDP rested on a series of illusions. Most obvious was the demonstrable fact that unions and interest groups did not speak politically for the people they purported to represent. Unions are extremely important institutions defending members' interests against the strength of capital, but they do not necessarily reflect the preferences of their members in things electoral. Hargrove's CAW, for example, could not get even half its members to vote for the NDP, despite all the CAW leadership's proselytizing and organizing. The same observation applies to the union movement in general, as a series of voting studies and polls have shown. The NDP may think of itself as the party of the unions, but it is more a party of the union leadership than of the rank and file. Union leaders deliver members' money, workers, and strategic advice in varying quantities to the NDP; they do not deliver votes. The voting pattern of unionized employees closely mirrors that of other Canadians.

Interest groups may purport to speak for certain segments of Canadian society, but not when it comes to voting. The National Action Committee on the Status of Women, to take an egregious case, no more reflects the interests, let alone the voting intentions, of Canadian women than a company president reflects the interests or voting intentions of his or her company's employees. The ultimate example of the illusion was the NDP caucus's decision to engage in street protests at the Summit of the Americas, believing quite falsely that the protestors represented the "people." The caucus, bewildered by crushing electoral rebukes, believed the "emerging left" was out there in the streets of Seattle, Washington, Prague, Davos, Los Angeles, and Quebec City, or wherever protestors gathered to contest "globalization." The Canadians who participated in these protests were, in fact, mostly the same union and interest-group leaders, buttressed by student activists, neo-Marxists, eco-feminists, and other assorted fringe groups, who, although showered with periodic media attention, left the vast majority of Canadians unmoved.

The more "ordinary" Canadians perceive the NDP to be tied to unions, interest groups, and protestors, the less capable the NDP becomes of reaching beyond the leadership of these organizations to build wider support in the country. The 1997 National Election Study caught this reality: "With almost one voter in two (48 per cent) actually wanting to see unions have less power, views about unions cost the NDP almost two points. Clearly, the party needs to weigh the organizational advantages of its ties with organized labour against the electoral costs."

It is an utter illusion, therefore, for the NDP to believe that even tighter ties to organized labour and the pursuit of a more "radical" agenda favoured by the heads of the CAW and Canadian Union of Public Employees will lead to wider public appeal. Indeed, the NDP would be much wiser – if it is serious about politics, which is in turn about the democratic exercise of power – to sever its financial and organizational links to trade unions. The party should demand campaign-finance reform, prohibiting corporations and unions from contributing to political parties. Quebec already organizes politics this way; the Manitoba and Ontario provincial NDP parties support the same rules. Freeing itself from union dependence would encourage the NDP to modernize its thinking about the economy and to reflect a wider range of Canadian concerns. Such a departure would not require the NDP to forget about the union movement, merely to be less reflexively dependent upon it. On the other hand, if the NDP is not serious about trying eventually to win political power, then it can continue to bathe in illusions, while the vast majority of Canadians ignore the party.

Ideologues will complain that making the NDP more electable is itself an illusion, because the cynical Liberals will steal a few progressive ideas, giving the NDP no credit and leaving the party as an echo not a voice. The Liberals have done this in the past, and will certainly do so again if pressed. But Sir John A. Macdonald once observed that politics is a "long game," and for the NDP the "long game" must be to restructure the country's politics along the broad lines of two parties: one left-of-centre, the other right-of-centre. Canadians politics, of course, will never be quite that neat, given that so many issues revolve around region, language, ethnicity, and symbols that defy left–right description. However, if the NDP does not fight the "long game" of contesting the moderate left with the Liberals through more resourceful leadership and creative, workable ideas, then the NDP will be forever consigned to the margins of Canadian politics. Since the party's inception, the NDP's marginality has never been so obvious – to the delight and political benefit of the Liberals. They govern without worrying about a credible NDP; they win seats the NDP might otherwise capture. The governing party cannot be blamed for the NDP's slide to marginality. Nor can anyone blame the Liberals if the NDP draws the wrong lessons from its enfeebled state and heads even further from the concerns of those "ordinary" Canadians that the party purports to, but increasingly does not, represent.

Alliance and Conservatives: Competitors in Folly

Canadian politics still function, more than a decade after the Meech Lake constitutional accord's demise, in the shadow of that national psychodrama. The Meech Lake debate pitted Quebec against the rest of Canada, gave birth to the Bloc Québécois, and abetted the formation of the Reform Party. Post-Meech, Canadian politics settled into a pattern of de facto one-party government. The Liberals emerged changed but intact from Meech Lake and its aftermath; the Conservatives never recovered. Jean Chrétien,

who worked to scuttle Meech Lake, became the principal political beneficiary of its failure.

Canadians passed judgment on Prime Minister Brian Mulroney
after he had spent nine years in office. If polls can be believed,
he departed politics as one of the least popular prime ministers,
though historians some day might look differently at the Mulroney
record, since the Liberals subsequently adopted many of his government's policies. When historians judge, they will have to
acknowledge two incontestable facts: that Mulroney was the only
Conservative prime minister in the twentieth century to win
back-to-back majorities; and that he assembled and maintained
a disparate, unwieldy parliamentary coalition through difficult
political battles. His 1984 election victory (211 seats) gave the
Conservatives the largest number of seats in every region; his
1988 triumph (169 seats) saw the Tories win more seats than their
rivals, everywhere but in Atlantic Canada and British Columbia.

This is not the place to retrace the political history of the
Mulroney government. Suffice it to say that the government's
popularity had seriously plunged midway through its first term.
The government recovered by 1987 and coalesced sufficiently
for the 1988 election victory, the catalyst being the proposed
Canada–U.S. Free Trade Agreement that enjoyed enough
support to restore Conservative fortunes in Quebec and western
Canada. Free trade completed, the government turned its attention to the constitutional agreement known as the Meech Lake
accord, the most controversial element of which was Quebec's
designation as a "distinct society." Mulroney and the ten provincial premiers reached an agreement in closed-door meetings; they
confirmed a final deal in another closed-door session. This deal
appeared to enjoy widespread initial support, but support slowly
eroded. Manitoba's governing New Democrats hesitated. Frank
McKenna, the newly elected Liberal premier of New Brunswick,
announced he could not support Meech Lake without changes.

Clyde Wells, the new Liberal premier of Newfoundland, opposed the accord. National women's organizations and aboriginal groups began mobilizing against it. But the hardest blow of all came from former prime minister Pierre Trudeau, who eviscerated the deal in articles and parliamentary testimony. Trudeau's intervention, more than any other, contributed to a sea of change outside Quebec against Meech Lake.

The national debate over Meech Lake played itself out intensely and at a highly symbolic level. The *Globe and Mail* and the Canadian Broadcasting Corporation sponsored a poll five months before Meech Lake's collapse, asking respondents about their knowledge of, and opinions about, the accord. Seventy-two per cent of respondents replied that they had "little" or "no" knowledge of the five elements of the deal, but the same percentage held "strong" or "very strong" views about the accord. Two weeks after the deal died in the assemblies of Manitoba and of Newfoundland, where Premier Wells refused to allow a vote, the same poll revealed that 63 per cent still had "little" or "no" knowledge of the deal's elements – but the same percentage had "strong" or "very strong" views about the accord. Most of those views were negative outside Quebec, but positive inside Quebec. The debate about Meech Lake was often conducted over technicalities among élites. Among the general population, it turned on clashing visions of the country, perceived historic grievances rooted in language or region, and the political reputation of proponents and adversaries.

The Meech Lake debate gravely weakened the Mulroney government. The most dramatic immediate consequence was the departure from cabinet of Mulroney's friend, Lucien Bouchard. He had been named Canadian ambassador to Paris by Mulroney, brought back as a Conservative white-knight candidate in Quebec, and made a senior cabinet minister. Bouchard had supported Premier René Lévesque's drive for Quebec sovereignty, but temporarily yielded up that dream after the 1980 referendum defeat and succumbed to his friend Mulroney's blandishments to help the Conservatives in the 1984 election. His hand gripped the pen for Mulroney's Sept-Îles campaign speech, in which he promised to create conditions for Quebec to sign the 1981 constitutional accords with "honour and enthusiasm." Mulroney did not specify how, but Meech Lake became the means.

As Meech Lake approached its death throes, Bouchard bolted from the government. Greeted as a hero in Quebec, he subsequently gathered around him a handful of other Conservative MPs and one dissident Liberal to form a coterie promoting Quebec sovereignty in Parliament. The Bloc Québécois's formation cracked Mulroney's Quebec coalition. The crack swallowed up the Conservatives in the 1993 election, when the Bloc won fifty-four Quebec seats and became rather incongruously Canada's Official Opposition. The Conservatives tumbled in Quebec from sixty-three seats in 1988 to one in 1993.

Meanwhile, various nettlesome issues and negative perceptions eroded the Conservatives' support in western Canada. Meech Lake's perceived kowtowing to Quebec damaged Conservative fortunes, but the rot had set in earlier. Within two years of the 1984 election, disquiet began growing in western Canada that the Mulroney Tories were not the West's answer to political and economic change. They seemed irresolute about the deficit and uninterested in lowering taxes. They took too long dismantling the hated National Energy Program, including the Petroleum and Gas Revenue Tax. Although western Canada had yielded a bumper crop of Tories, Conservative MPs from Ontario and Quebec outnumbered them. Western Canadians viewed themselves – again – as the tail wagged by the central-Canadian dog. The Mulroney Tories governed much like the old brokerage parties, paying special heed to Quebec. A firestorm erupted in western Canada in 1986 when the Mulroney government awarded a lucrative CF-18 maintenance contract to Canadair of Montreal instead of Bristol Aerospace of Winnipeg, despite the Western

firm's superior technical assessment. The government never plausibly explained why Canadair had won. Westerners reckoned
Quebec's interests and votes had once again triumphed in Ottawa
under Tories just as they had under Liberals. And they were right.

Western perceptions grew that Tories and Liberals were cut
from the same cloth, despite the Conservatives' huge political
presence in the region. The Conservatives, to give them their
due, attempted to respond to some historic western Canadian
grievances. They deregulated transportation rates. They negotiated better access to the U.S. market in the free-trade deal. They
pitchforked money into the embattled grain sector. They aided
the oil and gas sector when energy prices fell. Still, it struck
many Westerners, especially those wanting smaller government
and structural changes in the federation, that they were not
doing enough.

Those Westerners seeking more fundamental assaults on the
Canadian economic and political status quo began meeting informally during the Conservatives' first term, and the key figure
among them was Preston Manning. Many years before, he and his
father, Ernest, the long-time Social Credit premier of Alberta, had
jointly written a book calling for a realignment of Canadian politics along more ideological lines, with parties of the right and the
left. Now Manning began to promote the idea of a new party that
would reorient Canadian politics along these lines, and the idea
took hold at a series of meetings that gave birth to the Reform
Party. Not strong enough to threaten seriously the Conservatives
in time for the 1988 election, Reform's strength subsequently
soared as opposition to Meech Lake erupted in Mulroney's second
term. So, too, the persistence of huge fiscal deficits in Ottawa
fuelled anger at high taxation and government spending, not
enough of which seemed to benefit western Canada.

Political thunder on the right reflected more than traditional
western Canadian alienation. Those of a conservative persua-
sion had been influenced by the philosophies and the political

successes of British prime minister Margaret Thatcher and U.S. president Ronald Reagan. These leaders had campaigned against the very institutions of government they sought to lead. More sharply ideological than their Conservative and Republican predecessors, Thatcher and Reagan scorned any idea of a benevolent state. Traditional British Tories, with their sense of exaggerated *noblesse oblige*, conceived society as an organic whole in which the state played a constructive role in advancing society's purposes. Thatcher, on the other hand, rejected ideas of an organic society, insisting that society was made up of an agglomeration of individuals whose creativity and energies the state frustrated by excessively interfering in their lives. She scorned the old-style Tories, dismissing them as "wets," wrested the party from them, and carried her party to smashing electoral triumphs.

Reagan, for his part, was more avuncular than the didactic Thatcher, but he too insisted that Big Government programs often worked against the national interest and individual initiative. He decried generous welfare programs, meddling bureaucrats in Washington, and other manifestations of what Thatcher had called the modern "nanny state." Reagan's first presidential initiative made good on his promise to slash tax rates. These lowered rates, whatever their virtues, contributed, along with a massive increase in defence spending, to the largest peacetime deficits in U.S. history, a rather bizarre result for someone who had pledged to balance the books. Still, so-called "supply-side economics" rooted itself in Republican economic thinking and spilled across the border into Canada, where a new generation of conservative thinkers — magazine writers, newspaper editors, university professors, think-tank contributors, political activists — applied it to the Canadian condition. Canada, it struck them, needed its own dose of "supply-side" economics. The deficit remained staggeringly high. Interest on the national debt grabbed roughly a third of all tax dollars. Taxes had grown faster as a share of gross domestic product in Canada during the 1980s than in any other advanced industrial country. The Mulroney Conservatives had whittled and chopped at spending, and had privatized Crown corporations, but something more robust was needed. There remained too many manifestations in Ottawa of the "nanny state." Moreover, the federal government would always be dominated by the votes from central Canada. Only a structural change in governance through an elected Senate with effective powers and equal representation from every province could counter the East's political domination. That was the western Canadian twist on these broad conservative currents that swept into Canada from abroad. Conservative thinking in Britain and the United States had turned more ideological ("neo-conservatism," it was widely called); so it should in Canada. If conservative parties in those countries had been politically successful, why not in Canada too?

Meech Lake inflamed western Canada's sense of having been too long marginalized in Canadian politics. The West had its own grievances, yet Meech Lake focused only on Quebec's. The concept of Quebec as a "distinct society" collided with what had become a fixture of western Canadian constitutional thinking: that all Canadian provinces were equal. But beyond constitutions, the idea of a "distinct society" smacked of special treatment for Quebec, a province Westerners of almost all political stripes already considered Confederation's spoiled child. After all, had not Quebeckers been found disproportionately in higher government places since 1968? Had not bilingualism arisen to alleviate Quebec's concerns? Had there not been multiple examples of federal programs dishing out funds to Quebec companies and constituencies? Had the West not been forced to various constitutional tables to negotiate Quebec's agenda? The Reform Party capitalized on all these sentiments in rallying opposition to Meech Lake, and ideology and western Canadian alienation fused inside the Reform Party. The results were as devastating for the Mulroney government as the creation of the Bloc Québécois. The Mulroney government thrashed around in the second half of its second mandate after Meech Lake's demise trying to recapture lost political ground. Another round of constitutional negotiations led to the Charlottetown accord, a grab-bag of constitutional changes that attempted to wrap the essence of the Meech Lake accord in a larger package, including aboriginal self-government and Senate reform. Designed to satisfy Quebec and western Canada, Charlottetown failed in both regions in a national referendum.

Government agencies were suddenly disbanded, offered up on the altar of this new conservative thinking and in a panicky reaction to Reform's emerging strength. Modest tax cuts appeared. Nothing worked. The Conservative coalition, wrecked by the Meech Lake accord, could not be resurrected. Kim Campbell made everything worse after replacing Mulroney, by running a disastrously inept 1993 campaign. The Liberals won a majority, and two regional parties soared, the Bloc Québécois and Reform. Canadians have lived ever since with this new political constellation: one de facto governing party facing fragments – but only fragments – of a united alternative capable of threatening the Liberals.

Political scientists suggest that 1993 ushered in Canada's fourth party system, one characterized by the breakup of nation-wide parties and their replacement by essentially regional ones: the Bloc in Quebec, the Reform/Alliance parties in the West, and the governing Liberals anchored in Ontario. The first party system, they argue, endured from Confederation until around the First World War, when a nationalist party in Quebec and protest parties in western Canada appeared. These eventually faded, and the era of classic "brokerage" politics began, with the Liberals and Conservatives trying to form coalitions rooted in all parts of Canada. When in power the governing party – Liberals more often than Conservatives – balanced as carefully as possible the interests of all regions. That system, runs the argument, yielded at least somewhat to Conservative Prime Minister John

Diefenbaker's and then Liberal Prime Minister Pierre Trudeau's more pan-Canadian political appeals. Their parties espoused visions for the entire country that superseded appeals to regional concerns. Trudeau's Charter of Rights and Freedoms reflected this pan-Canadian appeal – that citizens' rights came before the prerogatives of governments, that courts not Parliament or legislatures were the best guarantors of liberties, and that Canadians everywhere shared the same rights. Mulroney, it might be said, reflected a mixture of the old brokerage style of governing with pan-Canadian appeals, reflected in Canada–U.S. free trade.

Political scientists' historical frameworks are probably too rigid, since each of the party systems they describe blended the new and the old. In any event, however, they are surely correct in describing what happened post-1993 as something quite new. Never before had two such clearly regional parties faced a de facto governing party. Never before had so many Canadians responded positively to political appeals based largely on regional grievance. The two parties lasted as strong political forces through three consecutive elections, whereas other regional protest parties had come and gone.

Some of Reform's founders saw the party as the vehicle for their rallying cry, "the West wants in." Preston Manning saw the Reform Party that way, too – but as something more. Reform would bring western Canadian sensitivities to government. It would champion issues in order to insert more western Canadian power into the federal government through a Triple-E Senate. It would introduce western Canadian political populism into government through more use of referenda, possible recall of MPs through petitions signed by constituents, more free votes in the Commons, and a search for guidance from constituents about how MPs should vote short of a referendum. Change the political structures and give MPs more power, Manning believed, and western Canadian interests would be advanced. So too, he believed, would those of Canada. Manning, a keen student of Canadian history, understood the shooting-star trajectories of other western Canadian protest parties. He was determined to prevent Reform from becoming another here-today-gone-tomorrow protest phenomenon. However, election setbacks outside the West revealed that he could not achieve his political objectives by his chosen means. He had learned certain important lessons from Canadian history, especially about the fate of western Canadian protest parties, but neglected the most important one of all: that political power in Canada has never been won – and cannot be won – by a fusion of alienation and ideology.

Manning always searched for a "political realignment," the words he chose for the book written with his father. A regional protest party could shake the existing political mould, but if history served as a reliable guide, the mould would harden over again. The political challenge therefore lay in breaking the mould with a protest party, but then replacing the mould with something else altogether. Manning believed assumptions about politics needed to change. So did underlying assumptions of what the state could reasonably accomplish. So did the structure of the Canadian federation. Canada's regions required better representation in Ottawa through an elected Senate, but provinces needed more constitutional power. They were closer to the people, and Manning argued that the task of political leadership consisted of understanding the "common wisdom of the common people." More profoundly still, he stood the Confederation myth on its head. Confederation had been as much about separating as joining. The original deal, he insisted, had deposited power over language and culture with the provinces. Canada's French- and English-speakers co-operated better when they enjoyed more space one from the other. Most attempts since the Trudeau government to give Ottawa the role of promoter and protector of "Canadian unity" through official bilingualism, cultural subsidies, multiculturalism, and other government programs, Manning considered mistakes based on a misreading of Canadian history.

Canada was more divided than ever because of excessive centralization. These, then, were the assumptions that guided the Reform Party. Manning believed they served western Canada, to be sure, but could be made saleable to the rest of Canada, starting with Ontario.

As Manning set out transforming the Reform Party from a vehicle for western Canadian grievance into one with national governing ambitions, however, a certain nervousness arose in his party. Some of the early Reformers feared that the West's legitimate grievances might be diluted in this pan-Canadian appeal, and these fears were legitimate, since broader coalitions in a diverse country meant by definition accommodating other, sometimes conflicting, interests. The questions Reformers grappled with were: how much dilution should there be, on what issues, by what means, and to what end? The answers, as events unfolded, were that the end was power, the dilution was minimal, the issues were restricted, and the means were faulty.

Manning overcame the rearguard nervousness by insisting that what served the West's interests would improve Canada too, a message Reform's true believers wanted to hear. They were heartened when, in 1995, Mike Harris's Conservatives captured power in Ontario, the focus of their federal aspirations. Here were "supply-siders," critical of excessive state intrusion in the economy. Here was a new breed of Ontario Conservatives, heirs to Margaret Thatcher and Ronald Reagan's view of government, far removed from the cautious, pragmatic Tories of Premiers William Davis and John Robarts. Here were politicians determined to bring fundamental change to government, not just better management. Premier Harris wisely refrained from endorsing any federal party, knowing his own ranks featured federal Conservatives, Liberals, and Reformers, but Reformers could not help believing that they had found new soulmates in provincial politics. Given a chance to hear Reform's prescriptions, they believed, this pool of Harris voters would gravitate to Reform and allow the party to take that giant step towards national political credibility. Once Ontario responded positively, some Quebeckers might sense how the political winds were blowing in the rest of Canada and begin paying some attention to Reform. The Reform Party fragment, part of the Mulroney coalition, would recast the Canadian political mould in its terms. De facto one-party governance would end.

Reform in 1993 had captured an impressive 20 per cent of Ontario's votes, to 18 per cent for the Conservatives. A fifth of Ontario's popular vote, however, translated into only one of the province's ninety-nine seats, a by-product of the unrepresentative first-past-the-post electoral system. The 1997 election promised better results. Reform spent more time and money preparing for 1997 than for 1993. It was now much better known. The Harris Conservatives had captured power between the two federal elections. Not even the most optimistic Reformer believed the party could supplant the Liberals as Ontario's largest federal party, but gains seemed inevitable. These gains, if subsequently built upon, would break the Canadian political mould on Reform's terms.

Instead, the election result broke Reform's heart. The party lost its only Ontario seat. Its share of the popular vote dropped by a point, while the Tories, who had stubbornly refused to die, raised their share to 19 per cent from 18 per cent in 1993. The damnable Liberals won 101 of the province's 103 seats and another majority government. Postmortems began immediately. Had the Reform television advertisement, asking whether someone other than a Quebecker could be Prime Minister, backfired? Was Preston Manning politically unsaleable? Why wouldn't the federal Tories accept their fate? What was it about Ontario voters? The questions were painful, the answers hard to find.

Populist parties – the ones organized internally on highly democratic lines – are paradoxically the most leader-centred. Traditional, hierarchical parties obviously featured a leader, but also a series of other power barons, who, by virtue of regional strength or longevity, carried weight within the councils of the party. Populist parties, by contrast, lacked power brokers between the leader and the rank and file. The leader of a populist party could only be ousted, or his policies rejected, by a mass mobilization of the rank and file, and that rarely occurred. While populist parties went through the motions of internal party democracy – procedures the membership took seriously – an effective leader almost always got his way, as Preston Manning did with the Reform Party. Only a spectacularly inept leader, as Stockwell Day turned out to be, could turn around these advantages for the leader of a populist party.

When Manning reflected on the disappointment of the 1997 election in Ontario – the party had won all sixty of its seats in western Canada – he hit upon a breathtaking strategy that Reform eventually endorsed. Reform should disband itself and be recreated as a new party, Manning recommended, with a broader appeal, a new name, and, if necessary, a new leader. Manning first set forth his arresting proposal after the election at a Reform convention in London, Ontario. To decide whether to endorse Manning's idea, Reform's populist, highly democratic, internal procedures required a vast consultation through a series of conventions and referendums. As Manning tirelessly explained, a new party would rid Reform of negative stereotypes and welcome a wider range of Canadians seeking fundamental economic and political changes. He listed the targets as if by rote: B.C. provincial Liberals, members of the fledgling Saskatchewan Party, Harris Conservatives, Quebec nationalists desiring a more decentralized Canadian federation, and, critically, federal Conservatives. Think Big, Manning exhorted Reformers. Build a bigger political house. Hard-core Reformers dissented, fearing as always the dilution inherent in coalition building, but Manning got his way – until the very end.

Think Big reflected the latest twist in Manning's search for the elusive political realignment that he and his father had outlined in their book. Prior to launching his Think Big campaign, Manning had invited federal Conservatives to discuss merging the two parties. The idea of merger appealed to a few federal Conservatives who could not envisage another way of defeating the Liberals. But when the Tories held a leadership race to replace Jean Charest, who had left federal politics to become leader of the Quebec Liberal Party, the leading candidates dismissed merger. Joe Clark, the winner, scorned merger and interpreted his victory as a vindication of that attitude. He and Preston Manning had been competing since university days in Alberta, including in the 1988 election, when Manning contested Clark's riding. Beyond their personal rivalry, Clark felt a widespread resentment shared by the senior Tories of the Mulroney era against Manning, whom they blamed for having fractured their coalition.

Clark had spent a lifetime in federal politics without a fixed ideological address. He was a Conservative all right, and had devoted his life to the service of the party, but he had always been intellectually malleable or, as his critics would say, devoid of creative thought. Clark had developed a reputation as an astute tactician, although just why remained unclear, given the tactical blunders in his career. Clark did understand political leadership as the art of brokering deals, although his lack of interest in policy often led him to pursue a deal for the sake of the deal rather than to attain a particular outcome. He had often described Canada as a "community of communities." The task of political leadership, as he understood and practised it, consisted of accommodating but not threatening regional interests. The Reform Party, he believed, threatened Canadian unity by its insensitivity to Quebec, a province he reckoned he understood. Repeated political rebuffs in Quebec never shook Clark's conviction that somehow he, a passably bilingual Albertan, was the sensitive

Canadian interlocutor whom Quebeckers had been seeking.

Clark was a Conservative Party man above all else, and he understood that Reform's greater political and financial strength – the Conservatives groaned under a $9-million debt – would allow it to call almost all the shots in a merger. Having just recaptured the Conservative Party's leadership, Clark was not about to preside over the party's disappearance. Academic studies underscored what practical experience taught: the majority of Conservatives who had not already left the party, if forced to choose between Liberals and Reform, preferred the Liberals. The 1997 National Election Study had found that "the Conservatives were the most popular second choice for Liberal voters, just as the Liberals were the most popular choice for Conservative voters." By 1997, the Conservatives had already lost supporters to Reform. There were not many more to lose in that direction, an elementary fact that Reformers who were suggesting a merger on their terms kept ignoring.

Reformers apparently did not know the membership of the party with which they proposed to merge. The 1997 National Election Study had asked a series of questions about values and policy, and concluded that, on most of them, the views of Conservatives and Liberals were closer than those of Conservatives and Reformers. The study asked all supporters of all parties where they stood on eight broad questions, ranging from the role of women to Canada–U.S. relations. Liberals and Conservatives offered almost identical responses on six of them. A Conservative–Reform merger was therefore implausible on Reform's terms. Even if a merger had occurred, by definition it would have pulled Conservatives towards the stronger Reform Party and therefore further away from median Canadian voters. As the authors of the 1997 National Election Study correctly concluded, "the formation of a united alternative to the right of the Conservatives could well help to guarantee the continued electoral dominance of the Liberal Party."

Formal merger talks therefore never had a chance, although Manning, who knew this perfectly well, felt obliged to peddle the fiction during the conventions and meetings to create what became the United Alternative. Even the new party's name seemed designed to beckon to federal Conservatives. A few of them did trickle into the United Alternative, including an Ontario cluster called the Blue Committee, made up of disaffected federal Tories fed up with Clark and his hostility to merger. Some of them doubled as prominent players in the Harris provincial Conservative Party. Their participation fuelled false hopes that, with the Harris Conservatives on side and some federal Tories moving over, the United Alternative could succeed in Ontario where Reform had failed. These Conservatives were invited to participate in policy committees that were charged with hammering out the new party's platform. They influenced the United Alternative to soften Reform's insistence on a Triple-E Senate in favour of a simply elected one and to accept federal language policy. These policy changes amounted to thin gruel. The United Alternative platform, although trumpeted as something new, read much like Reform's, and therein lay an insurmountable political problem.

Preston Manning argued for a new party, never believing its creation would open a Pandora's box. Manning had insisted from the launch of Think Big that everything should be on the table for review, including his own leadership. A compelling logic flowed from the initial premise that only a new party could attract additional Ontario support. If everything else were up for review, then why not the party leadership? Manning, a highly cerebral man, now faced the logical conclusion of his own reasoning. If members supported creating a new party, they should be given a chance to select a new leader. In retrospect, this looks like an extraordinary gamble; at the time, it seemed self-evident to Manning that he would replace himself. After all, he had been Reform's founder and only leader. He had slogged across the country and fought two national elections, shaking more hands, delivering more speeches, giving more interviews, enduring more bad food, flying more miles, challenging more Canadian assumptions than any conceivable competitor. The new party had been his idea; fairness demanded that he be given the opportunity to see where he could take it.

The United Alternative convention duly adopted the platform crafted by the committee. Members chose a new name – the Canadian Alliance – and the Reform Party, through an internal party referendum, voted itself out of existence, although 39.5 per cent of the 32,099 who voted opposed ending the Reform Party. Now came the leadership contest. Manning would run to succeed himself, of course. But would there be others? At Queen's Park, lair of the Harris Tories, ministers and strategists attracted by the Canadian Alliance almost universally concluded that Manning could not win Ontario. Accustomed now to exercising political power, and convinced that they knew how to win federally in Ontario, the Harris operators and their Bay Street contacts decided on a reverse-takeover strategy. Manning with his Think Big strategy had invited them into the new party; now they would assume command. Their brand of conservatism, triumphant in Ontario, would be extended to grateful Canadians everywhere. Such was their hubris as they searched for a candidate.

The trouble was that no one of stature wanted to run. Provincial ministers did not wish to leave office for the uncertain joys of leading a federal opposition party. When no bigwig stepped forward, backbencher Frank Klees believed he could count on the Harris crowd's support. Klees was a dim bulb, however, incapable of igniting any enthusiasm whatsoever. Klees may have been a loyal Harris follower, but that was not much of a claim to fame. No sooner had Klees announced his interest in the leadership than he was pushed aside by someone that the bigwigs around Harris, Bay Street financiers, and the editorial writers of the *National Post* considered one of theirs.

Tom Long seemed a dream candidate. He had been an intellectual and organizational architect of the Common Sense Revolution, the Harris Conservative Party's platform. He had impeccable, unalterably right-wing credentials, being a stout admirer of Thatcher and Reagan. He had been dismissive of Clark and the federal Tories as too soft on just about everything. He had access to people who could raise oodles of money. The *National Post* would make him their poster boy; the Harris organizers would provide organizational muscle. He was young and apparently effective on television. Sound bites held no terror for him. And, best of all, he was from Ontario, the Canadian Alliance's Holy Grail. Preston Manning had twice hit the wall in Ontario; Tom Long understood how to climb it. The trick to winning the leadership lay in quickly signing up members across Ontario and in Quebec and Atlantic Canada, where Reform had few supporters. Organizational muscle would be needed, but the Harris Conservatives could provide it. Money would be needed, but the Harris Conservatives knew where to find it, the provincial party being a vacuum cleaner for corporate cash. The premier himself, ostensibly neutral, called friends across the country. Tom was the man.

Another Conservative premier had other ideas. Ralph Klein of Alberta had spoken to the United Alternative convention, preaching unity on the right to defeat the federal Liberals. He had also warned the convention about something too many Canadian Alliance members subsequently forgot: that questions of personal morality and lifestyle choice were best left in the private sphere. Klein had plenty of social conservatives in his provincial party, but he did not govern with their interests in mind. Klein, like Harris, did not believe Manning could take the Alliance much beyond Reform's core support, and he had someone else in mind to lead the new party.

Stockwell Day seemed a wonderful political package. Athletic and handsome, he had lived in various parts of Canada and even spoke a smattering of French. He had been a successful Alberta Treasurer, lowering taxes and presiding over a reduction of the province's debt, courtesy of energy royalties and severe spending restraint. He certainly had the right ideological credentials as a foe of intrusive government and a proponent of lower taxes. He spoke smoothly, appealed to Reform's western Canadian base, but suggested that he could move the Alliance forward in Ontario, where Manning had failed. He had Ralph Klein's enthusiastic support, and that support would count in Alberta, and perhaps beyond. He was a social conservative, opposed to abortion, in favour of capital punishment, a Christian opponent of homosexuality. These were his personal views, but he insisted he would not foist them on Canadians as prime minister.

An exhausting leadership race ensued, won by Day. Tom Long proved to be one of the great Canadian political fizzles. His organizers' vote-buying schemes in Quebec wound up splashed across the national media. He had little appeal in western Canada, where he came across as Bay Street's boy. He spoke not a word of French. He unveiled a liturgy of ideological clichés. He ran out of time trying to sign up members.

Long's third-place finish on the first ballot of this one-member-one-vote contest surprised no one who had followed the contest. Manning's second-place finish stunned him. The gap between him and Day after the first round was astonishingly large. Manning's only chance lay in securing the support of Long supporters, after Long threw his support to him. Instead, many Long supporters did not bother to vote a second time. Those who did decided against marching en masse to Manning. Day's majority expanded on the second, decisive ballot.

Manning had intellectually accepted that he could lose the leadership, but really he did not believe it would happen. The logic of what he had set in motion destroyed him: a new party needed a new leader. If not, then why did they bother changing the party's name and a few of its policies? New wine in an old bottle would not entice new political buyers, who would see only the old bottle. Manning, for all his courage and convictions, or perhaps even because of them, was too associated with apparently ineradicable negative images. He had changed his hairstyle, subjected his eyes to laser surgery, taken voice coaching, altered his wardrobe, but none of these cosmetic alterations shook the impression outside the Reform Party that he was too strident, unilingual, dogmatic, and, well, too western Canadian for the rest of Canada. Manning told Quebec important truths too long obscured: that threats to secede would not budge the rest of Canada and that, if secession occurred, the rest of Canada would organize to defend its interests in ways Quebeckers would not like. As those who break taboos sometimes discover, for these truths he was applauded by some but viewed by too many Ontario voters as a threat to national unity. The moral traditionalism he personally practised and publicly espoused annoyed secular voters. In the 1997 election, after two campaigns with him as leader and almost a decade in the national limelight, Manning's Reform Party had become the least acceptable second-choice party. That standing meant slight possibilities for growth beyond Reform's core vote. The apparent improbability of future political gains under Manning overwhelmed the party's gratitude to him for past political service.

In electing Day, however, the Canadian Alliance dug itself deeper into a political hole. Although more "televisual" than Manning, Day was an intellectual flyweight and national political neophyte. Day had been elected with the organizational and financial help of social conservatives, who warmed to his own background as an evangelical preacher and moral traditionalist. The more he became identified with these causes, and the more he accepted support from groups espousing them, the less attractive he became politically outside these circles. Social conservatism has negative political appeal in Canada. For every vote gained by a leader who embraces it, more are lost.

Canadians are much less religious than Americans, as every cross-border survey shows. The religious right carries considerable clout in the Republican Party and subjects the party's presidential hopefuls to litmus tests on such issues as abortion, prayer in the schools, and support for church-based delivery of social programs. It is now almost impossible to win the Republican Party presidential nomination without making peace with the religious right. However, nothing of remotely comparable political strength exists in Canada. Many decades ago, religious rivalries and controversies roiled Canadian politics. What were sometimes considered French–English tensions were, in fact, Catholic–Protestant ones. Even today religious affiliation is among the telltale signs of how individuals identify themselves politically, Catholics for example being more likely to vote Liberal. But the salience of religion – that is, how strongly an issue is felt to be – has fallen dramatically. Canadian political leaders, whatever their private religious views and practices, almost never parade them publicly or use religious precepts to shape their political arguments. If Pierre Trudeau was right that the state has no place in the bedrooms of the nation, then it would also appear correct that religion has no place in the cabinet rooms of the nation either. That Day had been so overtly supported by the social conservatives produced much media commentary. His suggestion that he would countenance a national referendum on abortion, if enough Canadians signed a petition demanding one, left pro-choice voters wondering if Day had a hidden agenda to restrict access to abortions. One of Tom Long's reasons for supporting Manning was his political judgment that Day's social conservatism would not sell in Ontario, even though Day and Manning shared similar religious beliefs. The Alliance therefore saddled itself with a leader just as closely identified as Manning with the Reform Party core vote. Although younger and more athletic than Manning, Day gave the impression of being a less substantial and reflective politician.

The entire adventure in creating the United Alternative–Canadian Alliance had been to make a breakthrough in Ontario, but the Alliance predictably failed again in the 2000 election. The Alliance's share of the popular vote rose to 23.6 per cent from 19 per cent in 1997, but it won only two of 103 Ontario seats. In the 1993, 1997, and 2000 elections, the Reform–Canadian Alliance had contested 305 Ontario seats and won three. The Alliance was blanked east of Ontario. All the Alliance did was to cement Reform's hold on western Canada, by driving up Reform's 1997 popular vote in every western Canadian province.

Day had not delivered Ontario, but that alone could not explain the extraordinary rebellion that erupted against his leadership in the spring of 2001. Robert Stanfield fought three unsuccessful elections before departing as Conservative leader; George Drew, John Turner, and Preston Manning were given two unsuccessful electoral tries before leaving. But only six months after the 2000 election, a caucus rebellion destabilized Day's leadership. Three pillars of the parliamentary caucus – Deborah Grey, Chuck Strahl, and Val Meridith – publicly expressed dismay at their leader. Grey resigned as deputy leader; Strahl as House leader. Other caucus members demanded a leadership change. Ian Todd, Day's chief-of-staff, who had served Preston Manning too, quit. Scattered constituency associations passed resolutions calling for a new leader, or at least a review of Day's leadership, before the scheduled test at the party's April 2002 convention. Eleven Alliance MPs left the caucus, representing supporters in the leadership campaign of Day, Manning, and Long. Day fought back, of course, suspending the dissidents from caucus, revamping his advisers, reassigning caucus responsibilities, and vowing to remain as leader. The split, however, was spectacularly public, quite nasty, and could not be repaired (as was proven on July 19, when twelve Alliance dissidents formed their own parliamentary caucus, the Democratic Representative Caucus). Once a rebellion erupts, no leader can ever command unvarnished loyalty, as Diefenbaker,

Clark, and Turner all discovered. Day's leadership had been fatally compromised, not only in the eyes of many Alliance members, but also for Canadians, since a leader who cannot inspire loyalty in his own ranks can hardly inspire confidence in the general population, and a party that cannot unite itself is unfit to govern.

Day had made a series of embarrassing mistakes as Opposition Leader, which called into question his judgment and abilities. He did not listen to seasoned advice, relying instead on a coterie of family members and juvenile ideologues. He obviously had a much higher opinion of his own talents than almost anyone who worked with him, which explained why those who saw him regularly – Grey, Strahl, and Todd, among others – abandoned hope. Back in Alberta, former cabinet colleagues knew him as a silver-tongued airhead, clever with a phrase, pleasant in demeanour, devoid of substance. The 2000 election campaign revealed to Canadians what Alberta colleagues had known, and his performance as Opposition Leader confirmed it for caucus colleagues. Day was clearly out of his depth in national politics, but whether he stayed or departed mattered only marginally, because the Canadian Alliance was not going anywhere as long as it hewed to the same policies and offered the same vision of Canada that had been tried three times and had failed. In selecting Day, the Alliance had myopically dug deeper into the Reform Party's core vote for a leader, and all the subsequent angst about his leadership failings merely obscured the fact that, even if Day had performed better as Opposition Leader, the Canadian Alliance still would not be advancing in Canadian politics.

What It Takes to Win in Canadian Politics

The Canadian Alliance entered the twenty-first century as Canada's Official Opposition and bids fair to remain there without correctly analyzing its predicament. Few signs emerged after the election that the Alliance understood how it needed to evolve, a failure that suited the governing Liberals splendidly. As long as the Alliance, and the Conservatives for that matter, failed to understand how to win political power, Canada would remain a country of de facto one-party governance.

None of the opposition parties has absorbed the lessons of Canadian political history. The future never precisely replicates the past, but the past does offer clues about what it takes to be successful against the Liberals in Canadian politics. The most important clue is the nature of non-Liberal governments in the twentieth century. Only four of them lasted any length of time, and they all shared roughly similar characteristics. The Conservatives who defeated the Liberals these four times assembled a broadly based coalition, which is what parties must do in a geographically sprawling, regionally sensitive, linguistically divided, ethnically diverse country.

The Conservative governments did not endure more than two majority terms, although Diefenbaker did win two minorities and one majority. The Conservative coalitions eventually broke asunder. They did not cohere long enough to replace the Liberals as the country's dominant party. But they did come together for a while and provide an alternative to Liberal rule, thereby creating a competitive two-party system and forcing the Liberals to renew themselves. Nothing similar appears on the horizon of Canadian politics today.

These successful non-Liberal coalitions were comprised of four regional elements: traditional Tories in Atlantic Canada; Conservatives in Ontario, backed by Toronto financial interests; western Canadian populists (and business interests); and, critically, various hues of French-speaking Quebec nationalists. The Conservatives formed a majority government only once without significant strength in Quebec – in 1917 under Prime Minister Robert Borden. ("Significant" means either a majority of seats in Quebec or a healthy minority of them, as in 1930 when Prime Minister R. B. Bennett won twenty-four seats to forty-one for the Liberals.)

If history offers even a crude guide for Canadian political success, it can be easily demonstrated how far today's non-Liberals have been, and remain, from recreating any semblance of the only coalition in a century that has defeated the Liberals. The Conservatives show strength mostly in Atlantic Canada. Despite Clark's pretence that the Tories are a "national party," they won fewer than 10 per cent of the votes in the 2000 election in two of Canada's three most populous provinces, Quebec and British Columbia. Even in Clark's own province of Alberta, the Conservatives ran 7 per cent behind the second-place Liberals in the popular vote. The Alliance is the dominant party in western Canada. The Conservatives and the Alliance enjoy some support in Ontario, but not enough to threaten the Liberals' hegemony seriously. Even if all Conservative voters in Ontario had supported the Alliance in the 1997 and 2000 elections – a likelihood every serious poll and academic study debunked – the Liberals would still have won a majority of the seats. Neither the Conservatives nor the Alliance has even a small, solid base of support in Quebec. The Conservatives and Alliance therefore represent only elements of the coalition that history suggests is necessary to break the Liberals' dominance. Unless and until one of these parties, or a new political formation that melds the two, begins to reassemble all the elements of the successful non-Liberal coalitions, they will fail to threaten, let alone dislodge, the Liberals.

There was something else about these non-Liberal coalitions – with the exception perhaps of R. B. Bennett's in 1930. They were pragmatic arrangements rather than ideological formations, although the issues of the day differed – from creation of a Canadian navy to financing a natural-gas pipeline to deficit reduction to Canada–U.S. free trade. These non-Liberal coalitions favoured lower taxes and less government, as one might expect from conservatives. But pragmatism and brokering the interests of different regional and ethnic groups had more to do with their political success than the siren songs of ideology.

Diefenbaker, despite his erratic behaviour in office, certainly ought to have taught the Conservatives that lesson in 1957 and 1958. He was far from Bay Street's favourite candidate; indeed, Tory business bullhorns regarded him with a mixture of disdain and fear. He eschewed the usual business prescriptions founded on suspicion of government, and proposed using government to assist farmers, open up the North, and assist the less fortunate. Mulroney, although he jumped to politics from a corporate boardroom, did not get elected in 1984 on slashing the size of government. He campaigned on eliminating "waste and duplication" in government, the cliché of all parties trying to avoid discussing hard choices.

Successful parties, as we have said before, learn a quite simple lesson: Procrustean politics do not work in Canada. Parties that try to shape the country to their message rather than shaping their message to the country – the whole country, not just elements of it – are going to lose. This is not merely the lesson from the past. It resonates today, witness to which are three consecutive Liberal majorities and the repeated failure of the Reform, Alliance, and Conservatives to defeat them (and the increasing marginalization of the NDP). As long as the Alliance, in particular, chooses to practice Procrustean politics – trying to persuade the country to shape itself to the Alliance message rather than the other way around – it will remain on the cold benches of the Opposition and Canada will continue to have de facto one-party governance.

Ideologues will insist that what has worked for Conservative governments in Alberta and Ontario can be transferred with a few modifications to national politics. Tom Long's supporters in the Alliance leadership campaign shared this conceit, but it failed even in the closed confines of a party leadership contest. Obviously, anyone on the political right will relish the victories and subsequent governing approaches of premiers Ralph Klein and Mike Harris, and they will probably like B.C. Liberal Premier Gordon Campbell, who, although nominally a Liberal, espouses some policies inspired by the Klein–Harris successes, especially deep tax cuts.

Canadians searching for national alternatives to the Liberals have frequently fallen into the trap of believing that what works provincially can be transposed almost holus-bolus into national politics. Conservatives chose successful provincial premiers as federal leaders, hoping their provincial magic would assist the national party. Premier John Bracken of Manitoba, Premier George Drew of Ontario, Premier Robert Stanfield of Nova Scotia, estimable men and provincially successful politicians, failed as national leaders to defeat the Liberals. The same fate awaits Stockwell Day, the former Alberta Treasurer (or any successor), unless he studies the lessons of Canadian political history.

Provinces, especially the large ones, are diverse societies. Provinces have their cleavages, but no province is as diverse as Canada writ large. With the exception of Quebec and New Brunswick, provincial politics do not require leaders with proficiency in two official languages. They do not impose on leaders or parties the need to reflect and reconcile interests as diverse as those of, say, fishing villages on the East Coast, farmers on the Prairies, large concentrations of multicultural Canadians in cities, and so on. They do not demand of leaders that they play on the international stage. They do not require leaders or parties to handle complicated national files or to craft messages that will resonate everywhere in Canada.

If it were easy to leap from provincial success to national triumph, Canadians politics would be full of examples. Some successful provincial politicians have shone in the federal arena, but not many of them – and none at all who tried to transfer received wisdom gained in provincial politics into a kind of national vision to carry the entire country. T. C. Douglas, for example, went from being CCF premier of Saskatchewan to being the first national leader of the New Democratic Party. Douglas was an intelligent, honourable man, who made a significant contribution to his country, but he never raised the NDP beyond distant third-party status in national politics. A smattering of prominent Liberal provincial politicians entered federal politics in the twentieth century, but none ever led the national party. It is a comforting illusion, but nothing more, to suggest that what has worked in the smaller theatres of provincial politics can be the script for national success. The history of Canadian politics suggests otherwise – resoundingly.

Nothing inherent in Canada drives the country to one-party dominance. The problem, rather, is the failure to appreciate the nature of Canadian politics, the essence of which consists of trying to understand the whole country, not just parts of it, and to frame policies, choose leaders, and craft messages that have a chance of being appreciated in all parts of Canada. The consistent conceit of the Reform/Alliance Party, born in western Canada, has been that the essence of its message, if presented forcefully and often enough, with a new leader and a new party label, would finally resonate sufficiently beyond the West to bring the party to power, or close to it. Three electoral defeats ought to have dashed that conceit, and now those who worry about one-party dominance must wonder if the Alliance will understand where it has gone wrong. Only if the Alliance steps back, reconsiders some of its policies, and reshapes itself into a more moderate, less ideological party can it become a more electable political formation. Precisely the same challenge awaits sensible New Democrats. In both parties, however, the lessons of political success are apparently either hard to grasp or overwhelmed by ideologues for whom Procrustean politics is too self-satisfying to ignore.

In everything that transpired in the change from Reform to the Canadian Alliance, one essential ingredient was missing in overtures to the Conservatives: a genuine attempt to incorporate at least some core values and ideas from the Conservative Party into the Alliance. The Alliance basically informed the Conservatives: "We are stronger than you are, so join us." If the Alliance had been serious about a rapprochement with the Conservatives, rather than a takeover, it should have studied the history and policies of the Conservative Party and identified at least some policies that could have been brought to the new party. That would have reflected genuine co-operation rather than *force majeure*. Support for regional development, government cultural programs, and official bilingualism – these were among policies important to Conservatives. They were also important to Liberals. A party that realized, as the Alliance apparently did not, that it was the second preference of very few Canadians, would have worked to broaden its appeal. But the Alliance, egged on by ideologues inside the party and in the media, in provincial governments, and in think tanks, insisted on ideological prescriptions and so suffered a predictable political fate.

The Alliance ensnared itself in Procrustean politics for another reason. The Reform Party sprang from rebellion not against the Liberals in the first instance but against the Conservatives. Reform started with the Conservatives in power in the late 1980s. Many of its core supporters were former Conservatives. Once they fled the Conservative Party, they possessed the belief of the righteous that they had become custodians of true "conservatism," because the federal Conservatives had lost the faith. This arrogance of the ideologues was among Tom Long's favourite nostrums, that Joe Clark and the federal Conservatives had abandoned conservatism – whereas what Long and his provincial Conservative friends had done was settle into one wing of the historically large Conservative church and claim they now spoke for the entire congregation. In Alberta, to take the most obvious example, Reform decimated not the Liberals but the Conservatives. Replacing the Conservatives was therefore the first essential step to political legitimacy for Reform, but, having accomplished that objective, the Reform/Alliance parties refused to concede they had anything to learn from the Conservatives, let alone anything to offer to them except an inglorious assurance of their own demise.

To be fair, even if the Alliance had understood the lessons of Canadian political history – lessons that ought to have been drilled into them by successive defeats – Meech Lake's other political consequence rendered even more difficult the rebuilding of a non-Liberal coalition capable of governing. The Bloc Québécois effectively withdrew from national political competition at least half of Quebec's seats. The Bloc's support fell steadily, from 49 per cent of the popular vote in Quebec in 1993 to 40 per cent in 2000, and from fifty-four seats to thirty-eight. The Bloc remained, however, the preferred party of francophone Quebeckers in national elections. Not everyone who voted Bloc favoured Quebec sovereignty, although four-fifths of those who voted for the Bloc in 1997 did. The decline in support for sovereignty between then and the 2000 election accounted in large part for the Bloc's further decline, despite the party running an effective campaign.

The Bloc's vote can be interpreted as a kind of suspension of participation in national political politics and an extension of Quebec's domestic politics. A vote for the Bloc is a vote without consequence, and as such can be lightly given. The presence of a sovereignty party in Ottawa will not determine the outcome of Quebeckers' fate within Canada, for that will be decided within the provincial arena. A vote for the Bloc will not bring sovereignty closer, despite Bloc pretensions to the contrary, and Quebeckers know it. For much of its existence, the Bloc has acted as a mouthpiece for whatever the Parti Québécois decides. The Bloc nonetheless represents a handy and cost-free safety valve for francophone Quebeckers to express their dissatisfaction

with the status quo without having to decide in a federal election their preferred alternative to that status quo. Quite possibly,
it will take another referendum defeat to banish sovereignty to
the margins of Quebec political life, in which case the Bloc will
recede from Ottawa. Until then, however, the withdrawal of
Quebec seats from national politics renders creation of nation-
wide political coalitions difficult.

That difficulty does not erase the need for national parties to
think about the Quebec dimension of our national politics, even
if the tangible rewards for those efforts in Quebec might be slight.
Canadians prefer – and this is especially so for Ontarians – that
their national leaders and parties be present and active in all parts
of Canada. A party with little credibility in Quebec hurts itself in
Ontario, and perhaps in other parts of Canada too, because it is
not seen as being truly national. There is often little love for francophone Quebec in Ontario, but there is even less love for
anything that would potentially polarize the country along language lines, because such polarization might strain national unity.
Ontarians, who think contentedly of themselves as the pivot
around which unity turns, almost instinctively recoil from parties
that might imperil that unity. Ontarians will punish politicians they
think are getting too cozy with Quebec, but they react equally
badly to politicians who might turn Quebeckers against Canada.

The last three elections seem to have cemented Canadian
politics in a new pattern, since the results varied only at the
margin. With 172 seats in 2000, the Liberals won seventeen more
than in 1997 and five fewer than in 1993. The Canadian Alliance
inched up to sixty-six seats from sixty in 1997 and fifty-two in
1993. At that rate of progress, and assuming elections every four
years, the Alliance will achieve a parliamentary majority around
the middle of this century, although since the 2000 election the
Alliance slipped disastrously in public esteem. The Bloc has been
slowly declining, but remains the winner of a majority of French-
speaking Quebec seats. The Conservatives and New Democrats

barely cling to official party status. The new political pattern of the 1990s offered five parties to Canadians, with one party of governance.

Liberals, of course, consider this state of affairs natural and proper, since repeated success has engendered in them something close to a secular sense of the divine right to rule. Their most severe political test comes from the possibility that the Chrétien–Martin tensions over the leadership might publicly split the party. A lacerating public split, however, is highly unlikely. Liberals too often watched Conservatives tear themselves apart in internecine struggles not to have learned that parties incapable of managing their internal affairs properly are viewed by voters as incapable of running those of the country.

Less partisan observers cannot but lament this state of political affairs. Serious competitive politics, with a government-in-waiting, keeps the governing party more attuned to the country and accountable to Parliament. Assured of victories, the Liberals have foregone the need to renew themselves. Chrétien's decision to call a premature election in 2000, just three-and-a-half years after the last one, was an unqualified success as a matter of political tactics. But the decision completely aborted any internal party renewal. The striking characteristic of that campaign was how little fresh thinking the Liberals offered the country, and how many familiar faces resumed their places in the nation's highest offices. Red Book III, the Liberals' campaign document, was a pale imitation of Red Book I in 1993. The prime minister returned. So did most of his senior advisers and cabinet ministers. The vast majority of Liberal MPs were re-elected, including the massive and stolid Ontario contingent. When Parliament reassembled after the vote, it was almost as if a vacation and not an election had occurred. But little discernible enthusiasm for the Liberals marked the election. Voter turnout plunged to record lows. Even Liberal partisans found widespread scepticism among voters about the desirability of keeping Chrétien in office. The failure of any other party to emerge as a plausible governing alternative was the Liberals' best weapon, although a robust economy undoubtedly helped as well. And Chrétien's personal popularity, despite all the accumulated scars of political battle, still eclipsed that of any other leader.

The Liberals' re-election deepened the regional skewing of Canadian politics. The Liberal vote fell in all four western provinces, although the party won fourteen seats in the West, compared to thirteen in 1997 but down from twenty-seven in 1993. The West once again massively preferred other political options, only to find its preferences overwhelmed by Liberal dominance in Ontario and strength in Quebec. Consistent gaps between western Canada's political preferences and those of central Canada (and Atlantic Canada) further deepen the sense of estrangement in that part of Canada. It cannot be healthy in a far-flung federation for the preferences of one part of Canada to be more often than not rebuffed in national elections, and for the government of that federation to be elected on an unfettered first-past-the-post voting system that creates highly centralized parliamentary power based on the support of fewer than half the nation's citizens. The electoral system thus compounds the failure of competitive party politics. That bodes ill for the Canadian political community, because, if Canadian party politics congeals, as it partly has, into a series of unrelated regional contests, then the capacity of parties to think beyond their regions will wither, and so inexorably will Canadians' sense that they are part of a wider community.

A reflexive response to one-party dominance re-emerged after the election. If the system could not adequately capture the increasingly regional nature of Canadian political competition – indeed the system may even exacerbate it – then why not change the system? If Canadians are now set upon voting for completely or essentially regional parties such as the Bloc Québécois and the Canadian Alliance, then Canadians should recognize the inevitable and change the first-past-the-post system. Proportional representation, espoused by the NDP and toyed with by the Canadian

Alliance, would almost guarantee coalition governments. That system would also increase the likelihood of governments more representative of the whole country. After the 1980 election Pierre Trudeau realized his party's lack of representation in western Canada and offered cabinet seats to the NDP to fill that void, an offer the NDP rejected. This offer, which Trudeau with a majority in the Commons was not obligated to make, recognized the desirability of having federal governments that reflect all regions of a diverse country.

Changes to the electoral system are indeed worth debating, and this book elsewhere advances proposals for them. But changing the electoral system, let alone the constitutional changes that would be required for Senate reform, will be a prolonged, complicated, and perhaps ultimately futile exercise. That changes *should* be considered is evident to those who care about the state of Canadian democracy; that they will occur quickly is unlikely; that they will restore confidence in the nation's political institutions is possible, but not assured.

In the meantime, therefore, the obvious question arises: How can effective challenges be launched against the one-party dominance that contributes to Canada's friendly dictatorship? A large part of the answer lies in opposition parties reflecting on what put them in opposition. The old saying about one swallow does not a summer make can be paraphrased and applied to politics – one electoral defeat does not a blind alley make. Parties can lose one, or even two, elections without fundamentally rethinking what they are doing, although a second defeat should kick-start that reflection. But three defeats! In baseball, the third strike sends the batter to the bench; in politics, the third defeat should send the whole team to the clubhouse for a serious talk. Those who broke the old Conservative coalition passionately believed they would shatter the old patterns of Canadian politics and construct something new. They did all right, but what they created has now three times failed to defeat the Liberals. They changed the patterns of Canadian politics, only to cement the Liberals in office, which most assuredly was not the objective.

The easiest response to defeat is to blame circumstances and to believe that success will be at hand once circumstances change. Find a new leader. Wait for the economy to turn down. Get new advisers. Hire new pollsters. Work harder. Prepare better for Question Period. In other words, parties might say to themselves: do what we have been doing, only do it better, and things will improve with the passage of time. A private company that took this view after years of losses would go bankrupt; a party that follows this strategy will remain in opposition.

An even worse fate awaits those who interpret repeated defeats by accepting them as inevitable, thereby giving up any hope of governing. This sentiment has never been absent from the New Democratic Party, but the disastrous setbacks of the last three elections seem to have deepened it. The result is that the NDP seems no longer interested in governing or even in being a serious opposition party. They prefer to align the party with all manner of extra-parliamentary interest groups whose agendas become willy-nilly the NDP's. By moving further from the median Canadian voter, to say nothing of those on the moderate left of the spectrum, the NDP marginalizes itself further and will suffer appropriate electoral consequences. This marginality will be dismissed by those who sniff that electoral politics do not matter much anyway. However, it could be argued, to turn Lord Acton's famous dictum on its head, that the lack of all power corrupts absolutely. For it has been the dream of many social democrats – and in some parts of the world the reality – that political power is worth achieving to accomplish collective goals, and that, for all the heartbreaks and setbacks and compromises imposed by politics and "the crooked timber of humanity," the democratic pursuit of power is a worthy and not a corrupting objective.

Canadians' sympathies are evaporating for a party that refuses to be inspired by other successful social-democratic parties here and abroad, which have more or less accepted the free market, the reality of global trade and the need to regulate it through international agreements, the desirability of collaborative labour–management relations, and the limits of personal taxation. But these parties, having accepted these realities, work within them to achieve more fairness for more citizens, especially the disadvantaged. The signals Canadians are sending New Democrats could not be clearer. If these signals are misunderstood or ignored, New Democrats have no one to blame but themselves.

The Canadian Alliance and the Conservatives, unlike the NDP, do pretend to contend for power, but after three electoral defeats it should be apparent that neither is close to achieving it. Both in retrospect may have erred in selecting new leaders, although in the Alliance's case perhaps there was no other choice. In essence, both parties reached backwards. Joe Clark was obviously yesterday's man, having spent a lifetime in politics. Stockwell Day was the new, new thing, but his essential message resonated almost exclusively with the Alliance's existing political base. If the purpose of creating a new party was to broaden its appeal, the selection of Day – another Albertan and a social conservative to boot – merely solidified what was already secure, including the hostility of a majority of Canadians to the Alliance.

To the extent that leadership drives voting intentions and that new leaders carry less baggage than former ones, perhaps a serious electoral challenge to the Liberals must await the arrival on the political scene of a new figure capable of reassembling the only coalition capable of defeating the Liberals, one that stretches across the country and straddles the political spectrum. Failing that, perhaps Stockwell Day or someone else who becomes leader, will understand that he faces the same predicament as his predecessor: that only by broadening the party's appeal can he make it nationally competitive. Broadening does not mean repackaging, because the Reform Party already tried that and failed under Day's own leadership. Broadening requires resisting the temptation to believe that improved results would follow if only the mechanics of politics were better done. Maybe they would, because parties should always attend to their plumbing, but improvement by these means will not suffice. The Alliance must understand that it remains a fragment party whose pretensions to national leadership have been thrice mocked by Canadians, the majority of whom (this should be posted in bold letters on the walls of every Alliance MP's office) do not consider the Alliance even their second choice.

Of course the ideologues of the political right, like their brothers and sisters on the political left, will have none of these prescriptions. These ideologues, inspired by certain provincial successes but apparently blinded by repeated national defeats, have their institutional mouthpieces in the media. They will take heart from U.S. President George W. Bush's victory, ignoring the fact that it was built on fewer votes than Democrat Al Gore received and in a country with a somewhat different political culture. The United States, from the broader perspective of advanced industrial democracies, represents the exception, since almost everywhere else parties of the centre or centre-left govern: in Britain, France, Germany, New Zealand, Canada, Scandinavia. That Canada, according to probing surveys of Canadian values, has moved somewhat to the political right in recent years should not lull the Alliance into believing it will move even more sharply in that direction. If anything, now that federal finances are under control, the tendency will be for Canadians to seek additional investments in neglected social capital such as health care, education, and the welfare of children.

By means yet unknown, and almost certainly under different leaders, there must be a coming together of the Alliance and Conservative parties if Liberal hegemony is to be threatened. This cannot be accomplished by *force majeure*, because if what emerged was the Alliance with a new name but the same policies, the Conservatives would not consent, and, if they unexpectedly did consent on these terms, the majority of their voters would turn to the Liberals, leaving the Alliance no further ahead. The Conservatives, for their part, must recognize that they are finished as a national party as currently constituted. That they barely secured official-party status in the 2000 election should remind them of their marginal political status, even if Conservative fortunes improved in the first six months of 2001 while the Alliance battled over Day's leadership. If the ideologues have their way, of course, the coming together will be rendered more difficult, because they are less inclined to make compromises. A handful of them in Alberta demonstrated after the election their lack of interest in compromise and broadening. They reacted to defeat by recommending Alberta withdraw from various federal programs and create its own, thereby building a "firewall" around the province to protect it from intellectually alien elements. A surer recipe for continued political marginality in national politics could scarcely be imagined.

The dismissal of ideological prescriptions for political success in Canada, however, does not mean rejecting the importance of ideas in politics. Nor does it necessarily mean that politics must only be about which party can be sold as a superior manager, although competence in governmental management is important. Nor finally does it require the yielding of all principles to the temptations of expediency, although pragmatism, in contrast to expediency, is a prized Canadian political virtue. The distinction between ideology and ideas does require an understanding that ideas are not necessarily of value only as extensions of ideology. Some of the defining debates of contemporary Canada have been rooted in compelling ideas that did not fit any left–right ideological pattern. Think of official bilingualism, the Charter of Rights and Freedoms, an elected Senate, the Canadian flag, the Meech Lake and Charlottetown accords, women's and gay rights, abortion, capital punishment, equalization, the ongoing conduct of Canada–U.S. relations, military intervention overseas, the Goods and Services Tax, and so on. Even the need to balance the budget was an idea that ought to have mocked ideology, since prudent social democrats understood that accumulated deficits producing a large debt enfeebled the state's capacity to provide services, because so many dollars flowed into paying interest on the debt. And it might usefully be remembered that Conservative governments in Ottawa, Alberta, and Saskatchewan were among the worst offenders in piling up debt.

The new structure of Canadian party politics – the fourth party system – is a decade old. It succeeded in bringing new ideas into the political arena. It provided vehicles for regional alienation and disaffection. It reflected cleavages that constitutional reforms were supposed to narrow but wound up widening. It gave birth to two new parties, almost destroyed another, and marginalized the NDP. But for all the excitement and anticipation of change, the most important outcome of democratic politics in Canada was the de facto dominance of the Liberals as the country's apparently permanent governing party. This became the unwelcome consequence of all the agitation: that Canada's friendly dictatorship remained intact, while ideological and regional parties went this way and that, each wrongly convinced that their prescriptions would prevail, ignorant of the reality that Procrustean politics has never succeeded in Canada and, as long as Canada remains united, never will.

The Decline
of Voting

Canadians are increasingly turned off politics. Fewer of them are voting than ever. Voters are increasingly unhappy about or uninterested in the political choices on offer. Parliament, with its almost institutionalized one-party government, antiquated rules, piddling roles for backbenchers, and schoolyard theatrics, seems irrelevant, a source of national despair rather than pride. Respect for elected officials, as measured by polls, has plummeted to the depths reserved for used-car salesmen and journalists.

The electoral system produces a friendly dictatorship controlled by the prime minister and backed by a parliamentary majority, but the system lacks any effective checks and balances to prime-ministerial power. The parliamentary majority is built on fewer than half the votes cast, courtesy of a first-past-the-post voting system that systematically overrepresents in government some parts of Canada and underrepresents others, thus fuelling regional alienation. Canadians have a hierarchical political system in which the trappings of egalitarianism – one person, one vote; one MP for each constituency; one parliamentary vote for each MP – are mocked by the concentration of power in the hands of the prime minister. The rest of society is not organized as is parliamentary government, with the result that a gap of credibility, or at least of interest, grows between those who work within the political system and those who send people there.

Voting is not the only means of participating or showing interest in politics. People can consume information from the media or chat with their friends about current events. They can attend meetings, send money to political parties, join an interest group, participate in demonstrations, fire off letters to MPs or newspapers, or pull down information from the Internet – without ever voting. They can be keenly interested in their community or the wider world without necessarily paying attention to government and politics. They can feel that participation in a school council or a local sports team or a church or a non-governmental organization giving foreign aid is more worthwhile for them, and for their society, than bothering with government and politics. They can participate in what is called "civic society" – the network of organized links between an individual and the surrounding society – without being interested in politics.

The act of voting, however, has always been an important measure of civic engagement, and in Canada the incidence of that act has been falling. The 2000 election resulted in the lowest voter turnout in Canadian history. The vacuous nature of the campaign and the outcome's foregone conclusion – another majority Liberal government – undoubtedly contributed to the low turnout, but voter participation has been declining for a long time. Whether the 2000 turnout represented the culmination or a continuation of that trend obviously cannot yet be known, but the lessening of interest in the minimal political activity of voting – an activity that comes around only every four years or so – suggests a malaise within Canada's democracy. The decline scarcely ripples the conscience of the governing party. The Liberals, after all, captured three consecutive parliamentary majorities, each time with far fewer than half the popular votes cast, but they could care less about how many people actually bothered to vote. They won, and that is all they need to know.

The following chart illustrates voter turnout in federal elections over the last half-century.

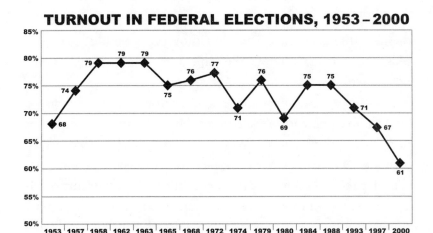

TURNOUT IN FEDERAL ELECTIONS, 1953–2000

Notes: Figure for 1993 is adjusted. Figure for 2000 is preliminary (as of December 19, 2000).
Source: Data from Elections Canada

Only 61 per cent of eligible Canadians bothered to vote in 2000, the lowest turnout by far since the Second World War and 18 percentage points lower than the post-war highs of 79 per cent in the elections of 1958, 1959, and 1962. It was occasionally argued after the 2000 election that this disappointing turnout nonetheless left Canada well above the United States, where turnout hovers around 50 per cent in presidential elections. Canadians enjoy nothing more than demonstrating their putative moral superiority vis-à-vis Americans, so that, even while lamenting the low voter turnout, Canadians could still consider themselves more civic-minded than Americans. This moral superiority, as usual, was misplaced.

Canadians and Americans count voter turnout differently. Canada measures voter turnout by comparing those who voted with those on the electoral list, whereas the United States compares voters to the total eligible population. We know that not everyone eligible to vote in Canada gets on the voters' list – indeed the gap between eligibility and those on the list has widened – so Canada is comparing voter turnout against a shorter yardstick than the United States. If Canada had used the U.S. method of calculating voter turnout – those who voted compared to the total eligible population, rather than those with names on the list – the 2000 Canadian election turnout would have been only 51 per cent, or about the same as for the 2000 U.S. presidential election.

Whatever the comparison – against those on the voters' list or total eligible population – Canada's electoral turnout is now at or near the bottom among Western democracies. Scandinavian turnouts are above 80 per cent, German between 75 and 80 per cent, Japan in the low-70-per-cent range. Canadian turnout is also below that of most Latin American democracies (where some countries insist on mandatory voting), Israel, South Korea, many Caribbean countries, and Pacific Island states, while remaining higher than that of Zambia and India with their widespread rural illiteracy. Voter turnout in some Western democracies, such as Germany, France, Finland, and Ireland, has also declined, but not as rapidly as in Canada, although turnout in Britain for Tony Blair's majority re-election in June 2001 fell almost to Canadian levels. Taking the larger Western European countries together, a decline in turnout can be measured over the post-war period in a series of small downward steps, whereas the Canadian drop has been sharper and of more recent vintage. The result has left Canada about ten points behind the United Kingdom (before the 2001 British vote), fifteen points below Germany, and thirty behind Italy. Canada in the last thirty years has slid from slightly below the average turnout rate in Western countries to near the bottom.

The sharpest drop occurred in the last four elections, from 75 per cent in 1988 to 61 per cent in 2000. A glance at the chart suggests two other trends. The first is easy to spot: a broad decline from the high-water marks of the late 1950s and early 1960s. The second is more speculative, but suggestive nonetheless. A few elections bucked the downward trend – 1979, 1984, and 1988. The Conservatives won all three elections, suggesting that more people will vote if elections are deemed to be nationally competitive, with the outcome somewhat uncertain before or during the campaign. The elections from Conservative leader John Diefenbaker's arrival in the 1957 campaign until the breakup of the two-party system in 1993 recorded higher voter turnouts than in the multi-party politics of the 1990s, which featured elections with assumed Liberal majority victories.

The breakup of the Conservative coalition into the fragment parties of Conservatives, Reform–Alliance, and Bloc Québécois therefore may have contributed to falling voter turnout, a superficially surprising result. The Reform–Alliance and Bloc were both protest parties of a sort, their members determined to shatter the old party system (and in one case the country). Their members and supporters would therefore be assumed to be possessed of such convictions that they would turn out in high numbers to achieve their parties' political objectives, thereby pushing up overall voting participation. Instead, the reverse occurred. The lack of a competitive national election, and its replacement by a series of different regional competitions – Conservative/Liberal in Atlantic Canada; Bloc/Liberal in Quebec; Liberal/Reform–Alliance/Conservative in Ontario; Liberal/Reform–Alliance/NDP on the prairies; Liberal/Reform–Alliance in British Columbia – contributed to driving down participation to record low levels, especially in English-speaking Canada. (A larger share of Quebeckers did vote in 1993 than in 1988, while turnout dropped elsewhere in Canada, presumably because of the excitement created by Lucien Bouchard's creation of the Bloc Québécois.) Put another way, one-party dominance such as Canada experienced in the immediate post-war years and since 1993 depresses voter turnout. Unless the fragment parties cohere into a competitive national alternative to the Liberals, not only will the Liberals gladly keep on governing, but Canada's voter turnout will remain among the Western world's lowest.

The same rough correlation exists provincially between competitive federal elections and turnout. Newfoundland aside – that province's turnout in federal elections has historically lagged far behind the rest of the country's – the two provinces with one-party dominance recorded the lowest turnouts. Some 58 per cent of Ontarians voted in the 2000 federal election, and the Liberals captured all but 3 of 103 seats; only 60 per cent of Albertans voted, and the Canadian Alliance won all but 2 seats. These provinces witnessed the Liberals and Alliance score some of their largest constituency majorities. By contrast, voter turnout in Prince Edward Island (73 per cent) and New Brunswick (68 per cent) were well above the national average, in part because Conservatives and Liberals hotly contested so many ridings.

What about provincial politics? Are Canadians also turning away from provincial politics as measured by voter turnout? The answer is a qualified yes. Average turnout dropped in seven of ten provinces over each province's last five elections, although provincial voting rates exceeded federal ones in every province except Alberta. Turnout in the last three federal elections averaged 66 per cent, compared to a 69-per-cent average turnout in five provincial elections in the 1997-to-2000 period. Provincial turnout rates until recently had closely resembled those in federal elections, so the recent falloff has been sharper in federal than provincial politics. There is, then, some evidence of a wider decline of interest in politics when federal and provincial turnout rates are considered together, although the provincial decline is less exaggerated. But the overall decline in both turnout rates suggests that something deeper than the absence of competitive national politics has been going on to turn Canadians off voting in federal elections.

Canadians know that, when they vote, they do not necessarily get what they voted for. They usually wind up with parliamentary majorities based on fewer than half the popular vote, and occasionally a government with fewer popular votes than another party. In 1979, for example, Prime Minister Joe Clark formed a minority government with 36 per cent of the national vote compared to 40 per cent for the Liberals. (British Columbia and

Quebec in recent years saw parties win legislative majorities with fewer popular votes than the Official Opposition.) The anomaly between votes casts and seats won derives from the first-past-the-post voting system. Only once in the last three decades has a party won 50 per cent of the popular vote – the Mulroney Conservatives in 1984 – and yet seven governments enjoyed a majority of parliamentary seats. In the 1990s, with voter turnout rates tumbling, the Liberals formed majority governments with 41 per cent of the vote twice and 38 and 39 per cent once each. Prime Minister Pierre Trudeau's three parliamentary majorities were built on popular votes of 46, 43, and 44 per cent. Here is another political fiction. Governments routinely insist that they speak for the "people," when quite obviously they do not. They may speak for more voters than any other party, but not a majority of voters.

These national distortions mask regional skewing. It matters greatly in the first-past-the-post system not just how many votes a party receives, but where. A party that bunches its votes is better off than one whose votes are spread evenly across constituencies. That bunching in recent years, especially in western Canada, helps explain why the Reform/Alliance has won so many more seats than the Conservatives, the most egregious example being the 1997 election, when Reform captured 60 seats and the Conservatives 20, although both won 19 per cent of the popular vote. Wasted votes also explain why the Liberals do so poorly in western Canada. Liberal votes are spread in the West, thereby producing a smaller share of parliamentary seats than their popular vote suggests.

The first-past-the-post system, imported from Britain, offers a singular virtue. It does produce, more often than not, stable parliamentary majorities. Canada has not been plagued with the instability of shifting coalitions and weak governments that have characterized some other countries. Nor does the first-past-the-post system remove from the voters and hand to parliamentarians the formation of a government, as in certain west European countries, where governing coalitions are negotiated after the votes are cast. Stability and the ability to get things done, even against the temporary winds of public opinion, led to the description of parliamentary democracy as an "elected dictatorship." The virtues of stability, however, are not offset by any reasonable checks and balances in the Canadian political system, and parliamentary government of the kind described in textbooks has evolved into a prime-ministerial government with no institutional impediments to prime-ministerial rule, except those that are blunt and usually ineffective.

The first-past-the-post system with its electoral anomalies may be contributing to Canadians' declining interest in things political. In wide areas of Canada, voters feel a kind of helplessness, knowing that their votes will not count. In the last three elections, supporters of the opposition parties understood that their parties could not form a government, regardless of the rhetorical hype during the campaigns. No matter how massive the Alliance/Reform majorities in Alberta and British Columbia, voters there had no chance of toppling the Liberals nationally, so long as that party dominated Ontario and stitched together enough support elsewhere. When voters in one region regularly wake up after elections to find their political preferences squashed by those of another region, and then discover that the winning party has formed another parliamentary majority on far fewer than half the popular vote, is it any wonder they might find themselves alienated from the political system and the government that benefits from it? On the other hand, in Ontario, where voter turnout was the second-lowest in Canada in 2000 (after Newfoundland), some Liberal supporters might have stayed home knowing the results were a foregone conclusion in many ridings. They might have been content with Liberal victories, but why bother, since their votes were not needed?

A technical reason might also be depressing voter turnout: the new electoral list. From Confederation until the 1997 election, Canadians were placed on the voters' list by door-to-door enumerations conducted in the campaign's initial weeks. In 1997, prodded by the Chief Electoral Officer, Parliament changed the enumeration from one compiled afresh for each election to a permanent list. The idea of a permanent list had been around for several decades before Parliament acted, but arguments against one had previously prevailed. A permanent list was deemed unreliable and costly, or so Parliament assumed – until legislators were persuaded that modern technology could produce a credible, low-cost permanent list. The Chief Electoral Officer argued that a list could be assembled using massive data banks for drivers' licences, death registrations, passport applications and renewals, and other computerized sources of information, augmented at election time with advertising to tell eligible voters whose names did not appear on the list how to get themselves enumerated. Better still, he insisted, the permanent list, once up and running, would save money, an appealing argument in the deficit-fighting years of the mid-1990s. The reservations of some distinguished political scientists – John Courtney of the University of Saskatchewan being one – were waved aside, and Parliament took the plunge.

Following the 2000 election, many parliamentarians regretted the change. Constituents had besieged candidates throughout the campaign because their names had not appeared. It had been assumed, wrongly as matters unfolded, that the teething problems that had emerged in the 1997 campaign would have been resolved by this point. The registration rate for voters had fluctuated between 90 and 95 per cent from the Second World War to 1993, but dropped sharply to about 85 per cent in 1997. In other words, although the total number of eligible voters rose with population increases between 1993 and 1997, the number of names on the list did not. Remember, also, that the share of Canadians eligible to vote as determined by the voting list contributes to the different way Canadians compare turnout to the United States, which contrasts voters to the total population.

Judging by the number of complaints during the 2000 election, however, the bugs had not been ironed out of the permanent voters' list. Some irate MPs returned to Ottawa determined to find out why and, if necessary, to scrap the permanent list and return to door-to-door enumeration, a system that had worked for decades. Their ire was well-placed. Not every change, whatever its inspiration, is for the better, and two tries with a permanent list suggest that too many Canadians are being disenfranchised. Then again, perhaps cause and effect are being turned upside down. It may be that the new system is less efficient than proponents argued, thereby depriving Canadians of their right to vote and so pushing down turnout. It could also be that a general disengagement from politics discouraged potential voters from bothering to check whether their names appeared, since they did not intend to vote anyway. Sharply lower voter turnouts in the 1990s represented just one manifestation of a declining interest in politics that certainly goes beyond any problems with the voters' list. Many years ago, Canadians were deferential to governments and politicians. Many more of them were committed partisans who voted the same way election after election, and took their political cues from party organizations, Liberal or Conservative newspapers, and partisans in their families, especially elders. Years ago, to know how someone would vote was to know how their father had voted. All this has changed in recent decades, although the reasons for the change are manifold and the subject of constant debate.

We know that fewer Canadians than ever before identify with a political party. They shop around politically, checking out leaders, images, and policies, changing their voting behaviour from election to election. This does not mean voters will randomly turf governments out of office just because they have been politically shopping. It may be, as in the last three federal elections, that those who bothered to vote had looked at all the options, however briefly, and decided that, on balance, the Liberals were the best political buy. But the weakening of partisan commitment does seem to have lowered voter turnout, not just in Canada but in other Western democracies. Weakening of commitment is linked to higher education levels and greater material well-being, since both reduce dependence on traditional ways of looking at authority.

Political scientists still lack a definitive answer to who is not voting. Provincial voter turnouts are easy to calculate, so we know that Newfoundlanders, for example, vote in fewer numbers than New Brunswickers. We also know that young people aged eighteen to twenty-five have historically voted less than middle-aged people and seniors. That, however, should produce higher voter turnouts, because the share of young people in the population is declining, but the reverse has occurred. We know that age and education are prime determinants in pushing people to vote, and yet, as the 1997 National Election Survey said, "turnout is declining in spite of socio-demographic changes that should cause it to rise." In explaining why voter turnout has dropped, we do not know with precision where it has fallen off among age and ethnic groups, or among partisans or independents. Some preliminary surveys of non-voters in the 2000 election suggested that, had the voter turnout been 10 per cent higher, the Liberals would still have won easily, since non-voters said their opinions roughly mirrored those who voted. But we cannot be sure, because they might have changed their minds had they actually voted.

A reasonable speculation, but only a speculation, suggests politics has become a spectator sport, even during elections. Parties used to do much more door-to-door canvassing, and they needed legions of dedicated volunteers for that activity. As fewer people volunteer for election work, these kinds of thorough canvasses become harder, if not impossible, to organize. The NDP of twenty or thirty years ago, for example, used to organize three door-to-door canvasses in key ridings, so that on election day the party knew with remarkable precision how to identify supporters and "get out the vote." This was the NDP's way of compensating for having less money for political advertising than their political foes. The shrivelling of NDP membership now makes three door-to-door canvasses impossible, except in a few ridings. Canvassing not only drew commitment from legions of volunteers; it at least fleetingly put the party in touch with voters through personal contacts with party supporters. Personal canvassing has given way to telephone canvassing, which parties believe is a more efficient use of a volunteer's time. But as anyone knows who has fended off dinnertime phone solicitations from groups trying to raise money, telephone canvassing lacks, shall we say, the personal touch.

Canadians are also far less deferential towards institutional authority of all kinds, including but not exclusively government. Political scientist Neil Nevitte of the University of Toronto has offered the most incisive analysis of this change in a book aptly titled *The Decline of Deference*, a work that built upon pioneering studies by U.S. political scientist Ronald Inglehart about structural shifts in attitudes caused by rising affluence.

Nevitte's thesis, confirmed in essence by other students of Canadian attitudes, suggests in part that more Canadians than ever have become "post-materialist." That means they have reached sufficient levels of economic comfort that they do not rely on government – or at least do not think that they do. Citizens can drive on a highway, walk on a sidewalk, assume their sewage will be flushed away, receive a pension, and avail themselves of a myriad of other public services without even thinking that these are organized by government. Rising material prosperity induces citizens both to take things for granted and to conclude wrongly that their individual well-being does not derive from government at all.

In Canada, as in other countries, Nevitte has found these "post-materialists" to be "consistently less deferential" towards authority. The greater their numbers, the less inclined the population as a whole will be to assume *prime facie* that governments understand problems, let alone have the answers to them. These attitudinal changes widen the gap between how governments do business and what the public expects of government. Prime-ministerial government is sharply hierarchical, despite the trappings of egalitarianism in the political system, whereas the rest of society is increasingly organizing itself differently. Studies of workforce participation and business strategies underline that greater satisfaction and results are earned by organizations that solicit participation and share information rather than those that rely on command-and-control management systems. Outside the political world, Canadians work and observe different patterns of organization than those they see inside their political parties and government. As Nevitte writes, "there is a sustained, and possibly generationally driven, public reaction against all hierarchical institutional arrangements that limit the opportunities for meaningful citizen participation."

The contrast between hierarchy and participation can only reinforce the already deep suspicions that Canadians feel towards their political system. Canadian political parties have recently tried to adapt to these suspicions in selecting their leaders. Three of them – Conservative, Bloc Québécois, and Alliance – now choose leaders by direct election of members, a method that widens participation, and the NDP is moving in a similar direction. But the new method of selecting party leaders has had no discernible effect either on the government – which is not surprising, given these parties' opposition status – or on how leaders, once elected, comport themselves. The methods of selection have changed; the relationship of leaders to led, inside their parties and with the general public, has not.

Campaigning Canadian political leaders have sensed this change and tried to articulate it. Liberal prime minister Pierre Trudeau spoke of "participatory politics." Conservative prime minister Kim Campbell pledged to "do politics differently." Reform leader Preston Manning, when he arrived in the House of Commons in 1993, tried sitting in the second row to symbolize that he would lead his new party differently in Parliament. It is now almost a given, following the referendum on the Charlottetown accord, that any major constitutional change must be voted upon by the people. The Alliance has pledged to hold national referendums on important issues if sufficient people – the definition of how many remains vague – demand one. Opposition MPs, and even some dissident Liberal backbenchers, clamour for more free votes in the Commons, so that individual judgment rather than party discipline can be brought to bear on issues. And yet, these pledges and fitful changes in behaviour have left the political system fundamentally unchanged, except for the apparent convention that any constitutional change must be approved through a national referendum.

Once elected, the government organizes itself in a traditionally hierarchical shape, with all power flowing from the prime minister, and within the institutions of government no effective check or balance exists against that power. When asked in 1990 in the World Values Survey whether they trusted the government in Ottawa to "do what is right," only 20 per cent of Canadians said "always" or "almost always," less than half the share of Americans giving similar answers. Those results undoubtedly reflected the unpopularity of Prime Minister Brian Mulroney's government and the relatively greater popularity of U.S. President Ronald Reagan. Still, a series of Canadian polls taken throughout the 1990s have shown only a slight improvement in the respect of citizens for politicians and governments. Two different surveys in the last five years, which asked Canadians to rank occupational groups in order of trustworthiness, placed politicians far down the list, bunched together with lobbyists, journalists, and lawyers.

In addition to declining deference, the definitive academic study of the 1997 election found supporters of all parties showing high levels of cynicism about politicians and the responsiveness of government. Liberal supporters were the least cynical, as we might expect, followed by Conservative and New Democrat, with Reform voters the most cynical of all. But on a scale from 0 to 1, the average cynicism score was 0.7, with even a majority of Liberal supporters displaying large amounts of cynicism. The study's authors found that cynicism did contribute to the low voter turnout in 1997, a turnout that was 67 per cent. If cynicism about politics contributed to a 67 per cent turnout, we can only conclude that cynicism was alive and well and doing its corrosive work in the 2000 election, in which turnout was 61 per cent.

In theory, higher levels of education should contribute to more interest in politics. Here is one of the great conundrums of contemporary politics. We know that better-educated people follow politics more closely than less-educated ones. They show greater awareness of issues and consume more political news. And yet at the very moment when Canada has more well-educated people than ever in its history, voter turnout is falling. People may be interested in things political, but that does not apparently translate to electoral politics as they are organized in Canada.

Various surveys have shown that another reason people do not interest themselves in politics is because "politics is too complicated." A historical correlation exists between deference and low education and income status. Citizens who felt they must rely on government counted upon élites to deliver benefits, and they were disinclined to question those élites unless the benefits eroded or were eliminated. The old patronage system of Canadian political parties was rooted in this patron-client relationship, in which elected officials delivered jobs, money, and government benefits in return for political support.

Remnants of those old assumptions about politics remain in parts of Canada, with the federal Liberals being the past masters at playing that kind of politics with make-work programs, Transitional Jobs Funds, regional development agencies, to say nothing of studied favouritism in the apportionment of jobs that remain the government's prerogative. Judged by the sweep of Canadian political history, however, the amount of patronage today has shrunk to a fraction of its former size. Rising incomes and higher levels of education have meant fewer Canadians depend on government programs for their livelihood. That same combination also raises levels of interest in societal questions, and emboldens people to think more for themselves about what should be done. The vast proliferation of interest groups, the rapid rise in the use of the courts to provide legal remedies for political questions, the persistently high television ratings for news and public-affairs programs, the readerships for new newspapers such as the *National Post*, the explosion of the Internet, all suggest that Canadians are participating in their society, or at least seeking information about it, without that participation being reflected in commensurate interest in the political system. Quite the contrary.

Less Government, Less Interest?

Perhaps some of the declining interest in government flowed from the shrunken size of government in the 1990s. The share of federal government program spending dropped to about 12 per cent of gross domestic product, the smallest since the 1950s. Taxes had risen throughout the 1980s and for most of the 1990s, but the taxation trend began slowly turning down at decade's end. Liberal and Conservative governments had run deficits without inter-ruption from 1973 to 1995, pushing up the federal debt to such levels that debt repayment gobbled up a third of all federal revenues. Canada had the second-highest ratio of debt to gross domestic product of the seven largest industrial nations. Despite nine years of fitful efforts to contain the deficit, the Mulroney Conservatives left office with one of $42 billion, the same as the one it had inherited. The Liberals in Opposition had relentlessly attacked Conservative efforts, and promised in the 1993 election only to reduce the deficit. Not long after taking office, with interest rates rising, the Chrétien government got religion about the problem, forgetting what they had promised during the campaign – an old Liberal habit. They cut back federal spending more sharply than the Conservatives, including major reductions in transfers to provinces. And they raised a variety of taxes.

Federal spending cuts ended or reduced some government programs. Having pilloried the Conservatives for privatizing Crown corporations, the Liberals, once in office, reversed field and privatized more. They also embraced "alternative delivery systems," bureaucratese for public services delivered by means other than civil servants. They created arm's-length organizations to deliver government programs, thus depoliticizing what had been government decisions. These changes were driven by fiscal enfeeblement and in some cases by a genuine belief among policy-makers and politicians that government services could be delivered more efficiently. The changes also seemed to catch the drift of public opinion: cynicism towards government; more emphasis on personal initiative. They also reflected the Liberals' attention to the Reform Party's attacks on Big Government, since the Liberals, that most malleable of political parties, lean with the political winds.

Reductions in government spending did produce periodic outbursts of anger. Seasonal workers in Atlantic Canada protested tougher eligibility for Unemployment Insurance, ironically renamed Employment Insurance by the Liberals. Provinces berated Ottawa for cutbacks to transfers, especially for health care. Cultural groups bemoaned their reduced subsidies; the Canadian Broadcasting Corporation lost about 40 per cent of its public money; public-sector unions protested layoffs; farmers complained, as they frequently do. But the Liberals had correctly read the public mood. After years of insouciance about deficits, Canadians came belatedly to realize the importance of fiscal prudence. Quite likely the pennies dropped for Canadians when they experienced stagnant real incomes. Even if their pre-tax incomes rose, their after-tax incomes did not. Too many families, working harder but getting no further ahead financially, began to understand that deficits are a form of delayed taxation. The higher taxes they paid were the inevitable response to yesterday's fiscal errors.

The Liberals successfully made the political case for deficit reduction. The Tories could not shake the nagging feeling among Canadians that their party slashed government programs for the ideological delight of it and that, without the leash of public opinion, the Tories' ideology would carry them beyond a point where Canadians were prepared to go. The Liberals, on the other hand, portrayed themselves as reluctant deficit-fighters – plausibly or otherwise. They had not campaigned on slaying the deficit. They took a "devil made us do it" approach in their public relations, relying on the credibility of Finance Minister Paul Martin and the popularity of Prime Minister Jean Chrétien. The Conservatives ate their hearts out when Canadians rewarded Liberals for carrying Tory policies farther, faster.

Whatever the politics of deficit-reduction, the scope of government shrank. Plenty of government policies and programs remained to excite interest or opposition, but there were somewhat fewer of them after the years of fiscal restraint. Canadians might not like their air carriers, but they could not complain to public authorities, because Air Canada had been privatized. So had their major freight carrier, Canadian National; their airports; their national energy company, Petro-Canada; their air-navigation system; and certain forms of government inspections. Programs such as manpower training had been handed to the provinces.

Agencies at arm's length from government ran the national parks and collected taxes. Citizens might receive improved service from these new ways of delivering service – a contested point – but the changes did shrink the size of government, disengaging services from the public sector and therefore from direct political involvement and accountability. The removal of these services from the public domain might produce efficiency gains, but the result also might have contributed to citizens' lack of interest in a government that no longer delivered these services.

The necessary restoration of Canada's federal finances hardly provided the stuff of political drama. Politics in the 1990s was about limits, not growth; about shrinking, or at least changing, visions for government. Politics became an accountant's game of which party's math added up, which could be better trusted to cut, which had greater credibility in pursuing much the same policies. The old clash between left and right petered out, and the struggles unfolded between two visions of smaller government. The majestic visions of Canadian politics were but memories – from Sir John A. Macdonald's National Policy and Sir Wilfrid Laurier's peopling of the Canadian West to John Diefenbaker's Northern Vision, from Pierre Trudeau's "Just Society," bilingualism, and the Charter of Rights to Brian Mulroney's free trade deal with the United States. No prime minister, except perhaps Mackenzie King, ever entered the history books for tidy management, although knowing the worth of a public dollar and who provided it ought to be a skill prized even by historians. Fiscal restraint's humdrum politics was unlikely to galvanize Canadians and rekindle their political interest, except for dwindling handfuls of leftists still misreading John Maynard Keynes and red-meat ideologues of the political right for whom the government that governs least governs best.

In a quite insidious way, the staggering levels of government debt heightened voter scepticism. About a third of every dollar citizens sent to Ottawa went not to deliver services or programs, but to pay interest on the national debt. Taxpayers understandably wondered why they received services and programs equivalent to roughly two-thirds of the value of their tax money, because holders of Canadian debt in Canada and abroad took the other third. Debt repayment produced perverse income redistribution effects, as people on the political left ought to have known but apparently did not. Lenders had money, and these tended to be institutions and individuals already awash with cash. Lenders were then repaid, with interest of course, by the entire taxpaying public, including those on low and middle incomes. Debt produced redistribution of income all right, but in precisely the wrong direction.

While the federal government taxed more but returned less in services and programs – federal program spending as a share of gross domestic product fell steadily throughout the 1990s – it found its sovereignty beset by competing pressures. Supra-nationalism required yielding up sovereignty to international treaties and organizations; demands for more local autonomy produced clashes with provinces. Federal governments faced this dilemma everywhere, as citizens responded to the loss of control over some policies with a demand for more local control over others.

To a lot of Canadians, Ottawa must seem to be merely a vast cheque-writing machine, sending money to provinces but not delivering programs. Ottawa distributes tens of billions of dollars to provinces for equalization, health care, regional development, integration of immigrants, manpower training, and minority-language education, but provincial governments deliver actual programs on the ground. The average hospital patient or university student, for example, may at best be only vaguely aware of Ottawa's role in financing these institutions. This is the domestic equivalent of the international "democratic deficit," because politicians raising the money are not those responsible for spending it. Conversely, as provincial governments will quickly retort, if the federal government hands over less money, provincial politicians will face the sharp point of public anger for providing fewer services or raising additional taxes. The domestic "democratic deficit" contributes to Canada's endemic federal-provincial squabbles, the rhetoric from which provides the background noise of politics, leaving citizens confused about who is responsible for what and often in a mood to wish a plague on all politicians.

Less Sovereignty, Less Interest

The 1990s also coincided with the arrival of international trading agreements that fettered governments' capacity to act. The Canada–U.S Free Trade Agreement, the North American Free Trade Agreement, and the creation of the World Trade Organization were all designed to liberalize trade. This objective necessarily meant curbing governments' ability to interfere with the free flow of goods and services among contracting individuals or companies. Government policies that directly subsidized domestic production were curtailed if those products entered other markets. Investment regimes were modified to provide "national treatment" for foreign investments; interventionist energy policies such as the National Energy Policy could no longer be contemplated; patent protection for pharmaceutical products was extended, delaying the market entry of cheaper generic drugs. These agreements effectively withdrew governments from areas of economic policy to give the market freer reign. Citizens who complained learned that government assistance risked running afoul of these agreements. So not only did the government shrink, parts of what remained were prohibited from even contemplating, let alone implementing, a range of policies that at least some citizens might have been drawn into politics to achieve.

Trade agreements highlighted an inherent problem with supra-nationalism – the so-called "democratic deficit." Historically, democracy grew up within nation-states, so that citizens could control who governed them, and decisions, once made, could be undone by a change of government. Democratic accountability is weakened when citizens learn that people and institutions they do not know or elect are making major decisions affecting their lives. Supra-national institutions make sense for regulating inter-national trade and settling disputes among countries, but they are staffed by civil servants and other "experts" who citizens do not know and could not identify. The European Union, whose supra-nationalism vastly exceeds anything in North America, has the European Parliament, with members elected directly in each member-state. But turnout for European Parliament elections is far below that for national elections. Euro MPs meet in Strasbourg, much farther removed physically and emotionally than Rome for Italians or Madrid for Spaniards, and European media less rou-tinely report the Parliament's deliberations than those of national parliaments. European Commissioners appointed by member states make many of the Union's most important decisions.

The North American free trade agreements were ratified by parliaments, and, in Canada's case, extensively debated in an elec-tion campaign. But once ratified, the agreements could not be altered; use of the withdrawal clause was hardly an option. The market's "invisible hand" did its inexorable work, bringing about changes in the lives of Canadians. As companies entered a more fiercely competitive world and cross-border flows of capital intensified, governments seemed relegated to the sidelines. These new arrangements might have been economically necessary to raise aggregate living standards, but they also left Canadians feeling that perhaps governments had lost some of their importance.

The same could be said for another major economic change – the deterioration of the Canadian dollar. Canadians felt the impact of that deterioration every time they travelled to the United States or purchased a U.S. good or service. Exporters rejoiced in the sliding currency, since it made their products easier to sell in the United States. The only bright spot for the Canadian economy in the 1990s lay in booming exports to the United States, since Canada has now become for all intents and purposes an economic colony of the United States – or to put matters less pejoratively, one economic region among many within the Greater United States. Decisions of the U.S. Federal Reserve are of more consequence for the Canadian economy than those of the Bank of Canada, whose monetary policy since the currency began sliding from par with the U.S. dollar in 1976 has focused on ensuring a leisurely and controlled deterioration rather than attempting to support the loonie's relative value. Whether Canadians liked the loonie's slide or not, they were instructed that nothing could be done because of international "market forces" and, of course, the government's traditional hands-off relationship to the Bank of Canada. Arguably, the loonie's deterioration shaped Canada's economy much more than free trade in the 1990s, but in both instances citizens were told that neither they nor their governments could do anything.

"Market forces" extended beyond trade agreements and the currency. Canadians were repeatedly told that, because capital whizzed around the globe at the flick of a trader's switch, the country had to pull up its socks and become more competitive in attracting investment and conquering export markets. Wall Street bondholders and investment bankers, Chicago commodity traders, the proverbial "gnomes of Zurich," became, as never before, players in the lives of Canadians, although only a handful of Canadians had ever met any of these players. They imposed apparently ruthless judgments on all countries, not just Canada, in deciding which deserved money and investment, and at what price. Some of these capital movements were sheer speculation, as some countries discovered when traders feasted on their currencies, but other movements reflected pitiless calculations of profit maximization.

These real or anticipated external pressures shaped domestic political decisions. For example, the Chrétien government's first serious attack on the federal deficit occurred against the backdrop of fear of international financiers' negative reaction to continuing Canadian fiscal laxity. Provinces shaped their budgets with one eye to their credit ratings. A staple of any federal budget is the immediate dispatch of a minister or senior Finance Department official to Wall Street to explain and defend the budget; provincial officials make the same trips after their budgets. These real or anticipated external pressures can have salutary effects, as in providing further justification or political cover for difficult but necessary domestic decisions, such as deficit reduction. But constant reference to forces over which Canadians have apparently no control – and Canadians' sense that their elected officials have no control over these forces either – heightens the sense that their governments are marginal.

A feeble rearguard reaction against "market forces" and free trade animated the New Democratic Party and its trade-union allies. But the NDP's sagging political fortunes underscored the fact that North American free trade had become an irreversible reality, endorsed by the four other parties and by the majority of Canadians – according to pollsters. The Liberals themselves had moved from opposing Canada–U.S. free trade in the 1988 election to becoming free trade's prophet in another one of the party's policy pirouettes. The Liberals not only signed NAFTA, they negotiated free trade deals with Chile, Costa Rica, and Israel, unsuccessfully proposed one with the European Union, pushed for free trade in the western hemisphere and the Asia–Pacific region, and negotiated freer trading arrangements with the Caribbean countries, thereby tacitly admitting what one Liberal cabinet minister, Brian Tobin, stated publicly: Prime Minister Brian Mulroney had been right about Canada–U.S. free trade.

Since it was too late to reverse North American free trade, the fight focused on potential expansions of free trade to the Asia–Pacific region and Latin America. Assortments of anti-free-traders – anarchists and trade unionists, anti-poverty activists and environmentalists, socialists and feminists – protested at meetings in Vancouver, Seattle, Washington, Quebec City, and wherever else governments or international institutions met to consider international economic arrangements. The protestors had some effect, especially in securing media coverage, since the conflict between them and the police proved more interesting for the television cameras than the dry material of communiqués and substantive negotiations. Through media coverage, the protestors did force at least some negotiators – even if those negotiators refused to acknowledge it – to widen their discussions to include labour standards and environmental protection. Many protestors, however, cared little for those niceties, since they did not favour free trade at all but rather a return to various forms of government economic interventionism.

Whatever the protestors' modest influence on the international negotiations, and despite the media attention lavished on their doings, they had negligible impact on how Canadians viewed free trade. Poll after poll in the late 1990s – a decade after the Canada–U.S. agreement – showed Canadians had accepted the reality of free trade. Whether willingly or grudgingly, Canadians embraced the new economic realities. The economic transformations of the 1990s had been rapid, arguably faster than even free trade boosters had imagined. Canada's trade with the United States rocketed to 87 per cent of total Canadian trade in the decade after the agreement, despite Team Canada missions to Asia and Latin America and predictions at the time of the Canada–U.S. agreement that free trade would produce larger, fitter Canadian companies ready to conquer markets beyond North America. Instead, Canada's trade became even more dependent on the United States, and no one seemed to mind. Without booming exports to the U.S., aided by the deteriorating value of the Canadian dollar, the indifferent economic decade of the 1990s would have been a disaster.

Trade agreements themselves were the most obvious and sometimes controversial manifestations of "globalization," a word whose meaning varied almost as much as its use. To free trade's foes, globalization meant, in a loosely generic way, the sprawling power of corporations to cut governments down to size, oppress the poor, rape the environment, cripple unions, and suck dry the Third World in a rapacious, relentless quest for profit maximization. Trade agreements, the International Monetary Fund, and the World Bank were three horsemen of the capitalist apocalypse, with compliant governments riding the fourth horse. Not many Canadians accepted this description, as election results and polling analyses revealed. But globalization also brought restraints on government activities because of other sorts of agreements. Environmental agreements such as those protecting the ozone layer and the proposed one on greenhouse-gas emissions required, or would require, domestic policy modifications. United Nations treaties or declarations on everything from the treatment of children to provisions for refugees and human rights became yardsticks by which domestic policies were judged.

International agreements, therefore, not only restricted government actions, they sometimes forced or prodded them to do things that, without international pressure, they would not have done. But beyond these agreements, treaties, and declarations, globalization meant Canada's greater interconnectedness with the world and the accompanying need for Canadians to equip themselves and their governments with the tools to understand and compete with that world. Canadians would have been forced to change habits to compete even without trade agreements, because Canada depends more on foreign trade as a share of gross domestic product than any other G7 country. The country's competitive position vis-à-vis others is therefore integral to its economic well-being. Adjustments to domestic practices and laws must be made if that position deteriorated.

Marshall McLuhan, a Canadian, coined the phrase "global village." He was thinking of the speed and reach of modern communications, but he died before the advent of the Internet and the World Wide Web. The technology of the Web, and that of satellites, digital reception and transmission, cellphones, cable, information services, all-news television, and a myriad of other technologies, combined to render impotent or outdated many of Canada's policies for regulating content. By the late 1990s, the Canadian Radio-Television and Telecommunications Commission gave up trying to regulate the Internet, acquiesced to just about every merger proposal before it, and looked increasingly like an institutional throwback to another era. Canada continued to fight the United States's opposition to a range of Canadian cultural policies, although Canada insisted cultural policies had been exempted from the Canada–U.S. free trade agreement. Maybe they had, but that only meant the United States would carry the fight against them to other forums such as the World Trade Organization, where it won in the late 1990s a case against Canadian restrictions on so-called split-run Canadian versions of U.S. magazines.

International treaties and agreements, and Canada's increasing interconnectedness with the rest of the world, therefore narrowed somewhat governments' room to manoeuvre. The movement of capital and international "market forces" mocked governments' capacity to restrain them, or sometimes forced governments to act to get rid of them. The free market's greater sway and other pressures fettering governments' scope for action seem to suggest to at least some citizens that governments are simply less important actors than before. This change might strike some citizens as all to the good and certainly overdue. It might also signal that political involvement is less important too.

A citizen is less likely to become interested in politics if he or she learns that options are limited or non-existent because of "market forces," international agreements, trade treaties, applied or threatened foreign pressure, and the realities of "globalization." The argument from elected officials that "we have no alternative" may prove handy, and sometimes even be true. It may allow them to pursue policies domestically that they would otherwise resist, pointing to international obligations as justification. The shift from quotas to high tariffs for dairy imports, the extension of pharmaceutical patents, the recasting of support programs for industry, and the guarantees granted asylum-seekers are but a few examples of the "we have no alternative" changes. But since politics is ultimately about choices, the elimination or narrowing of plausible choices does not encourage citizens to maintain an interest in politics.

It might be tempting to draw a straight line between the internationalization of Canada and the decline in respect for government and politics. But as with many complicated phenomena, the shortest distance between two points is seldom a straight line. It would seem more likely that internationalization per se is not the cause, but rather that the domestic shifts it engendered forced politicians to redefine what governments can accomplish in the modern age.

Interest Groups Rise: Parliamentary Politics Declines

Protestors against globalization were easy to dismiss, despite the massive media coverage accorded them. As we have seen, their influence on Canadians' views of globalization and free trade was marginal; their own agendas were divergent to the point of incoherence. But the street protests did point to a wider phenomenon: that Canadians, far from being a deferential people, were among the world's leading participants in extra-parliamentary politics. Neil Nevitte's comparison of attitudes in 1990 found Canadians more willing than Americans and Europeans to engage in four kinds of public protest: unofficial strikes, unlawful demonstrations, boycotts, and petitions. That willingness did not mean Canadians were downing tools everywhere and taking to the streets (56.9 per cent in Nevitte's analysis said they would never join at least one of the four protest behaviours); rather, their interest in things political remained high, even while their confidence and interest in conventional party politics and government declined. The act of voting or participation in political parties seemed only marginally useful in pursuing political agendas for the environment, women, aboriginals, refugees, multiculturalism, trade unions. Government decisions affecting these groups ultimately did count, but direct action, court challenges under the Charter of Rights and Freedoms, or public-relations campaigns seemed a better place to start. Parliamentary government was the last link in the chain; indeed, parliamentary government struck many of these groups as an obstacle to change, a place to be pressured rather than a place to look to for leadership.

The rise of single-issue political action groups has been the most noteworthy change in Canadian politics in the last two decades. The influence of these groups on changing public policy has been immense, and not just on domestic policy. Modern means of communications, especially the Internet, have allowed them to mobilize constituencies across Canada and around the world.

Foreign policy used to be the preserve of diplomats. The Canadian foreign service, for example, sets its own entrance examinations, and entry into the service from other than the bottom is difficult. This highly élitist notion of foreign service perfectly fits a hierarchical model, in which specialists are deemed to possess unique experiences and training from which they derive particular wisdom not granted those outside the tribe. But two recent examples among many illustrate how non-governmental action groups have diluted the élite's grip on foreign policy and influenced government policy.

The most obvious was, of course, the international campaign to ban land mines. This campaign coincided with the Canadian government's own foreign-policy objective – part of Foreign Affairs Minister Lloyd Axworthy's "soft power" approach to international affairs – but that policy would not have succeeded without heightened public awareness raised by non-governmental campaigners in Canada and around the world.

The second was East Timor, a speck of land in the vast Indonesian archipelago that few Canadians could have identified on a map. However, across Canada, courtesy of the Internet, a group grew up calling itself the East Timor Alert Network. It harried the government, publicized Indonesian oppression of East Timorese residents, and linked up with activists in many other countries. They succeeded, along with foreign correspondents' coverage of East Timor, in so raising the profile of East Timor's plight that the Canadian government became more involved in international efforts on the island than would otherwise have been the case, given East Timor's location and lack of importance to Canada.

Environmentalists, too, have formed networks and associations across Canada to press their concerns through a variety of direct-action methods and legal cases, bringing pressure to bear on Canada from like-minded groups in other countries. Anyone remotely familiar with forestry policy in British Columbia, to take just one example, appreciates how environmentalists outside Canada have influenced government to change harvesting practices, expand parklands (now 12 per cent of the province), stiffen reforestation requirements, and take old-growth forests out of production. In forestry, as in other environmental areas, groups have used courts to push governments to expand protection or to enforce their own laws.

Aboriginals, arguably more than any other group, have provided in recent years the most obvious example of extra-parliamentary political action. Aboriginals have treated with government because they had no choice, given the Indian Act and their excessive dependence on government social programs. They had to deal with government because no land-claims negotiations could succeed by definition without government, since aboriginal demands included a mixture of taxpayer's money, control of Crown land, and self-government. Parliament has had little to say about land-claims negotiations that are conducted between negotiators for aboriginals and civil servants. Parliament will see treaties for ratification once they have been negotiated, by which time they cannot be changed, or so governments instruct their legislatures.

Governments quite often act in aboriginal affairs following court decisions. Once aboriginal rights became enshrined in the Constitution, aboriginal groups increasingly took their claims to courts. Courts, in turn, invariably affirmed, and, in many cases expanded, aboriginal rights, leaving governments with the job of negotiating these rights in practice. *Sparrow, Marshall,* and *Delgamuukw* were among the best-known cases affirming aboriginal rights. Each one provoked furious opposition from non-natives, leaving governments struggling to negotiate agreements that respected court rulings while defending the interests of taxpayers.

Direct parliamentary participation held little appeal for aboriginals. Aboriginals seldom ran as candidates, except in the territories. Their voter turnout stood far below the already low Canadian average. In the Charlottetown referendum, which had been hammered out with full aboriginal participation, on-reserve aboriginals' turnout rate was 8 per cent. A majority of those who bothered to vote rejected the very accord their national leadership had secured. Aboriginals consider parliamentary politics a "white man's" game, a not unreasonable perception from scattered and small communities with sad memories of past treatment and their own quite different political mores. Aboriginal communities that govern themselves by trying to forge consensus look askance at the institutionalized and ritualistic divisions between government and opposition parties in Parliament. Georges Erasmus, the former grand chief of the Assembly of First Nations, once recalled how as an adolescent he could not figure out why elected officials would form up into two groups and spend almost an hour per day shouting at each other. Aboriginal communities have their own divisions, to be sure, but they play themselves out quite differently than in parliamentary government.

By the most elastic definition, aboriginals comprise only 4 per cent of Canada's population. They are not sufficiently numerous anywhere in Canada outside the Northwest Territories and Nunavut to form a majority in even one parliamentary constituency, unlike blacks in certain U.S. congressional districts. Even if aboriginals wanted to play the "white man's" parliamentary game, they reckon the demographic odds are stacked against them. In recent decades, the intellectual and political thrust of aboriginal leaders has been to recover power from parliaments in the drive for self-government. Leaders know they can exercise real power in aboriginal communities, whereas they might exercise little or none in parliamentary governments.

There have been exceptions, of course, and Len Marchand was one. He served in Pierre Trudeau's cabinets and, after receiving his patronage post in the Senate in 1984, he chaired a committee than recommended dedicated House of Commons seats for aboriginals. The committee studied the New Zealand experience, where Maoris elect a fixed number of their own legislators during national elections. The Marchand report proposed several models for these aboriginal constituencies in the House of Commons. The report stirred little interest among aboriginals, received a frosty reception elsewhere, and took its place on oblivion's dusty shelves. But in 1992, the Royal Commission on Electoral Reform and Party Financing took up the issue. It, too, recommended direct elections of aboriginals by aboriginals to the House of Commons.

Blowing the dust off the Marchand Report and the pertinent sections of the Royal Commission, however, would make more sense as part of an elected Senate based on proportional representation, since that kind of voting system treats minorities more generously than a first-past-the-post system. Intellectual tidiness might suggest that aboriginals should be treated the same as other Canadians – one person, one vote, in other words. However, court rulings, common sense, and even the vaguest familiarity with Canadian history, suggest that aboriginals do have distinctive traditions and that attempts to obliterate this distinctiveness are doomed to fail; worse, these attempts produce even greater social dislocations and deeper alienation from non-aboriginal fellow citizens. Conversely, the drive for self-government sometimes ignores the common citizenship of aboriginals and non-aboriginals.

Professor Alan Cairns has persuasively argued in his book *Citizens Plus* that a balance must be found between respecting aboriginal distinctiveness through self-government and enjoining aboriginals to appreciate common citizenship. At present, parliamentary government does not encourage aboriginals to believe participation makes realistic sense. If, however, certain elected Senate seats were set aside for their voters, this hostility to "white man's" government might be somewhat attenuated. Participation in this fashion would not negate self-government, because aboriginal governments would be busying themselves with delivering municipal- or province-like services: social services, education, housing, land-use regulations. But formal participation in the nation's parliamentary life might reassert a few fraying bonds of common citizenship, because aboriginals without some form of dedicated representation will remain at the parliamentary margins, takers rather than framers of government decisions.

Critics (and I used to be one of them) will argue that the multiplicity of aboriginal groups – or "nations," to use contemporary parlance – would defy sensible allocation of candidates for dedicated aboriginal constituencies. But this attitude reflects an unwarranted paternalism, because we non-aboriginals in existing parliamentary constituencies regularly sort out representational challenges on the traditional bases of party affiliation, gender, ethnicity, income status, candidate experience, and so on. As for the argument that aboriginals should be treated like other Canadians, this is true up to a point, but courts, the aboriginals themselves, and increasing numbers of non-aboriginals accept that special arrangements are necessary to respect aboriginal differences. Finding the proper balance between communality and difference will never be easy, but without some special action within parliamentary life the common threads of citizenship will remain thin.

Aboriginal organizations began playing an important role perhaps two decades ago in Canada. There is nothing new about interest-group politics, although it has usually been more prevalent in the United States than Canada. The authors of the *Federalist Papers* in the early United States considered themselves high-minded preachers of civic virtue, and James Madison, in particular, rued the influence of "faction" in political life. Republican virtue, however, soon yielded in practice to the messier politics of interest groups, logrolling, horse-trading, and patronage. Ever since, U.S. politics have featured a mixture of the virtuous and the sordid. Americans have seldom been uncomfortable with interest groups in their political life. They welcome them as organized expressions of particularistic concerns, the notion being that, in a wide-open democracy, with free speech guaranteed by the Constitution, the clash of interests will ultimately produce sound policy. Or so the theory goes, although the incessant search for money in U.S. politics often means that those with the largest financial resources get the most attention.

Canadian democracy, until recent decades, viewed interest-group politics more suspiciously. The Crown was supposed to stand above particular interests, as were the Crown's representatives in Parliament. Political parties, more tightly disciplined in the Canadian Parliament than in the U.S. Congress, were supposed to reconcile interests within cabinets and parties. This was another gentle fiction of the parliamentary imagination. Parties did pay more attention to some groups than others, depending on circumstances and levels of political (and financial) support. But in the decades when Canadians displayed greater deference to elected officials, the influence of interest groups in Canada paled in comparison to the United States. Even today, partial public financing of elections and free-time political advertising removes from Canadian parliamentarians the frantic, incessant search for money that frames the life of U.S. legislators.

Now, however, a vast honeycomb of interest groups envelops parliamentary government. Interest groups began proliferating when the size of government exploded in the 1960s and 1970s. This proliferation both reflected and encouraged the growth of government. New Ministries of State or sections of government departments were created just to deal with particular concerns: Minister of State for the Status of Women, Minister of State for Multiculturalism, Minister of State for Small Business. If, somehow, a group missed getting its own section of government with attendant programs, it had been falling down on the job.

The dizzying list of organized interest groups is much too long to recite, but they stretch from the powerful Business Council on National Issues, bullhorn for large corporations, to anti-poverty and social-action groups. They can be categorized, in part, by how they are financed. Some, such as the BCNI, the

Canadian Labour Congress, or industry associations, are funded by member companies or unions, whose employees or members have no say in the spending. Then there are groups funded by individuals' contributions, such as the National Citizens' Coalition or the Sierra Club. Finally, there are those entirely or partly funded by government, such as aboriginal organizations. Non-smokers and refugee advocates, brewers and printers, aboriginals and multicultural groups, bankers and trade unions, film producers and cable companies, doctors and nurses, university faculties and universities themselves, airlines and automobile drivers . . . if an interest group or a cause lacks a federal presence, they either do not count in political debates, or have simply decided to locate their national offices outside Ottawa.

The rise of interest-group activity does not reflect a decline in political involvement. Rather, the proliferation of interest groups displays an apparent conviction that political results can best be influenced or achieved outside the framework of political parties. There are too many variables to trace a direct cause and effect, but the rise of interest-group politics roughly coincided with the years of declining respect for government and politicians. Interest groups target specific issues, and these might be of more importance to particular sets of citizens than the broad range of issues with which parties must grapple. Many citizens feel interest-group politics offers a more effective use of their time and money than the messy, time-consuming business of party politics.

Whether interest groups do, in fact, represent the people they claim to do is often another matter. To take a few obvious examples. The National Action Committee on the Status of Women purports to speak for Canadian women, a laughably false assertion given the gap between NAC positions and how Canadian women vote. The NAC's influence with political decision-makers is next-to-nil, given the strident and often insulting tone NAC adopts towards government representatives. The Canadian Labour Congress is the trade-union movement's official voice, but elections keep demonstrating that the unions' links with the New Democratic Party do not mean that union members vote NDP appreciably more than other citizens. Ovide Mercredi and Phil Fontaine, grand chiefs of the Assembly of First Nations, kept claiming to speak for aboriginals across Canada, although they were both deposed after one term in office. The Business Council on National Issues might claim to speak authoritatively on a subject such as the decline in the value of the Canadian dollar, but some of its members benefit from a low dollar, while others are penalized by it. The Canadian Taxpayers Federation's name suggests it speaks for all "taxpayers," which it manifestly does not. The Federation's campaign for lower taxes and less government might reflect the wishes of some Canadians, but a series of polls suggested that lower taxes was not the highest priority of the majority of Canadians. The National Citizens' Coalition, a right-wing pressure group, targeted thirty-nine MPs for defeat in the 1993 campaign, but an academic study found that the targeted MPs' vote rose in thirty-six of those ridings.

Interest groups are never satisfied. They seldom say thanks to or praise government; when they do, the congratulations are ephemeral. Interest groups must always be unhappy, because if they pronounced themselves completely satisfied, their sources of funding would dry up and they would disappear. Even if a government does something of which an interest group approves, the group can always justify itself by claiming it must keep watch, in case another group or political party threatens to unravel the gains. Interest groups must therefore live in a permanent state of agitation, always pressing new claims on government or recycling old ones. They must also justify themselves to their members, and that often requires being seen and heard in the media.

The media are complete suckers for interest-group spokes-men. The media never ask just how representative these people are. The media seldom question the wisdom of their prescriptions. The media value those who are accessible on short notice, speak in sound bites, ratchet up rhetoric, and provide the kind of confrontational debate that the media so desires. In return, the interest groups feed the media with information favourable to their cause. Budget day is the yearly apotheosis of media–interest group relations, as various interest-group spokesmen troll the media areas, eager to provide commentary. They certainly receive considerably more attention on budget day than any member of Parliament, except for the party leaders, although interest-group spokespeople offer reactions as utterly predictable as those of MPs who read from speaking notes provided by the parties' research offices and government departments.

Hand-in-glove with these organized interests go lobbyists or, as they prefer to be called, "government relations experts." These have grown like Topsy in the last two decades. People with knowledge of government and connections inside the bureaucracy and the governing party, they represent their clients' interests, being paid through monthly or yearly retainers. In recent years, a bevy of senior civil servants has fled to lobbying firms or become consultants to government departments. A year-long cooling-off period supposedly prevents them from lobbying their old department directly, but no prohibitions apply after that period. In the meantime, they are free to give advice to others dealing directly with government departments. Lobbyists live, by definition, in the shadows of political life, since they and their clients usually believe influence is best exerted away from the public limelight. This shadowland produced sufficient concern about untoward influence that the government created a registry for lobbyists, who must list the interests or companies they represent. The registry has at least cast some light into the shadowlands, but not much. Lobbyists still go about their daily business far from public scrutiny.

Whom they lobby illustrates the nature of contemporary government. When surveyed, lobbyists and interest groups consistently placed members of Parliament at or near the bottom of their lists. Knowing how government actually operates, as opposed to how it works in textbook definitions, lobbyists press their clients' case, if possible, to the Prime Minister's Office, then to senior ministers and top bureaucrats. They may make the rounds with MPs, but more as a courtesy or an insurance policy, because they understand that MPs have no power and only scattered influence.

Organized letter-writing campaigns, still a favoured tool of some misguided groups, have almost no effect. They are targeted at MPs who, although without power, are not perfect fools. They know an organized campaign does not reflect public opinion by virtue of the fact that it is being organized. Smart lobbyists and interest groups understand that civil servants form policy. They take general directions from ministers. Under guidance from the Prime Minister's Office, the Privy Council co-ordinates everything important in the government. Interest groups (but seldom lobbyists from the shadowland) will parade before parliamentary committees, but these committees are like the House of Commons writ small, in which government MPs are allowed some latitude for individual expression but no deviation from the governing party's line.

It can be argued that interest groups enrich democracy. They provide avenues for citizens to participate beyond the act of voting, which gives them a chance to express a blunt, broad choice among a range of issues and personalities once every four years or so. Without interest groups, certain voices might not be heard. Governments can easily be cocooned in Ottawa, wrapped up in the rituals of parliamentary life and the administration of vast bureaucracies. Interest groups provide them with information and feedback; indeed, part of the new vogue of "consultative" government requires civil servants to meet frequently with interest groups.

Interest groups may enrich democratic debate, but they can also damage democracy if their claims are not treated with necessary scepticism. Interest groups purport to represent the "public interest," but they only represent narrow perspectives and do not always even reflect the views of those on whose behalf they claim to be speaking. That is why they cannot be a substitute for representative democracy in which MPs must balance competing claims, assign some kind of priority, and make decisions. Only MPs and political parties are ultimately held responsible by the public, through elections, and, in a looser sense, by public opinion between elections. The disengagement from the electoral system, however, makes participation in politics through interests groups an inadequate surrogate for parliamentary politics.

The Rise of the Courts

The declining interest in politics and the lowered respect for government among Canadians coincided with the most revolutionary change in Canada's constitutional arrangements since Confederation – the Charter of Rights and Freedoms. It would be facile, and therefore misleading, to fall into the trap of direct causality: to argue that the advent of the Charter produced the declining interest in parliamentary government. The Charter contributed to that decline, but far too many other forces were working in Canadian society to make it possible to draw a direct link between the Charter's arrival in 1981 and citizens' changed attitudes towards government. It might even be argued that the Charter simply provided a different outlet for citizens' involvement in politics, as they took their competing claims and clashing aspirations to courts instead of legislatures. What has certainly occurred is the shifting of some political debates into the courts, a legacy of the Charter.

Canadians quickly fell in love with the Charter. They have now lived with the Charter for two decades, and it eclipses in popularity all other national institutions. Perhaps popularity, a word that suggests something transitory, is not adequate. The Charter became the country's most important symbol. Just ten years after the Charter's arrival, in 1991, an Environics Research survey showed that, outside Quebec, 75 per cent of respondents considered the Charter a "very important" national symbol, compared to 71 per cent for the flag, 69 per cent for the anthem, 38 per cent for multiculturalism, 31 per cent for the Canadian Broadcasting Corporation, 25 per cent for the monarchy, and 22 per cent for bilingualism. Inside Quebec, the Charter still topped the list of national symbols: 64 per cent for the Charter, followed by bilingualism (52 per cent), anthem (39 per cent), flag (38 per cent), Radio-Canada (31 per cent), multiculturalism (29 per cent), and monarchy (5 per cent). Subsequent public-opinion surveys revealed roughly similar results, with the Charter leading all other national institutions or policies, including those that have been around for much longer.

The Charter was the political creation of one man: Prime Minister Pierre Trudeau. The idea for a bill of rights in the Constitution, as opposed to a statutory Bill of Rights, had been promoted by various academics, but Trudeau, first as justice minister, then as prime minister, put the idea on the country's political agenda and kept it there, finally succeeding in achieving his dream as part of the constitutional patriation negotiations of 1980–81. He effectively sold Canadians on its virtues by insisting that the Charter spoke to national values and put Canadians' fundamental rights above the threatening grasp of governments. He described the Charter as integral to the "people's package" of constitutional changes, in contrast to the self-interested agendas of power-hungry provincial governments. The Charter meant that individual rights were inherent, not dependent upon

Parliament, a significant change from the traditional Canadian philosophy, derived from British law and practice, that rights derived from the common law and the Crown, whose powers were exercised through democratically elected representatives in Parliament. The corollary struck citizens as axiomatic: If Parliament was no longer the institutional defender of their "rights," then its importance as a national institution must decline. Or, put another way, since the Charter's philosophy was founded on a suspicion of government, once citizens fell in love with the Charter, that affection confirmed and deepened those suspicions.

Trudeau's argument for a Charter reflected a growing world-wide concern for human rights, a concern once used in the moral battle against communism, but more widely interpreted by groups fighting for self-government, social justice, and equal treatment before the law. Robust democracies such as Britain and Australia rejected the worldwide trend for constitutional bills or charters of human rights, but these countries found them-selves increasingly isolated. Even Britain became bound by certain European rights codes to which it subscribed upon joining the European Community.

The Charter reflected and encouraged another broader trend in Canada – towards the "Americanization" of politics. The Charter is inspired by suspicions of state power that find their expression in the U.S. balance-of-power – or checks-and-balances – system of government, which allocates to courts a wide latitude for overseeing government decisions. This kind of power had found no echo in Canadian courts in the pre-Charter era. Courts before the Charter had been exceedingly deferential to legislative prerogatives, contenting themselves in constitu-tional matters with deciding disputes over power between the federal and provincial governments. Prime Minister John Diefenbaker's Bill of Rights was a legislative statute, not a con-stitutional document, and, as such, did much less to give courts U.S.-style latitude than the constitutional Charter.

The Charter also reflected and abetted the end of the old élite-accommodation model of governing the Canadian federation, whereby governments made decisions behind closed doors, then explained them to citizens. The Charter gave interest groups and individual citizens a sense of their "rights" that did not depend upon governments. It turned over to the judiciary many political decisions and increased the amount of "rights talk" in political discourse, often thereby making political compromises more difficult. The old élite-accommodation model disintegrated because it could not adequately reflect the desire for political influence of a plethora of new groups reflecting social, economic, and demographic trends. The changes to Canada's immigration policies in 1976–77, for example, opened the doors to many more immigrants from Third World countries, thereby increasing the number of "visible minorities" who found themselves severely underrepresented among the élites who made the country's political decisions. The huge entry of women into the workforce both changed the nature of the family and propelled many of them against the glass barriers that existed in all walks of Canadian life. Women, too, found themselves underrepresented in the élite groups. Organized women's groups rejected the model of élites making decisions. Aboriginals began demanding respect for their inherent rights, including self-government. The Charter, with its "equality" clauses specifically directed to each of these groups, became an instrument for their affirmation.

Parliament struggled to keep up with these social, economic, and demographic changes, but the political system was unable to become sufficiently representative quickly enough to satisfy these demands. This failure sent groups searching outside government for redress, and the Charter provided an important avenue, through court challenges, to governmental sins of omission or commission. There were historic grievances over past mistreatment of linguistic minority groups or ethnic groups such as

Japanese Canadians that Charter proponents insisted would never have occurred had a Charter been in place. A yearning for something unifying, ennobling, and enduring also emerged from the constitutional impasses of the 1960s and 1970s that featured interminable federal-provincial bickering and an apparent lack of national cohesion – a desire perfectly met by the Charter, which spoke to rights, values, and principles.

The governance of Canada's heterogeneous society has always been a supreme political challenge, and that challenge is now more difficult than ever with the multiplication of groups clamouring for attention, each with its own agenda, sense of entitlement, and grievances rooted in historical memory. The political culture of contemporary Canada, within which public policy must be conceived and executed, reflects the self-evident facts that judges are considered more trustworthy, capable, and desirous of advancing the public interest than are politicians; courts are considered more appropriate institutions for rectifying wrongs and offering solutions than legislatures; the Charter is a surer guide to respect for and expansion of human liberties than parliaments; legal cases are a better vehicle for confrontations from which will flow ringing affirmations of rights than are messy compromises required by parliamentary debates, party politics, and national elections.

The Charter encouraged a generation of Canadians to look upon it as a supplement or even a replacement for parliamentary institutions in order to achieve political ends. Courts are now immersing themselves in, or being asked to concern themselves with, issues that are largely if not exclusively political – in the non-partisan sense of questions that members of civil society in their capacity as citizens might be interested in and affected by. These would include, to mention but a few, Sunday shopping, street soliciting, mandatory retirement, tobacco advertising, tax law, spousal benefits, employment insurance, abortion, fishing

quotas, the number of electors per constituency, refugee administration, and provision of hospital services for the disabled.

An innocent observer of public discourse in contemporary
Canada must be aware of, if not amazed by, the escalation of
"rights talk," a phrase used by Harvard Law Professor Mary Ann
Glendon in her book of the same name. The assertion of "rights"
is now widespread in almost every kind of political debate in
Canada; indeed, it would appear that, unless a political claim lacks
some justification in asserted "rights," the claim lacks moral force
and political weight. What Professor Glendon noted despairingly
about her own excessively litigious society has crept into
Canadian discourse and infected the political culture. A few illus-
trations of this changed discourse will make the point. When the
government cut VIA Rail services, those opposed to the cuts
insisted that Canadians had a "right" to a national rail service.
When Air Canada, then a Crown corporation, stopped flying to
certain Canadian cities, mayors and others opposed to the decision asserted that their cities had a "right" to air service. On the
East Coast, Canadian fishermen claimed a "right" to fish stocks.
Even the fish themselves became bearers of "rights." In the
Supreme Court's *Singh* decision, non-citizen, non-landed immigrants were given "rights," even though they had not been
accepted as legitimate entrants into Canada. Smokers frame their
case in terms of the "right" to smoke; those who oppose them
insist upon their "right" to enjoy a smoke-free environment.
These obvious exaggerations do not always impress courts when
they are advanced in legal arguments, although, as in the *Singh*
case, sometimes the result is surprising. But the Charter era has
changed the framing of essentially political arguments for public
consumption, even if the arguments never reach a court of law.

A distinguishing characteristic of this "rights talk" is the degree
to which discretionary decisions of government and the normal
and sometimes healthy tensions in a pluralistic, democratic society

are elevated to those of apparently fundamental human rights. When issues are so elevated, compromises and accommodation become more difficult, because rights are involved. These rights, by virtue of being rights, cannot easily be compromised. They can only be defended to the maximum. These asserted rights also seldom have obligations or responsibilities attached to them, at least in the eyes of those making the assertions. Rights "exist," therefore they "are" – political statements whose underpinnings are apparently immune from examination, because the use of the language of rights has raised the moral stakes. This "rights talk" can gravely deform the nature of political discourse, and, as such, can be considered the particular contribution of the new generation of Charter-conscious lawyers to our politics. Lawyers have always been overrepresented among politicians, in part because politics is about argument and laws, the stuff of legal training. Not surprisingly, many of the greatest Canadian prime ministers have been lawyers. Since Mackenzie King left politics in 1948, every prime minister save two (Lester Pearson and Joe Clark, who governed for only six years between them) has been a lawyer.

Like economists, social workers, sociologists, political scientists, or other intellectual species, lawyers frame issues in the terms most familiar to them. "Rights talk," like the fascination with the constitution itself, places public debate within a framework where lawyers can shine. The new generation of lawyers has come of age under the Charter; law-school courses on the Charter are filled to capacity, and many of those graduates seeking social change reckon the Charter puts a premium on their skills and provides a more satisfying outlet for achieving their political objectives than party politics. Pre-Charter constitutional law was the dull stuff of federal-provincial arbitration; constitutional law now expands into social, economic, and human-rights policies. Indeed, law schools have taken over from sociology, political science, and philosophy departments as academic hotbeds of social change, where students grapple with critical legal theory, feminist law, human-rights law and the "equality" sections of the Charter. Not surprisingly, some of Canada's law faculties have been torn apart by differences among professors and students, with their clashing political agendas and legal theories. Whether this framing of political objectives within a Charter framework produces an appropriate venue for resolving disputes, determining political priorities, and conveying a realistic sense of what can be expected from public policy is quite another matter.

Supreme Court justices and other judges across Canada did not ask for the Charter of Rights and Freedoms. The Charter emerged from the political debates of the time. It was enacted by politicians, and therefore constituted a political act. The Supreme Court did not seek its greatly expanded powers – as the Court has explained in decisions. Criticized by some for judicial activism and by others for excessive timidity, the Court has tried to steer a middle ground, insisting that it wishes a "dialogue" with legislatures. That "dialogue," however, more often resembles a one-way set of commands, since legislatures are reluctant to tell the Court it has erred. Canada has moved, in Professor Peter Russell's excellent phrase, from a parliamentary democracy to a "constitutional democracy," in which citizens view courts, not legislatures, as the ultimate protectors of the values, rights, and institutions underpinning that democracy. Politicians are well aware that Canadians display little respect for them but place judges on a pedestal. They also know, or ought to, that citizens consider courts more trustworthy than legislatures. They are therefore reluctant to use the Charter's "notwithstanding clause" that empowers legislatures to stay court rulings for up to five years. That clause, a distinctly Canadian innovation not found in other constitutions, was an integral part of the interlocking political compromises that attended the Charter's birth. It has as much legal force as any other Charter section, but it lacks political credibility, and as such has seldom been used. Should parliamentarians carefully use the "notwithstanding clause," a true "dialogue" might exist, because a genuine "dialogue" between individuals or institutions implies the ability of one side to say that the other is wrong, and over time either to make that assertion stick or find a compromise.

Standing up for "notwithstanding" could sometimes be justified, because what the Supreme Court and other courts cannot do effectively is consider the costs of decisions and whether the extension of benefits or the elaboration of new rights are the most urgent matters requiring the attention of government and society among inevitably jostling priorities. Judges deal with cases at court; cabinets must balance dozens of simultaneous claims. Judges may try to find the balance within a case; politicians look for balances among many dossiers. Judges may have the interests of two, three, or four parties to a case to consider; politicians often must take account of the interests of a multiplicity of groups. The weakness of the judiciary in balancing competing claims, especially on the public purse, is perhaps of little consequence in an age of munificence. It can become burdensome in the age of limited government resources.

Precisely because courts need not consider the entire range of issues vying for public attention, individuals and groups are increasingly using courts to press their claims. If they can get a case before court and achieve a favourable ruling, which requires the government to act, they can push an issue onto the government's agenda instead of watching it languish. Governments, too, sometimes prefer courts to rule, because court decisions take the heat off elected officials who, forced to do something contentious or unpopular, can defend themselves by saying they had no choice. As we have seen, the same defence is provided by international agreements that require politicians to make contentious domestic changes. In both instances – court rulings and international agreements – governments claim they are merely following orders imposed by bodies other than the legislatures they control.

Arguments over Charter interpretations abound, and will continue; the argument about the Charter itself is over. Charter advocates won that debate against sceptics in 1980–81, and their victory has never since been seriously challenged. Soon after the Charter entered into force, it became clear that the Supreme Court judges under Chief Justice Brian Dickson took their new responsibilities seriously. Those who believed that the Court would tread warily and slowly into the Charter age were quickly proven wrong, as the Court began laying down markers about Charter interpretation, preferring a "large and liberal" interpretation and rejecting any attempts to interpret the "original intent" of the Charter's creators. The Court interpreted its mandate as defending the interests of "insular minorities" and brushed aside as "administrative inconveniences" arguments about costs. The Court has periodically been assaulted by those wanting even more expansive interpretations of the Charter. These critics want more, not less, "judicial activism," having largely given up on parliamentary government as a venue for progressive social policies. These critics have been exclusively outside Parliament, because even some Charter enthusiasts, such as former Ontario Attorney General Ian Scott, understood once they achieved elected office how much more trying the Charter had made their life as politicians. Inside the political arena, the only spasmodic criticisms of the Court have come from the Reform Party, whose former leader Preston Manning decried excessive judicial activism. But his criticisms were never sustained, in part because, after delivering them, he discovered that Canadians remained unmoved.

What the Charter has certainly done, for better or worse, is create a new arena for political debate and citizen involvement. It sometimes seems as if the Supreme Court and not Parliament is handling some of the country's most controversial issues. Citizens seeking social change, or even seeking to block changes, now have recourse to the Charter and they have not been shy to use it. With legislatures and the politicians who run them in disrepute, courts and the judges who preside over them enjoy a respect that political actors can only envy. In the Age of the Charter, respect for the political process has declined, just as, in the highly litigious United States, courts are more respected than legislatures and judges are more esteemed than politicians. In the court of public opinion, Parliament and those elected to it have been the losers; courts, and the judges who preside over them, are the winners.

False Promises

Some provincial education ministries have reintroduced "civics" into the high-school curriculum. Why civics was dropped in the first place is an excellent question, but the same question might be asked about lots of subjects and teaching methods abandoned in the "child-centred" educational reforms of the 1960s that have taken so long to undo. In any event, civics examines the reciprocal obligations of citizens and state, and for a long time young people were instructed that an obligation of citizenship required voting. Why?

Why indeed? In a rational-choice world, voting does not necessarily make sense. People make a rational choice, or what they hope will prove to be one, in buying a house or car, taking a job, deciding which movie to watch, where to take a vacation, or how to invest their savings, because the decision will directly influence their interests. Some form of direct link, therefore, is presumed to exist between the decision and the outcome. Economists are particularly wedded to rational-choice theories, believing individuals will try to maximize well-being and firms to maximize profit through rational decisions in a free market. Voting is different. The outcome of an election very seldom depends upon one vote. When politicians exhort people to vote because "every vote counts," this amounts to political fiction. Every Canadian election usually brings recounts in only a handful of ridings, recounts mercifully handled under uniform national guidelines and therefore not subject to the shenanigans surrounding the Florida recount in the U.S. presidential election of 2000. Even these Canadian recounts, however, seldom turn on one vote. Since rational-choice behaviour suggests that an individual's vote almost never determines the outcome, the theory should lead to widespread abstentions. It should also logically spark inquiries not into why voter turnout has fallen, but why it was once so high.

Canadians do vote, albeit in declining numbers. Rational choice hardly explains why. Moral obligation offers a better answer, as University of Montreal political scientist André Blais has argued. If people believe in a democratic system, they feel a moral or civic obligation to support democracy by voting. They also read into their vote a series of preferences about how society should be organized, or at least who should wield power in a democratic system. The act of not voting can be construed as an abandonment of democracy, but, in the vast majority of cases, not voting reflects rather a distaste with the choices on offer or a sense that the outcome scarcely matters. In this latter sense, as we have seen, competitive Canadian national elections do tend to produce higher turnouts than uncompetitive ones, such as the last three that have given Canada de facto one-party governance and pro- duced our current friendly dictatorship.

There has been a distressing tendency for political parties to say one thing in elections, then do something else in power, a ten- dency that deepens cynicism about politics. Very few Canadians who voted Liberal in 1980 would have guessed that they would get a National Energy Policy or patriation of the Constitution with a Charter of Rights and Freedoms. Brian Mulroney, in cam- paigning for the Conservative leadership, had dismissed free trade with the United States, a policy recommended by his leadership rival John Crosbie. Similarly, Mr. Mulroney had derided Tory

leader Joe Clark for "playing footsie with separatists," then he pro-
ceeded as Conservative prime minister to bring a variety of
former separatists into his government. Nor could anyone have
gleaned from his sunshine speeches in the 1984 election campaign
that deficit reduction would become one of his government's
overriding preoccupations. Jean Chrétien had promised in
Opposition to eliminate the Goods and Services Tax, although
he hedged that promise in the Liberals' Red Book campaign document. His party's fierce opposition to Canada–U.S. free trade and
generally negative reviews of that agreement's possible widening
to include Mexico would not have led anyone in 1993 to believe
what an ardent free-trader he would become as prime minister.
Having castigated the Mulroney record, the Liberals pursued
many of his government's initiatives once they were in power.
Nor could anyone have reasonably foreseen from the Liberals'
promises how resolutely they would attack the federal deficit.

   Broken promises and policy flip-flops obviously sour citizens'
perceptions of politicians' trustworthiness. There is something
curious about this perception, because current political practice
seems to require parties to publish more complete records of their
intentions than before. Not long ago parties sprinkled their promises throughout a campaign, feeling they needed the element of
surprise, in case their opponents stole their ideas. A promise every
other day would give the party momentum, feed the media fresh
headlines, and therefore heighten coverage of the party. The 1990s,
however, saw a remarkable change in both federal and provincial
politics, bringing Canadian politics more into line with British
practice, where at the beginning of the campaign parties publish
quite detailed "manifestos," specifying their proposals in detail.
The Liberals' 1993 Red Book was a prototype for what would
follow. Aware that Canadians felt Jean Chrétien devoid of intellectual ideas – "yesterday's man," his critics said – the Liberals
produced a packaged list of promises. Everywhere Mr. Chrétien
campaigned, he carried his Red Book, like a preacher carrying a

Bible, and replied whenever questioned about his intentions, "They're in the Red Book." The Reform Party and Canadian Alliance did likewise in every campaign, producing an attractively packaged and reasonably detailed outline. Ontario Conservatives campaigned in 1995 on the "Common Sense Revolution," a document outlining in impressive detail what they intended to accomplish. Arguably the most detailed document of all came from Conservative John Hamm of Nova Scotia. It offered in mind-numbing detail what he proposed to do in just about every department of government. Premier Gordon Campbell, in winning the British Columbia election, outlined two hundred promises, some of them in considerable detail.

The publication of these detailed campaign documents did not lessen political cynicism about politicians and their promises. The 1997 National Election Survey found solid majority support for these two statements: "Politicians lie to get elected" and "Political parties don't keep their election promises." A plausible case can be made that the Liberals did, in fact, keep many more of their Red Book promises than they broke or abandoned, but that was not the general impression conveyed by the media. Mike Harris did cut provincial income taxes by 30 per cent, as he had promised. But the prevailing view among Canadians remains that politicians cannot be trusted to do in power what they promise. When that view shapes public opinion, it is little wonder that at least some citizens reckon voting to be a waste of time. A widespread sense pervades Canadian politics that, once in power, the government can do what it wants and does not have to pay attention to public needs and that citizens between elections possess few, if any, means of influencing their government. No wonder a healthy majority of Canadians agreed in 1997 that "those elected to Parliament soon lose touch." Yet three times in succession Canadians re-elected a government, while simultaneously telling pollsters that politicians had lost touch. Perhaps that apparent paradox is explained by cynicism: voters were simply choosing among a series of unappetizing options. Perhaps, too, the paradox is explained by the statistical fact that, in 1997, the Chrétien government won with only 38 per cent of the voters on the list, or only about one-quarter of the total eligible population.

Bowling Alone in Canada

Voter turnout dropped faster and more recently in Canada than in other major democracies, but some of the disillusionment Canadians feel about politics can be found in other countries; Canadians are apparently not alone in their cynicism about government in the modern age. Comparative studies of attitudes and values elsewhere suggest that some other electorates are even more sceptical of politicians and trust governments less. A study of fourteen electorates from 1980 to the mid-1990s showed a decline in respect for parliaments in eleven, with Canada obviously being among the five countries (along with Britain, Germany, Sweden, and the United States) recording the sharpest declines. A trio of leading political scientists, having studied these international trends, reached this disturbing conclusion: "If party attachments represent the most fundamental type of citizen support for representative democracy . . . then their decline in nearly all advanced industrial democracies offers strong and disturbing evidence of the public's disengagement from political life."

A welter of explanations has been advanced for this decline. Robert Putnam of Harvard University offered the most influential – and controversial – explanation. Putnam argued that the decline in political interest flowed from the erosion of civic society. Politics was among the most obvious sign of citizens' engagement in the wider society, but if citizens' engagement was declining in non-political institutions, it would seem logical that citizens would participate less in political life, too. Putnam analyzed a myriad of civic associations, everything from parent-teacher associations to Rotary Clubs to bowling leagues (hence the title of his book, *Bowling Alone*), and detected a marked reduction in participation. This led, he continued, to a shrivelling of "social capital," or the network of links that binds citizens to their society and encourages them to be engaged in it. When people look for reasons behind social malaise, Putnam suggested they examine this erosion of social capital; and when people wonder why traditional means of political participation are declining, they should start with the erosion of social capital. He stood on its head the assertion about cynicism concerning government – which he did not deny. Perhaps, he wrote, "we are disaffected because as we and our neighbours have dropped out, the real performance of government has suffered. As Pogo said, 'We have met the enemy and he is us.'"

Putnam's thesis, a much more sophisticated one than summarized here, caused an intellectual sensation. He was much lionized, especially by "communitarians" in the United States who had been worried by the decline in civic engagement, and even invited to Camp David for discussions with U.S. President Bill Clinton. His thesis was also subjected to rigorous attacks, including some from those who believed participation in civic society had simply taken different forms than the traditional ones Putnam analyzed. Internet chat rooms, to take one example, brought together people with common interests. They did not need to leave their homes, as bowlers did, to engage in their pastime. There were now time constraints on families when both parents worked. Perhaps the previous generation, forged by war and Depression, had been the exceptional one, because those extraordinary times shaped common experiences as nothing before. Still, Putnam's thesis startled Americans, because it seemed to explain their social malaise and it appeared so historically counterintuitive in a country where, as Alexis de Toqueville observed, the act of joining seemed a distinguishing and altogether healthy characteristic of society and democracy.

No one, to the best of my knowledge, has taken Putnam's template about "social capital" in the United States and applied it to Canada, although research in that direction is underway. We would know one difference immediately. Participation rates in U.S. "civic society" had been influenced by declining church attendance, since church activities in the wider society – Hadassah bazaars, Mormon welfare programs, Anglican and Catholic "outreach programs" – put churchgoers in contact with secular society. Since Canadians are less religious than Americans by every observable measurement, including church attendance. So one important way for Americans to engage in "civic society" would be correspondingly less evident in Canada.

What about the other major factors Putnam identified to explain the U.S. decline? They would all seem evident in Canada. Putnam ascribed no more than 10 per cent of the decline to time pressures on two-income families, which would be no less intense in Canada than the United States. He suggested another 10 per cent was related to suburbanization, commuting, and urban sprawl – the spreading out of the population. Canadian central cities are, broadly speaking, more attractive and densely populated than U.S. ones; indeed, the largest number of Americans now live in neighbourhoods described as "suburban" by the U.S. Bureau of Census. Suburbanization may be less evident in Canada, but only slightly, witness to which are the sprawling subdivisions around all of Canada's major metropolises.

Putnam laid more stress on electronic entertainment – above all television – in explaining the decline in civic engagement. He suggested it accounted for about 25 per cent of the decline. The average Canadian household watches twenty-one hours of television per week. Canadian children often spend more hours watching television than they spend in school, and every study has concluded that television long ago supplanted newspapers as the principal medium by which Canadians receive their political information and news. Nothing would therefore suggest that Canadians are less susceptible to television's influence than Americans. Canadians are often described as "news junkies," because viewer ratings remain high for national news and current-affairs programs. Canada's private television networks that make their money from imported U.S. programs still command impressive audiences for their nightly newscasts, and both CTV and the Canadian Broadcasting Corporation/Radio-Canada offer all-news stations twenty-four hours a day.

The lack of television news therefore cannot explain declining rates of political participation, although perhaps the way that news is presented and explained can offer clues. Television news concentrates on conflict over consensus, accentuates personalities over issues, seizes on screwups rather than successes, gives full voice to chronically unhappy interest groups, and presents most political news in a breathless, urgent tone that leaves viewers believing that history began this morning and that governments are lurching from crisis to crisis. Indeed, citizens are so often told that something is a "crisis" by electronic and print media alike that they might actually come to believe it.

It is a curious paradox that the last decade or so has seen, at one and the same time, declining engagement in politics and the appearance of new media outlets providing information about politics and government. The *National Post* hit the newsstands and quickly established itself as a serious, entertaining, quirky, and conservative voice across the country with a circulation well above 300,000. The combined Monday-to-Friday circulations of the *Globe and Mail* and the *National Post* stood in early 2001 at about 700,000, and since about 180,000 copies were being given away for free or at knock-down prices, causing both papers to lose money in the circulation wars, Canadians could not complain about the lack of national newspapers. The *Post* paraded its ideological colours, delighting those who shared them and repelling those who did not, but the paper did treat Parliament as serious business and, still lacking enough advertising, provided acres of space for writing about politics and public issues.

On the television side, speciality channels proliferated, some of which offered public-affairs programming. The Canadian Broadcasting Corporation launched Newsworld and its French-language equivalent, RDI. CTV News started a twenty-four-hour-a-day news channel, Newsnet. The country's cable owners provided CPAC, a channel devoted to providing unfiltered coverage of conferences, seminars, parliamentary debates, press briefings, and the daily scrum after Question Period. Parliament required cable companies to carry the parliamentary channel. AM radio stations, struggling to compete with FM, adopted all-news formats with open-line shows and frequent news bulletins. Newspapers all rushed to go "on-line" with Web sites, although none of them has yet made a penny on these investments.

So a nation of "news junkies" found even more news at its disposal, but this development did not increase engagement or even understanding. The 2000 National Election Survey found a shocking 25 per cent of Canadians could not answer even one of four simple questions about prominent political people recently in the news. Chicken-and-egg explanations seem plausible. The electronic media's breathless, episodic coverage of government did little at best to enhance serious interest in politics and at worst may have turned off even more citizens. But was it also the case that people were withdrawing their interest from things political for other reasons and therefore did not pay attention to the additional information being provided by the media?

It would seem that the expansion of news catered mostly to those already informed. Existing consumers of news simply piled more atop their existing stock of information. The same applied to users of the Internet, which opened the world of cyberspace to citizens. The Internet provides direct access to information. Those who use the Internet can cut out the media, politicians, or any other interpreter of information. They can go directly to the source, pulling down unfiltered material: reports, budgets, departmental programs, press releases, speeches. They can rummage through cyberspace, searching for information about government from sources other than the government itself. The Internet's potential to create a democracy of the informed, however, remains a pipe dream. Studies of Internet use thus far conclude that seeking information stands far below use for personal entertainment and e-mail. A study of the Internet as an information source about politics through the 2000 U.S. Presidential election, done by the Annenberg School for Communications at the University of Pennsylvania, showed that the already well-informed were using the Internet as an additional source of information, but that the poorly informed were not using it at all. The Internet at this early stage of its development is not a technology for mass audiences, but rather for a series of selected, specialized audiences. It has deepened rather than bridged the "digital divide" between people comfortable with information technology and those who are not.

Putnam ascribed about 50 per cent of Americans' declining civic engagement to generational change – the "slow, steady, and ineluctable replacement of the long civic generation by their less involved children and grandchildren." Here again, the Canadian evidence is suggestive if not conclusive. Canadian pollsters have certainly discovered Generation Xers (the phrase was invented by a Canadian, Douglas Coupland), who value personal fulfillment more than civic engagement. "Self-actualization" seems more important than co-operative civic ventures. But this leads back into a paradox: that this is the best-educated population in Canada's history; that education is supposed to be an indicator of political involvement; but that the rates of traditional political engagement, including the act of voting, are moving sharply downwards. At best, Canadians are simply engaging in politics differently; at worst, they are giving up on it altogether.

Some of the 1980s decline in Canada undoubtedly related to the unpopularity of Prime Minister Brian Mulroney, but nothing suggests an upsurge in confidence since he left office. As we have argued, Canadians' waning attachment to political parties mirrors an international trend. Massive declines in party membership have been recorded in most Western democracies. Citizens' "de-alignment" with parties has been extensively measured by political scientists. Their unanimous conclusion: citizens in all democracies are showing less attachment to organized parties. What sets Canada somewhat apart is the relatively recent abandonment of party affiliation. The "de-alignment" started in Western European countries and the United States before Canada, but Canada caught up fast with the breakup of the old Conservative–Liberal party system in the early 1990s. The share of the Canadians who feel a "great deal" of confidence in political parties in Canada dropped from 30 per cent in 1979 to 11 per cent in 1999. Confidence in the House of Commons as an institution slid from 49 per cent in 1974 to 21 per cent in 1996. That means only one in five Canadians displays considerable confidence in the House of Commons, and only one in ten in political parties whose existence makes parliamentary life possible. The lower the interest in politics, the less likelihood Canadians will bother enough to press for change. The less they press for change, the longer our friendly dictatorship will last.

Now What?

W hat can be done to reconnect more Canadians to their country's democratic institutions? Are Canadians destined to live under a friendly dictatorship? The answer is probably yes, unless enough citizens reflect upon what has happened and consider changes that will restore at least some of the lost confidence in those institutions.

Sceptics will reply that no one should bemoan the lost confidence. Right-wing ideologues never put much faith in government anyway, believing that government should recede from citizens' lives in as many areas as possible. The Liberal Party, having won three consecutive elections, appears naturally content with the status quo. Michael Marzolini, the party's pollster, argued in the spring of 2001 that a low voter turnout in federal elections was not a cause for alarm, because it signalled a general contentment with the current state of affairs. This is what a Liberal pollster is supposed to say.

Whatever the appropriate role for government, it is important that government does its job well and that citizens feel engaged in shaping that role. Canadians get the government they deserve. If they disengage from caring about government, then they have no one to blame but themselves for the results. The literature of political reflection overflows with those who, while not giving up on democracy, nonetheless lament its limitations, especially the apathy and ignorance of citizens. They sometimes have a point, but democrats must believe that an engaged citizenry does produce a healthier democracy.

It is natural and healthy in a pluralistic society that people participate in civic society beyond government, because not all
forms of civic engagement depend on the formal political
process. That citizens attempt to expand their life chances or
improve their society by means that do not involve direct government action enriches democracy by establishing a variety of
points of engagement. Lenin, that great democrat, wanted a
"people's democracy" that obliterated all forms of civic engagement not controlled by the state, and the twentieth century
learned what tragedy and horror that form of democracy delivered. Engagement beyond government is indispensable for
pluralism to flourish, and pluralism lies at the heart of liberal
democracy, in which competing voices are heard and multiple
identities exist. But disengagement from government can be a
recipe for apathy or cynicism, both of which corrode the civic
ties that bind people through government to their neighbours
and fellow-citizens. No other institution beyond government
represents the entire citizenry, with all its complexities and competing aspirations, and therefore no other institution can be the
crucible for shaping the rights and responsibilities, duties and
laws, priorities and challenges, values and aspirations – in short,
the overall framework of society.

Canadians obviously care about democracy, now enshrined
in the Charter of Rights and Freedoms as a core Canadian value.
But do they care enough to improve its functioning? The
Churchillian quip, now cliché, about democracy being the worst
form of government except for all the others, remains true but
inadequate, because it suggests resignation and appeals to the
status quo. There is much to admire in Canada's democratic traditions, and even in certain aspects of its democratic institutions,
but they are not good enough for the twenty-first century.
Parliament, the party system, and the electorate are out of sync
with what Canadians want and expect from government, in large

part because today's friendly dictatorship inadequately reflects the complexities of the country and the democratic urges pulsating through the rest of Canadian society.

No magic cures exist for this state of affairs, which, as we have argued, finds echoes in other democratic countries. There is no one, sweeping reform that can reverse the trends of disengagement overnight. Sheer circumstances alone might help, such as in a change of political leadership. Or there could be a national catharsis or international crisis, neither of which would be desirable. It might help, of course, if students received more instruction in civics, if more of the media treated politics as something beyond theatrics and remembered that journalism at its best is about the public interest, and if Canadian history moved from fashionable fascination with particularities and refocused some attention on wider themes, but these are old laments that cut against the grain of contemporary developments. Perhaps all that can be reasonably expected is a modest rekindling of interest, and for this to occur there are changes that could, over time, bring more efficiency and vigour to Canadian democracy.

Reforming Parliament

Start at the top of the friendly dictatorship, the prime minister. Of course, it would take someone other than the current occupant of that position to imagine, let alone consent to, a dilution of the prime minister's powers. Even his successor, Liberal or otherwise, might easily succumb to the temptations of the imperial prime-ministership. But there are ways of thinking about the prime minister's role that would not deny its centrality in the political system but would nonetheless provide more democratic outlets for dissent and impose useful checks and balances on his power.

It is absurd, for example, to consider all government legislation in the parliamentary system to be matters of confidence, on which the government must stand or fall. Not everything the government proposes flows from key election promises and must therefore be deemed central to the government's program. Among those promises, some are obviously more critical for the government's core agenda than others. The imperial prime minister might wish his backbenchers to cause no trouble and therefore vote as he instructs them, but the fear of trouble rests, in part, on the assumption that everything must be a matter of confidence. If governments decided that not every defeat meant calling an election, or that not every adverse vote necessarily reflected badly on its performance, then the assumptions would change. Defeat would not necessarily be ascribed to weakness or lack of direction, but perhaps to the strength of honest disagreement, which is, after all, at the heart of democracy. Canadians would prefer an approach of this kind, as they have consistently told pollsters. MPs would temporarily be "somebodies," because they could periodically and publicly exercise their judgments out from under the whip of party discipline – and be seen by their electors to be doing so.

The notion of a Parliament full of free spirits, on the other hand, is a pipe dream, and a dangerous one at that. Politicians group themselves in parties because they share more in common with each other's outlook than with those of another group. Parties require a reconciliation of divergent views, an indispensable requirement for such a diverse country as Canada. Only the naive believe that permitting more free votes in the Commons would revolutionize the institution. Even if they were accorded liberty of action, most MPs in a given party would vote alike because, broadly speaking, they share more in common with their colleagues than with those in another party. Remember, too, what was explained earlier: MPs get elected more on their party label than on their personal standing. It is usually opposition MPs who publicly clamour for more free votes, meaning that they hope backbenchers will join them in voting against the government, thereby causing political embarrassment. But free votes cannot be like unilateral disarmament. Opposition parties must loosen their whips, too, and thus far in this dialogue of the deaf the opposition parties have been no more eager than the government to relax party discipline. That said, parliamentary discipline has become so stifling that it turns off voters, turns away the media, and turns back people of quality who might otherwise consider running for public office – for who among the creative and committed wants a job in which you just do as you are told day after day?

It would be quite wrong, however, to turn back the clock to a time long ago when only party caucus members selected the party leader, as is done now in the British Conservative Party and in Australia. The argument favouring such a change – advanced in 2001 by former Liberal prime minister John Turner – rests on the desirable idea of holding the prime minister and other party leaders to stricter, ongoing account. Such a system would indeed provide an internal party check on prime-ministerial power, but it would also be highly undemocratic, since only caucus members would sit in judgment on the leader. The caucus tends to be stronger in certain parts of the country than others, and is therefore somewhat or very unrepresentative of the entire country and the party membership from coast to coast. A party wants and needs to involve its members, because they form the backbone of its support during and between elections. The most important decision a party can make is the selection of its leader, and to deprive the membership of that choice is to cut off the rank and file from that most important decision. Parties should, however, be open about the financing of these leadership campaigns, since revealing the sources of contributions is voluntary under the current rules. This means most candidates shield their contributors from public scrutiny. Where no light is shed, suspicions can lurk about those to whom leadership candidates, and eventual winners, are beholden.

(Speaking of no light being shed, the Access to Information Act has been crying out for an overhaul for years. In the spring of 2001, the Liberal government appointed a committee of highly qualified Canadians from outside government to study the Act and make recommendations, belatedly fulfilling an election promise. Whether the committee's eventual recommendations will be acceptable to a government notorious for viewing the existing Act with suspicion remains to be seen. Governments have usually viewed the Act as a threat to themselves rather than an opportunity for citizens to learn more about government. That pervasive mentality does not lead to optimism that either the Act itself or the government's general attitude towards release of information will be substantially changed, but citizens can only live in hope, and express their annoyance if those hopes are dashed.)

It suits the imperial prime minister to exercise so much power in appointing so many people to positions in the government. That is how all Sun Kings operate, because fealty is owed to the person making the appointments. But that is not necessarily how the best people are chosen, nor does it inspire citizens' confidence that the proper criteria are always being applied in making the selections. In the matter of the ethics counsellor, for instance, his selection by the prime minister mocks the old Roman question: Who will guard the guardians? The current system allows someone appointed by the prime-ministerial guardian to be guard, which inspires no confidence whatsoever in the citizens. Just as justice must be seen to be done, so ethics, applied in accordance with published regulations and requirements, must be judged by someone who is appointed by someone other than the person potentially being judged. The same applies to the auditor general, a servant of Parliament but appointed by the prime minister.

There are better ways, too, of filling many government positions than the existing system, whereby the prime minister's
appointments secretary compiles lists, vets them with ministers and
party worthies, then submits them to the boss for prime-ministerial
approval. For starters, this system often results in unpardonable
delays in making appointments, as ministers and the prime minister sort out the political calculations. Those calculations themselves
should not enter into many decisions, but patronage being what
it is, they do. Canadians are fed up with crass political patronage.
The defence offered by the party in power – that their supporters
are talented individuals who should not be denied a chance at
government appointments just because of their political stripe –
is transparent nonsense. If they were indeed talented, they would
not be denied opportunities under a more objective selection
process. One could imagine a variety of other processes. The
Public Service Commission could be asked to collect and select
names for certain posts. Canada could adopt a variation of the
British system, whereby applications are publicly sought, then
chosen by non-political boards. The boards of directors of public
agencies, selected by this method, could then select the chief
executive officer, which is the normal procedure in the private
sector, universities, and hospitals.

The same rationale would apply to the selection of the governor general, now chosen exclusively by the prime minister. Not
surprisingly, before Adrienne Clarkson's arrival at Rideau Hall,
the office was held by a string of former politicians with political
or personal links to the prime minister of the day: Roméo
LeBlanc, Ray Hnatyshyn, Jeanne Sauvé, Ed Schreyer. Again, one
could imagine the selection being made by all party leaders acting
in concert or, better still, by the 150 Companions of the Order of
Canada, recipients of the nation's highest-ranking civilian award.

Were the Senate elected, one could imagine a ratification
process for prime-ministerial appointments to key government
positions. Similarly, Supreme Court judges under the Charter

now make so many decisions of great moment that the proposals for vetting their appointments that have been advanced by the Canadian Bar Association, among others, should be considered. Judges will squawk at the prospect, insisting that talented individuals will resist being subject to public scrutiny. U.S. President Harry Truman's quip about being able to withstand the heat in the kitchen comes to mind upon hearing these objections. There is very little evidence in the United States that Senate ratification has deterred individuals from wanting to be nominated for the Supreme Court. The vast majority of U.S. Senate hearings do result in ratification; those that produce stormy, partisan debate have usually been justified by the weak qualifications of the applicant or, as in the case of Judge Robert Bork, by a well-known and highly debatable interpretation of the constitution. Canada does not need to go as far as the United States in giving an elected Senate ratification powers, but it could adopt the Bar Association's proposals for a more extensive and public canvass of potential Supreme Court justices.

Proportional Representation?

Laments about low voter turnout and apathy often lead to demands for reform of the electoral system. These demands have usually been consigned to academic treatises, conferences of political scientists, and occasional editorial scribblings. The Royal Commission on Electoral Reform, established by the Mulroney government, was specifically enjoined from considering any changes to the voting system, a rather large hole in the dough-nut for a group supposed to improve electoral politics in Canada. Quite obviously, a victorious prime minister, elected under the existing system, is the last person in Canada who might think another system would be better. Inertia and habit, too, are the enemies of change, since Canadians know best the existing first-past-the post system. For the vast majority of citizens unfamiliar with other political systems, it is the only one they know. Here is where civic society can play an important role in debating alternatives, so that perhaps one or more of the opposition parties will advocate change and, if elected, feel compelled to do something.

Just what should be done, however, is the question. Informed Canadians understand some of the weaknesses of the first-past-the-post system that have been canvassed in these pages. Many MPs arrive in Ottawa having won fewer than half the votes cast in their ridings. The system is blunt – one choice only, with no ranking of preferences. The government invariably wins a majority of seats with only a plurality of the popular votes, then governs as a kind of elected dictatorship. One or two regions usually find themselves overrepresented in government, while other regions are underrepresented or shut out entirely, a situation that fuels regional alienation, especially in recent decades in western Canada. The first-past-the-post system thus suffers from a double flaw – it elects MPs who are not necessarily representative of the majority of their electors, and it produces governments that are not themselves reflective of the wishes of the electorate. The winning party usually, but not always, has captured more votes than any other party, but seldom a majority of them, yet it then governs as if it had won a majority, because no effective checks and balances can block a government, let alone cause it to think again. The prime minister, as we have argued, is the principal beneficiary of this voting system, because he wields unbridled power.

There is no perfect electoral system, and no one system can be taken from one country and adopted holus-bolus for another. Each country is different and must adapt its political system to its history and needs. In Canada, the antidote often advanced for the obvious weaknesses of the electoral system is some form of proportional representation in voting. When Parliament resumed after the 2000 election, the idea of proportional representation surfaced briefly in the House of Commons. The New Democratic Party used one of its "opposition days" – day-long debates with subjects selected by an opposition party – to recommend creation of a Commons committee to study proportional representation. The motion was defeated by the Liberal majority, but the Canadian Alliance showed only tepid interest in the idea, the Conservatives were uninterested, and the Bloc Québécois was strongly opposed, perhaps because their Parti Québécois masters had won a majority in the Quebec National Assembly with fewer votes than the Liberals.

Academic studies of voting systems around the world illustrate that turnout is higher in most countries that use proportional representation than in those using first-past-the-post. Proportional representation would seem to cause fewer voters to believe that their votes are being wasted, because parliamentary seats are more closely allocated according to the popular vote than in the first-past-the-post system. Proportional representation apparently leads more citizens to apply a kind of rational-choice model to their voting, because they feel their vote will make more of a difference.

Proportional representation's greatest virtue lies in matching voters' intentions more precisely with electoral results. First-past-the-post systems seldom match intentions with results. Consider the Liberals' record. In only one election since 1968 has the Liberals' share of the popular vote matched their share of Commons seats – in 1979, when they won 40 per cent of the votes and 40 per cent of Commons seats. In every election when they formed the government, the Liberals won a higher share of Commons seats than their share of the popular vote, the most obvious example being 1993, when they captured 41 per cent of the votes but 60 per cent of Commons seats. The same mismatches have plagued the Conservatives and NDP, which explains why the NDP pushes proportional representation. The Conservatives, still thinking of themselves as a national alternative to the Liberals, presumably hope that some day they may again profit from the first-past-the-post system by winning power with fewer than half the popular votes. Only the Reform/Alliance has enjoyed an almost perfect match between popular votes and Commons seats.

Proportional-representation systems are used around the world. By one estimate, variations of the system are found in about half the world's democracies, including most of the countries of continental Europe and Latin America. The most common form of proportional representation is the list system, in which parties present a list of candidates, either nationally or in regional districts. Winning candidates are then selected according to their position on the parties' lists, with parties allocated seats on the basis of their share of the national or regional vote. For simplicity's sake, we can see how such a system might work in Canada by considering Ontario with its 103 Commons seats. Under a proportional-representation list system, if the Liberals won half the popular votes, they would be entitled to 51 or 52 Ontario seats, whereas that share of the popular vote under first-past-the-post has given the Liberals almost all of Ontario's seats. The other parties under the list system would be given their share of Ontario's seats according to their popular vote. If such a system had been used across Canada in the 1997 election, for example, the results would have been dramatically different. Instead of a Liberal majority, the results would have been Liberals 115, Conservatives and Reform 59 each, NDP 36, Bloc Québécois 29, Greens 2, others 2.

Israel has the world's purest form of proportional representation for Knesset elections. The unhappy result is a kind of Mad Hatter politics, with a swirl of small parties vying for a few Knesset seats and multiparty coalitions in which the large parties of Labour and Likud bribe small, often religious, parties for support. Even the Israelis have introduced a floor, requiring parties to win at least 1.5 per cent of the popular vote to qualify for seats. Most other countries set the minimum threshold higher – 4 or 5 per cent – for parties to qualify for representation, in an attempt to weed out fringe parties.

A smaller number of countries use a mixture of single-member constituency elections and proportional representation, a system sometimes called mixed-member proportional representation. Under this system, voters are given two ballots – one for their district, one for national party lists. The aim is to retain the connection between some elected officials and voters in individual constituencies, but to offset the frequent mismatches of votes and seats with a parallel list system. Germany offers the best example of this mixed system, since German elections result in stable coalition governments whose composition does reflect closely the popular vote results. Germany requires a 5-per-cent minimum vote for list seats, thereby eliminating fringe parties.

New Zealand made the radical leap from a first-past-the-post system to the mixed-member proportional-representation system for the election of 1996. New Zealand had abolished its upper house, so that a government with a parliamentary majority held unfettered power. Governments had used that power in the late 1980s and early 1990s to implement far-reaching free-market reforms. New Zealand's parliamentary majorities, like those in Canada, were built on a minority share of the popular vote. There, as in Canada, cynicism about politicians rose, an increasing number of voters became frustrated with the results of an electoral system that did not reflect their wishes, and, of course, some disagreed strongly with the reform agenda of successive governments. These pressures led the government to create a Royal Commission on election reform which, to the considerable surprise of New Zealanders who had anticipated suggestions to fine-tune their existing system, recommended not just scrapping the first-past-the-post system but leaping all the way to the mixed-member system. There would continue to be single-member constituencies under the proposed new system, but voters would have two votes – one for local candidates, one for parties on the national list. The resulting system, argued the Royal Commission, would retain the best feature of the Westminster system (local MPs) with a more accurate representation in Parliament of the voters' overall wishes.

Politicians never like to admit they make mistakes, but they are human and so make them. David Lange, Labour's Prime Minister, made a whopper during a televised leader's debate in 1987, which, as events unfolded, proved crucial to electoral change in New Zealand. Labour was not committed to scrapping first-past-the-post, but Lange blurted out during the debate that, if elected, Labour would put the Royal Commission's recommendations to a national referendum. Lange later explained that he had misread his notes because he was not wearing his glasses, but the words had been spoken, the commitment given, and, in due course, New Zealanders did vote in a referendum for the new system. Advocates for change were well-organized, but it is doubtful they could have won had not the economic changes imposed on New Zealand been so radical and raised so many questions about the lack of checks and balances within New Zealand politics.

The eventual change in voting system moved New Zealand from Canada's end of the electoral spectrum – highly centralized parliamentary power, a quite unrepresentative voting system – towards the other end of permanent coalition governments, since the mixed-member proportional representation all but guarantees that no party can win a majority of parliamentary seats. New Zealand has now held two elections under the new system. Both produced coalition governments, one led by the conservative National Party, the other by Labour. New Zealanders agreed when adopting the new system that they would review it after two elections, but it is hard to imagine a return so soon to the old first-past-the-post system.

There is a third variant of proportional representation used, among other places, in Ireland and the Australian Senate – the single transferable vote. The system is extremely complicated and involves multi-member constituencies, voters marking ballots (if they choose) on the basis of preferences among candidates, a mathematical calculation about how many votes are required to win a seat, then, in order to fill up the rest of the seats, the allocation of second preferences among candidates who did not score enough first-preferences to be elected. As we said, the single-transferable vote system is extremely complicated, and for that reason advocates of proportional representation in Canada seldom recommend it.

Of all of the variations of proportional representation on offer (there are even variations we have not discussed), the one that has percolated into Canadian thinking has been the German model of two ballots – one for individual districts, the other for a national list. This would seem to be the New Democratic Party's preference. It was also recommended strongly by the Pepin–Robarts task force on national unity established by Prime Minister Pierre Trudeau after the election of the Parti Québécois in 1976. The task force's proposal would have retained the first-past-the-post system for all existing constituencies, but added sixty additional MPs chosen from regional lists. The aim was clearly to mitigate the over- and underrepresentation of regions in the House of Commons. If, for example, in the last election western Canada had received, say, fifteen of the sixty list seats and the Liberals had captured a third of the votes in that part of Canada, they would have elected five MPs off their list from western Canada. Conversely, if the Reform/Alliance had won 20 per cent of the Ontario votes, and Ontario had fifteen of sixty seats, then Reform would have elected three MPs from the Ontario list. In other words, the hybrid system recommended by Pepin–Robarts was intended in effect to "top up" the first-past-the-post results, thereby producing a Parliament slightly more in line with voters' actual intentions.

Like all the task force's recommendations, this one died when Trudeau threw the whole report into the trash bin. He disliked just about everything in the report, set as it was on the premise that there was a need to decentralize the federation to deal with Quebec nationalism and other forms of regional alienation. Occasionally, someone blows dust off the report and recycles its electoral recommendations into a speech or academic paper, which are absorbed by a tiny audience – and forgotten.

The problems with proportional representation, however, outweigh its advantages. The proportional-representation system definitely matches voters' preferences with electoral outcomes better than does first-past-the-post. As such, it would mitigate regional alienation arising from the under- and over-representation of voters in particular regions, especially western Canada. By matching voters' preferences with electoral outcomes, proportional representation would produce minority governments most of the time, and these would be an obvious check on the power of a prime minister.

But there are better ways of achieving the objectives of electoral reform – a more representative electoral outcome, greater interest in politics and reasonable checks on prime-ministerial power – than adopting any of the variations of proportional representation.

Proportional representation almost always leads to minority governments. The singular virtue of the first-past-the-post system is the government's ability – with a parliamentary majority – to get things done, and that virtue is diluted in a system that produces constant minority governments. Better checks are needed in Canada against the parliamentary power of the majority, but there are more effective and democratic ones than constant minority governments.

In the most extreme forms of proportional representation, voters only indirectly affect the outcome. In countries with pure list systems, the parties find out how many seats they have won, then, through secret negotiations, cobble together a group of them that can form a government, with sometimes surprising results. In New Zealand's first election under the new multiple-member proportional-representation system, for example, a party called New Zealand First held the balance of power. For weeks, the party negotiated privately with both the larger National and Labour parties, with opinion evenly split in the country about which party New Zealand First would support, and on what terms. The composition of the government was therefore decided behind closed doors by a party that had won many fewer votes than the larger ones. In countries such as Italy or France under the Fourth Republic, coalitions formed and re-formed; none of them lasted very long as parties jockeyed for power and political advantage. The results of all this jockeying gave rise to chronic instability and voter distaste for partisan manoeuvring. Rather than enhancing voter interest in politics, the coalition-forming political dances deepened disillusionment, which is one reason why the French under the Fifth Republic moved away from proportional representation to a two-stage election that guarantees deputies are selected by at least half the votes in each constituency.

Other proportional-representation systems, paradoxically, can lead to the opposite result – semi-permanent governments that are difficult to change. In Germany, for example, once a smaller party locks itself into a coalition with a larger one and announces before the election it will enter a coalition with that party after the election, it becomes difficult to unseat the coalition. That is what happened during the many years when the small Liberal Democratic Party supported the Social Democrats, and later when the Liberals switched their support to the Christian Democrat–Christian Social Union formation. Now the German Greens have become the third party, and as long as they remain in a coalition with the Social Democrats – the so-called "red–green" coalition – it is difficult for Germans to dislodge them.

We can leave aside these two possibilities under proportional representation systems – too much instability or too much stability – because they are not proportional representation's biggest problem.

The purest form of proportional representation breaks the link between individual MPs and constituents. Under this system, voters are not choosing an individual and holding him or her accountable, nor can they identify someone attached to their district to sort out problems with the government or promote local causes within the government. Instead, voters cast a ballot for a national or regional list, the winners from which may or may not have any local connections.

These lists tend to be weighted towards party worthies; that is, the longest-serving or most powerful people in the party get themselves towards the top of the list and are therefore almost guaranteed election. The intra-party fights about who winds up where on the list are almost as consequential as electoral battles against other parties. Proportional representation can perpetuate a kind of caste system within political parties. Of course, some proponents of proportional representation argue that it allows parties to position minority candidates – women (who hardly qualify demographically as a minority), visible minorities, aboriginals – high on the list, thus guaranteeing their election and making the parliamentary system more "representative." One advocate of proportional representation has pointed out that, among fourteen West European countries using a list system, women comprised in 1997 an average of 23.6 per cent of legislators, compared to 20.6 per cent in Canada. But that difference is hardly persuasive, and the reason Scandinavian legislatures boast a much higher share of women legislators than Canada relates to many factors other than their use of a proportional-representation voting system.

It will be argued that the mixed proportional-representation system – constituency voting and national lists – gets around the problem of not eliminating the link between electors and individual legislators. But it creates another problem in the process. There is no getting around the fact that this hybrid system creates two classes of MPs – those elected locally and those from a list. The ones elected locally must submit to the drudgery of constituency work; those elected off the regional or national lists do not. The "top-up" proposals of the Pepin–Robarts system – 60 additional MPs chosen from regional lists – would have created this two-tier system without substantially altering the regional makeup of parliamentary parties. The two-tier system might allow parties to "top up" their parliamentary representation with more "minority" MPs chosen from the lists; it might also be a temptation for party worthies to ride a magic carpet of automatic re-election to Parliament.

The biggest danger of all with proportional representation in a diverse country such as Canada, however, lies in the temptation to form small parties on the basis of region or language. Parties trying to cement themselves in all parts of Canada have been among the country's strongest forces for national integration. Canada was, in essence, a political creation. It did not arise, as some European countries did, as political reflection of a common language or religion. Its boundaries did not emerge from war or from monastic dynasties. It was not a natural outgrowth of economic links. Canada was, and remains, above all a political statement, requiring the reconciling of sometimes deep divergences into something approximating a national whole. The task of that reconciliation has never been easy, but it would have been even harder without national parties, because within them, and through their national competition, they were forced to think about the interests of the whole country, not just bits and pieces of it, if they wished to govern.

This kind of national bonding is less obviously required in geographically small, linguistically and ethnically homogeneous countries such as those in Scandinavia. But in more diverse countries, proportional representation often leads to splintering of parties formed along regional, linguistic, religious, ethnic, or single-issue lines. If only 5 per cent of the national vote is required for election of legislators, small parties can crop up that appeal to small slices of the electorate. These legislators enter governments, or sit in opposition, largely to defend just the interests of the slice of the electorate that sent them there. In today's Canadian Parliament, the Bloc Québécois represents just this kind of party. It campaigns, of course, for Quebec secession, but since that is not on offer in federal elections, the Bloc's appeal devolves into a "defence of Quebec's interests." The Bloc frankly could care less about issues of importance to the rest of Canada; indeed, when after the 1993 election the Bloc became the Official Opposition under Lucien Bouchard, the party said it would interest itself in national matters. But soon it reverted to concerning itself overwhelmingly with issues of interest to Quebec alone.

Imagine, then, a voting system that encouraged the formation of similar parties in different parts of Canada – the B.C. Party, the Alberta First Party, the Western Canadian Party, the Ontario Fairness Party, the Atlantic Canadian Party, the Newfoundland Party. Or perhaps the Marijuana Party, the Right-to-Life Party, the Greens, or other kinds of single-issue parties. Many years ago, when Canadians often split more sharply than they do today along religious lines, a proportional-representation system might have given rise to Catholic or Protestant parties, or French-speaking and English-speaking ones that mirrored the religious divisions. The always-difficult task of finding compromises and reconciling differences within Canada would have been far harder under proportional-representation systems. Any change to Canada's political system has to keep the imperative of national bonding at the top of its objectives, which means a system that encourages national parties. Proportional representation, whatever the variation, would not meet that test were it to become the only means by which legislators were selected;

in fact, it might move Canada further from that overriding objective. And, as we argued, the "top-up" proportional-representation system of the Pepin–Robarts commission creates two tiers of MPs, without doing much to address the under- and overrepresentation of regions in the House of Commons.

A New Electoral System

Thoughtful Canadians have remained troubled by the first-past-the-post voting system, or at least by the direct or indirect consequences of that system – cynicism about government, the centralization of power in the prime minister's hands, the lack of effective checks and balances to that power, government out of touch with voters, and the regional alienation fuelled by skewed election results under- and overrepresenting votes. Is there a better way of marrying some of the virtues of the existing system – and there are some – while eliminating some of its negative consequences?

The best way of thinking about changes is to reflect on what any new system would try to accomplish. An effective government should be one that can get things done. That means some degree of stability and longevity. The first-past-the-post system, whatever its liabilities, delivers effectiveness, defined by the stability and longevity of parliamentary majorities.

Effective governments should also be accountable. In a theoretical sense, governments are accountable to the House of Commons, but in practice this becomes a gentle fiction when a government controls a parliamentary majority. Elections are the ultimate test of accountability, but these occur only every so often and are extremely blunt instruments. As we have argued, the other methods of theoretical accountability in Parliament – Question Period, opposition attacks, the Senate – are all weak. And the prime minister's control over everything that matters in government – from cabinet selections to caucus management, from appointments to insistence on strict party discipline for MPs – creates a friendly dictatorship within Parliament. So the existing system produces a form of effective government all right, but not a sufficiently accountable government, which in turn tips the balance from effectiveness towards imperiousness.

Effective governments should also be representative governments. There is no perfect solution to the search for balance between effective and representative government. A pure proportional-representation system will produce precisely representative government, but at the probable cost of effective government – in the sense of one with stability and longevity, which can get things done. Canada's first-past-the-post system, coupled with a docile Senate, will produce effective government, but at the cost of marginalizing power for dissenting voices and throwing up parliamentary majorities based on fewer than half the popular vote.

Representative government should mean at least two things. First, it should encourage all regions of the country to believe they can be reflected in the national government. This is not always the case, as we have seen, in the first-past-the-post system, especially since the fracturing of the political system into five parties, only one of which shows some strength in all parts of Canada. Second, it should allow citizens to believe that their MPs represent them and can be held accountable between and during elections. This direct link between voter and politician is an important asset for the parliamentary system, even if MPs are not going to conduct themselves as Edmund Burke promised he would to the electors of Bristol. MPs, much maligned as a breed, do listen to what constituents are saying, even if the rigidities of the government party in Parliament stifles their ability to speak freely. They can and do work with groups and individuals in their constituencies on projects and problems. They are – or can be – an avenue for the redress of grievances, slicing through bureaucracy, lobbying for help. They do talk to the party leadership – the Prime Minister's Office and cabinet ministers, and sometimes even directly to the prime minister. Any proposal for change should guard this valuable asset of democracy, although the value of this coin has been diminished by the life of a trained seal that MPs are forced to endure. If they were given occasional opportunities to vote as they saw fit, as suggested earlier in this book, perhaps they could emerge from being the "nobodies" former Prime Minister Pierre Trudeau accurately described them as being. The trouble is that MPs themselves often live in a world of gentle fictions, insisting that they are speaking for all their constituents when they have, in fact, been elected by fewer than half of them, courtesy of the first-past-the-post system.

Thinking, then, about how to combine effectiveness, accountability, and representation requires one to remember that Canada does have two chambers of government that could theoretically help achieve these objectives. The existing appointed Senate assists in achieving none of them, but changes there, coupled with a new method of electing MPs, could transform, or at least improve, Canada's existing government and perhaps, just perhaps, break the cycle of cynicism and apathy citizens now display towards government. The trick is to retain the virtues of government effectiveness and personal accountability of MPs to voters within a system that also enhances accountability and representation. Both chambers can be used to achieve that better balance.

One way of ensuring that voters get the MP they want is to ensure that the winner does, in fact, secure more than half of the votes cast. In 1997, only 35.2 per cent of MPs won more than 50 per cent of the votes in their ridings. MPs may protest that, once elected, they speak for all their constituents, but of course they do not. Most of them feel obliged to help all constituents on individual problems with government, regardless of that constituent's political preferences, although Liberal MP Tom Wappel got himself deservedly into hot water when he wrote to a blind war veteran asking why he should offer to help when the veteran had not voted Liberal in the election. But when roughly two-thirds of the members of Parliament get there with fewer than half the votes, it gives the lie to the pretence that their presence in Ottawa reflects the preferences of their electors. A plurality of them, yes; a majority, usually no. Since unanimity cannot be the basis for any democratic system – forced unanimity being the tool of dictators – a majority will have to suffice for meeting a democratic test. But that test is not being met in about two-thirds of Canada's constituencies. Nor are voters given a nuanced way of expressing their preferences. They mark ballots for one – and only one – candidate, although they may, on balance, have a second preference as well.

There are two ways around this problem of MPs lacking a majority of the votes. The first is the French system – two rounds of voting. Under the French system, any candidate with more than 50 per cent of the votes is elected, period. In those constituencies where no candidate receives 50 per cent plus one, another election is held, with only the top two candidates from the first round on the ballot. The winner of that second election goes to Paris. The trouble with this system is, of course, that it forces electors to vote twice, at different times, and may as a consequence cause people not to bother a second time. It is hard enough in Canada to get people to vote once. Requiring them to vote a second time a week or two later might have the perverse effect of driving down the country's already low voter turnout. The Canadian Alliance and Conservatives discovered just this by-product in their two-round leadership voting system among party members. Fewer members voted the second time.

The best system, therefore, is called the Alternative Vote, which has the virtue of being simple and nuanced, requiring only one ballot, and producing a winner with a greater semblance of majority support than received by many MPs elected by the first-past-the-post system. Australia uses this system for its lower house, and it works well there. Elections would still be held in single-member constituencies. An Alternative Vote ballot, however, invites voters to list candidates in order of preference. If one candidate receives more than half the first-place preferences, he or she is elected. If not, the candidate with the fewest number of first preferences is eliminated, and his or her second preferences are then assigned to the other candidates. This process carries on until one candidate has an absolute majority.

The Alternative Vote system therefore avoids the problem of MPs being elected with less than majority support, although some winners under this system would do so with a combination of first- and second-preferences. It would therefore improve the representative capacity of MPs, since they and their constituents would know that the election was decided by at least half of the votes cast. It would be simple to understand and not require a second round of voting, thereby minimizing additional expenses. It would retain the links between MPs and their voters. It would allow, or encourage, voters to think about the relative virtues of candidates and parties, freeing them from the yes/no, winner-take-all, first-past-the-post system. It would invite voters to believe that their votes mattered more, since, even if their preferred candidate could not win – as a Liberal would not in Red Deer or an Alliance candidate in downtown Toronto or a New Democrat in Calgary – the voters' second preference could be consequential in determining the outcome. The wasted-vote syndrome would be correspondingly diminished. An Alternative Vote system might force parties to think about crafting at least some of their messages for potential supporters of other parties, since their second-preference votes might be needed in some constituencies.

It is difficult to predict which party would benefit most from an Alternative Vote system. Quite likely, the Canadian Alliance as currently constructed would not. Every public-opinion survey has shown that the Alliance is the least favoured second choice among

Canadian voters. Of course, that is the Alliance's largest problem, and an Alternative List system might force the party to think about broadening some of its policies, which would be no bad thing if it ever hopes to be elected, or to enter a union with the Conservatives. The Liberals, Conservatives, and even New Democrats might do better under the Alternative List system, but their fortunes under the new system would depend upon leadership, the issues of the day, their policy approaches. The new system might play itself out quite differently in various parts of Canada.

On balance, an Alternative Vote system would favour strong national parties, because they would be the ones with the broadest appeal in all regions of the country and therefore would be most likely to win more second-preference support. If one believes that strong, nationwide parties are important forces for national integration, this would be a highly desirable result of an Alternative Vote system. The Alternative Vote system, were it to help nationwide parties, would not do anything however to change parliamentary life, in which the Prime Minister rules all. Nor would it alone give further expression to regional sensitivities. It would make individual MPs more representative by ensuring their election with more than half the votes cast, but it would not allow the regions of Canada to feel that their voices were heard and their perspectives accorded some power in Ottawa. For these objectives to be met, something more is required – an elected Senate.

An Elected Senate

The Canadian political system lacks the most important check of all, a second chamber with credibility and effectiveness by virtue of the fact that its members are elected. The Senate, despite the undeniable qualities of some senators, is an affront to federalism and democracy. The Senate's weakness encourages the friendly dictatorship, because the institution invariably dances to the prime minister's tune. The senatorial appointments system expands the prime minister's arsenal of patronage and ensures docility.

The original error of the Fathers of Confederation in opting for an appointed Senate has never been corrected. Whole Canadian forests have fallen to provide the paper on which have been written critiques of the Senate and proposals for reform. Constitutional committees and government-appointed task forces have intermittently suggested changes. The federal government under Prime Minister Pierre Trudeau drew up a blueprint for major unilateral Senate reform in 1977–78, only to be instructed by a unanimous Supreme Court that unilateral federal changes would be unconstitutional. Even a sprinkling of senators themselves have decried the appointed nature of their own institution. But the Senate's sheer convenience for the prime minister, coupled with the damnable complexities of changing it, has produced the status quo triumphant.

No one should enter the quicksand of Senate reform without remembering all the proposals swallowed up by previous debates. Senate reform requires constitutional change, and Canadians have learned at their peril how arduous and often self-defeating that process can be. In an ideal world, Senate reform should be considered on its own, isolated from other potential constitutional changes. In the real world of Canadian constitutional politics, nothing is ever that tidy. Canadians discovered the last three times they embarked on constitutional changes – Trudeau's patriation of 1981–82, and Mulroney's Meech Lake and Charlottetown accords – that the federal government's original intention to restrict the agenda gave way to horse-trading with provinces and interest groups that resulted in a much wider package. Trudeau's original intention to repatriate the constitution from Britain with an amending formula and a Charter of Rights wound up being changed to include provisions enshrining provincial control of natural resources, federal equalization payments, and aboriginal treaty rights. Meech Lake had attached to it political promises for later conferences on aboriginal rights and Senate reform. The Charlottetown accord, designed to wrap the essence of the Meech Lake accord in a bundle of additional changes, became a multi-faceted series of proposals for Senate reform, guaranteed provincial seats in the House of Commons, aboriginal self-government, regular first ministers' meetings, a revised federal–provincial division of powers, to name but a few elements. Patriation, we remember, was never ratified by the Quebec National Assembly. The Meech Lake accord died for lack of support. The Charlottetown accord was rejected in a national referendum by a 55 to 45 per cent margin, securing majority support in only four provinces.

Prime Minister Jean Chrétien, sensing constitutional fatigue and appreciating the perils of constitutional debates, has steadfastly refused to contemplate any constitutional changes during his time in office. Asked occasionally about Senate reform, he has defended his lack of action by saying he had supported the Charlottetown accord as opposition leader. But as prime minister, he showed no interest whatsoever in initiating any discussion of change. Not only is constitutional change admittedly difficult, but the status quo of an appointed Senate suited him splendidly as an all-powerful prime minister.

Senate reform will come only if Canadians in increasing numbers demand it, and if political parties respond to those demands with commitments. Provincial governments could keep the heat on for an elected Senate by holding elections for Senate vacancies, even if the prime minister did not appoint the winners. Those elected would be mocking witnesses before the existing appointed Senate and suggest to Canadians what the Senate could become. The Canadian Alliance, to its credit, has always campaigned for Senate reform, but the other parties are either not interested or, in the case of the NDP, favour abolition. Abolition would be a foolish decision. It would remove even the potential for a check and balance against prime-ministerial power, and it would throw away the chance for a second chamber that represented regional interests in a far-flung federation. Abolitionists should look around the world. Other federations all use the second chambers for this purpose. They either have second chambers through direct election (the United States, Switzerland, Australia), indirect election by provincial legislatures (India, Malaysia), or appointments from state governments (Germany). Even unitary states such as France, Japan, and Italy have second chambers to check the power of the lower house.

There are a variety of models from which Canadians could choose for an elected Senate, if and when their governments decide to re-enter constitutional negotiations. An elected Senate would have many attributes, but four stand out. It would provide for greater expression of regional and even single-issue views, something highly desirable in a federation and a healthy democracy. It would attenuate the political weight of Ontario and Quebec. It would open up a new institution for democratic discussion of priorities and challenges. And it would provide a check and balance on parliamentary majorities controlled by the prime minister. With those four objectives in mind, none of which are met by the existing appointed Senate, reasonable people can debate alternative models for the composition, powers, and methods of election of the Senate.

The Charlottetown accord lost for many reasons. Adversaries attacked it like a swarm of angry bees, from every angle and with great ferocity. They could not agree on an alternative, because their objections were usually contradictory. But enough people were angry about particular aspects of the accord to doom its chances, despite widespread support by political and media élites. That said, the Senate reform proposals it contained were ingenious and constructive, and should form at least the basis for any further debates.

Without wading through all the details of that proposal, a few noteworthy ones stick out. The Charlottetown accord proposed six senators from each province, elected either directly by the people or indirectly by provincial legislatures. Elections would be held at the same time as Commons elections. It was left to the federal Parliament to decide the method of election – first-past-the-post or some form of proportional representation. The Senate was given different sorts of powers, ranging from an absolute veto to a suspensive one, depending on the kind of legislation. In the event of deadlock between the two houses, the members of both would vote together. The Senate would ratify prime-ministerial appointments. To compensate for the loss of seats in this Senate, Ontario and Quebec were given additional Commons seats, with Quebec guaranteed 25 per cent of Commons seats, regardless of its share of the national population. This clause provided wildly unpopular in parts of the rest of Canada, especially British Columbia, where critics pointed out that B.C.'s population was growing while Quebec's was declining.

The Charlottetown model should be altered in several important respects – but remember that these changes should occur along with a switch from the first-past-the-post to the Alternative Vote model for electing MPs. The Alternative Vote model would tend, on balance, to reinforce national political parties and make it more difficult for smaller ones to win representation. These smaller parties, however, can make a contribution to democratic debate by raising issues and perspectives sometimes smothered in the large national parties. An elected Senate should be designed to encourage these sorts of expression and to give members genuine power within the overall parliamentary system. The result of the combined change of a new voting system for the Commons and an elected Senate would encourage national parties in the Commons and allow the Senate to become the institution for more regional or particularistic expressions.

The combination would make Canada's democratic institutions more representative in two ways – by ensuring that MPs were elected by majorities and by allowing a wider spectrum of views to be represented in the Senate.

Therefore, an elected Senate should use a proportional representation system based on province-wide lists. To ensure a wider scope for the reflection of different views, there should be more senators per province than the six proposed in the Charlottetown accord. The questions then arises about whether all provinces should have the same number of senators – the so-called Equal Senate, as in the United States. The Australian Senate, elected on a variation of the proportional-representation voting system, also provides for the same number of senators from each state. But the populations of the Australian states are somewhat more similar to each other than those of the Canadian provinces. There is nothing in Australia remotely like the difference in population between Ontario and Prince Edward Island. Although devotees of a Triple-E Senate will not like it, the political fact remains that equality of the provinces in an elected Senate is almost certainly going to be a non-starter – unless, as in the Charlottetown accord, Canadians begin enlarging the number of MPs from the larger provinces, which somewhat defeats the purpose of greater representation for smaller provinces in an elected Senate.

An equitable Senate rather than an equal Senate is therefore one that will likely command the most support. My preference would be for four provincial tiers. Ontario and Quebec would have twenty senators each, British Columbia and Alberta fifteen, Saskatchewan, Manitoba, Nova Scotia, New Brunswick, and Newfoundland ten, and Prince Edward Island five. The three territories would have one senator apiece. There would therefore be 128 senators, to which would then be added a certain number (say ten) seats for aboriginal senators. The Senate would then have slightly less than half the number of members of the House of

Commons. A necessary wrinkle should be added – that French-speaking senators be given the right to veto legislation that might infringe upon the status of the French language, a reassurance to the country's official minority language group. The larger number of senators than those proposed in the Charlottetown accord would allow a wider spectrum of representation of different parties in the Senate, especially if the senators were selected by the proportional-representation system.

Simultaneous Senate and Commons elections are a bad idea, since Senate results would tend to mirror those for the Commons, even though, under proportional representation, the governing party's Senate results would be less favourable than in Commons elections under either first-past-the-post or the Alternative Vote systems. Six-year terms, with fixed election dates, with half the Senate being up for election every three years, would be a better model, thereby separating Senate and Commons elections and providing a kind of periodic barometer of public opinion.

The various kinds of power for the Senate envisaged in the Charlottetown accord, ranging from veto to suspensive veto, seem appropriate. Best of all, the provision of reconciliation committees of senators and MPs when the two houses disagree, or a combined vote of both houses in the event of deadlock, would provide a check and balance within the parliamentary system. The Commons would still have the upper hand, because it would have more members than the Senate; but an elected Senate would dilute the imperial powers of the prime minister and periodically cause a degree of negotiation over certain government bills.

Canadians will argue, as they have in the past, about an elected Senate's method of election, powers, and responsibilities. But Canadians should understand, as they contemplate their friendly dictatorship and declining interests in things political, that their country stands alone among the world's federations in having an upper house appointed by the prime minister. The appointed

Senate is a throwback to the House of Lords model that has been rejected everywhere else in the world. The Canadian Senate is therefore a hopeless anachronism and, as such, a wasted opportunity for more democracy, a wider range of views, additional access points for citizens to participate in democratic politics, and a reasonable but not debilitating restriction on the prime-ministerial power that is now wielded through absolute control over a parliamentary majority, itself built on an unrepresentative voting system.

Strengthening Parties

Changes to the way Parliament operates, and changes to the way legislators are chosen for the Commons and Senate, could help move Canada from a friendly dictatorship to a more accessible democracy that would encourage more Canadians to engage in the political process. More genuine political competition would also help, since competitive national elections do interest citizens more than those with foregone conclusions. Voter turnout is higher and more citizens become involved when governments seeking re-election are put to serious electoral tests. This has obviously not been true in the last decade, as the Liberals waltzed to three majority victories without a threatening challenge from any of the opposition parties. Liberal dominance, of course, was one unintended consequence of the new, fractured party system, in which four, not two, opposition parties face the Liberals in the House of Commons. The Liberals did not devise this system, but they profited from it handsomely. As long as divide-and-rule politics prevail, the Liberals will be in office for a very long time. Unless opposition parties learn from their recent defeats, or unless the Liberals unexpectedly self-implode, Canadian politics may come to resemble Japanese politics, in which one party (the Liberal Democrats) always governs. Politics in that country revolves much more around which faction within the LDP is in the ascendancy rather than whether another party might defeat the LDP.

For the Liberals to be challenged, changes will be required in three of the opposition parties – the NDP, the Conservatives, and the Canadian Alliance. The Bloc Québécois cannot be expected to change, since its objective is neither to form a government nor even to influence national opinion. It will probably take yet another defeat for Quebec secession in a referendum to eliminate the Bloc's presence, or at least substantially reduce it, thereby making additional political room in Quebec for federalist parties to win seats. The hard core of Quebec secessionists will probably not give up their dream even after a third referendum defeat, but a number of them will, and therefore will be open to considering at least some form of federalist option. But this freeing up of political room in Quebec may take a while yet.

In the meantime, the other parties face a simple choice. They can continue as they have for the last decade, failing in their own ways, or they can reflect on those failures and recognize that more of the same will produce equally depressing results. New Democrats are welcome to chase the illusion that a more radical party, aligned with protestors and fringe interest groups, and tied financially to the trade-union movement, will bring political redemption. Such a strategy might bring episodic moral victories and certainly reinforce the party's sense of self-virtue. If this is what New Democrats are content to achieve, then they can comfort themselves with these results, while watching even more Canadians turn the other way, as they did throughout the 1990s. Liberals will be watching, and praying, of course, that New Democrats learn nothing from their party's declining fortunes.

The Conservatives and Canadian Alliance have also been pursuing illusions, the most enticing being that each will emerge alone as the alternative to the Liberals. This was the dream of Reform leader Preston Manning, but the dream turned into the frustration of three failures to crack the entire mould of Canadian politics and the subsequent nightmare of the Canadian Alliance's vicious internecine warfare that enveloped the leadership of Stockwell Day. If three frustrating elections did not prove the point, that very viciousness of the internecine warfare killed any hope that the Canadian Alliance could grow. Parties that turn on themselves are usually signalling that they are unfit to govern and are locked into a cycle of recrimination and failure.

The Conservatives, too, have been chasing the illusion that they alone will become the chosen alternative to the Liberals. This illusion is based on the false proposition that they are somehow a national party, whereas they remain a fragment party, just like the Alliance – a part, but only a part, of the more formidable coalition assembled by successful Conservative leaders of the past. While the Alliance turned on itself in 2001, the Conservatives under Joe Clark returned to political respectability, but remained far short of threatening the Liberals.

The Conservatives and the Alliance must come together to have any chance of ending Liberal one-party rule, but they cannot do it under their current leaders nor with their existing policies. Stockwell Day cannot even command the loyalty of his own party; he could hardly therefore lead a broader coalition. Joe Clark has far too much baggage from past battles and issues espoused to bring about a reconciliation with the Alliance. Many Alliance members bolted the Conservative Party, of which Clark had been a leading member and once, briefly, the prime minister. Perhaps Clark was stubborn enough to convince himself that he could become the Canadian political answer to Lazarus by uniting the two parties, under terms dictated by him, and later to oust the Liberals.

What is required instead is new leadership in both parties committed to union, which will mean a meshing of policies. Neither the Conservatives nor the Alliance can be expected to forget all their policies, since these are sincerely held and were supported by slices of the Canadian electorate. But as long as each insists on refusing to dilute any of them, union will be impossible. Each needs to understand the virtues of compromise – a virtue cherished by Canadians. Compromise will mean for the Alliance an understanding that ideology is a trap for Canadian political parties and for the Conservatives an appreciation that the Reform/Alliance brought into Canadian politics some important, fresh ideas that deserve continued exposition, such as certain democratic reforms, a somewhat smaller state, and a clear-eyed view of how to respond to Quebec secessionist threats.

Beyond the opposition parties drawing sensible conclusions from their repeated failures lie changes that all parties should espouse to heighten the confidence Canadians have in political life. The most obvious are the means by which parties are financed. At present, parties are too dependent on corporate or union interests. The Liberals receive more money from corporations than they do from individuals. The Conservatives and the Alliance, too, are always going cap in hand to corporate Canada for money, just as the NDP always chases trade unions for contributions. None of this is democratic in two respects. First, neither shareholders nor union members are consulted about whether they want their money used in this fashion. Second, this method of financing parties makes them appear excessively beholden not to the public interest but to certain elements within in. Parties have demonstrated their ability to raise money from individuals, and it is from them that contributions should come to finance party activities. If necessary, to fill the gaps left by eliminating corporate and union contributions, the limits for individual donations should be raised, along with the refundable contributions to candidates from the public purse.

Parties, too, have to produce ideas that in turn might generate citizen interest. Each parliament party with official status (twelve seats) is given money after an election to finance a caucus research office, the funding being determined by the number of seats the party holds in the Commons. These offices usually service the daily needs of MPs as they prepare for Question Period, committees, speeches, or householder mailings. They seldom, in other words, have the time, money, or mandate to focus on broad issues of public policy. The Germans have a better system. In that country, the Social Democrats and Christian Democrats are equipped with foundations, or mini-think-tanks, paid for at least in part from public funds, that produce ideas, sponsor conferences, and put the parties in touch with ideas from other elements of German society and abroad. Although organized and financed differently, Britain has similar institutions, associated with the Labour and Conservative parties, that consider ideas that go beyond today's headlines or parliamentary squabbles. If Canadians want their political parties to think more deeply about policy, they could look to the German and British models, and give them more resources to do just that.

Final Thoughts

Institutional changes to Parliament, the electoral system, and political parties will not by themselves answer the need to improve Canadian democracy, although they would help. Democracy is also a matter of attitudes and values, and of how citizens relate to the rest of society. Democracy is premised on equal rights and responsibilities, but its full flowering is hard to imagine if government is controlled by self-perpetuating political élites and excessively influenced by the economically powerful. Nor can Canadians warm to a system that is depicted ritualistically in the nation's media as the equivalent of an endless man-bites-dog story, wherein the spectacular drives out the routine, and whatever is negative drives out everything that is positive. Never has less understanding, let alone sympathy, been evinced by the media for political men and women. It is little wonder that Canadians, who must rely largely on the media for information about government, even in the Internet age, are so cynical, when that cynicism pervades their principal sources of information.

Canada's democracy is not a wreck. It could, however, stand plenty of improvement, as *The Friendly Dictatorship*'s diagnosis and prescriptions suggest. Canadians are cynical about politicians and the democratic process, and some of that cynicism is well-founded. My experience over a quarter of a century of writing about politicians suggests, however, that the majority of men and women in politics are no more or less worthy than any other cross section of Canadians. There are scoundrels to be sure, and politics, as other occupations, attracts an assortment of decidedly second- or third-rate minds. Not all of them are as hard-working as they ought to be. There are careerists for whom it is hard to imagine another line of profitable work. There are blowhards and those for whom the elixir of power goes to their heads. But circles of the eternally virtuous exist only in heaven.

We do ourselves a disservice by denigrating all politicians as a kind of national sport. We ought to be vigilant in monitoring them. Happily, Canadians have developed a nicely satirical brand of humour about politics that prevents people in public life from getting too big for their britches. We ought to get angry when they screw up, but we ought also to give credit when they do things right – which they do. We need not venerate them, but neither should we hack them apart. A humbling question for cynics is whether they could do any better; more humbling still, for them, would be their replies.

Politicians come, after all, from among us. They are our representatives, although we could reform our electoral system and governing institutions to make them more representative. If we give up on them, we are in effect giving up on ourselves, or at least on a part of the democratic belief that we can make a better country through the institutions of government. Citizens will always disagree about what would constitute a better country, and how to achieve it. That is the essence of democracy. The more effective, accountable, open, and representative our democracy, the greater the chance that, through the clash of ideas and the interplay of political forces, we can inch, however slowly, toward that better country.

Concerns for democracy are really concerns for Canada. Citizens can contribute to a better country – and a better life for themselves and families – in a myriad of ways that do not involve politics. No institution, however, plays such a central role in defining society's values and priorities as does government. The institutions of government are our institutions, as citizens and taxpayers. The electoral system that sorts out who runs those institutions is our system, as citizens and voters. If we care enough about those institutions and that system, we can change them and so improve the functioning of our democracy. Apathy and cynicism are soulmates. They are on the rise, but they are democracy's foes and, as such, worth combating.

Suggestions for Further Reading

Kenneth Carty, William Cross, and Lisa Young, *Rebuilding Canadian Party Politics*, U.B.C. Press, 2000.

Harold Clarke, Jane Jensen, Lawrence Le Duc, and Jon Pammett, *Absent Mandate: Interpreting Change in Canadian Elections*, Gage, 1991.

John Courtney, *Do Conventions Matter?: Choosing National Party Leaders in Canada*, McGill–Queen's University Press, 1995.

Tom Flanagan, *Waiting for the Wave: The Reform Party and Preston Manning*, Stoddart, 1995.

C. E. S. Franks, *The Parliament of Canada*, Toronto, University of Toronto Press, 1987.

Edward Greenspon and Anthony Wilson-Smith, *Double Vision: The Inside Story of the Liberals in Power*, Doubleday Canada, 1996.

Richard Johnston, André Blais, Henry Brady, and Jean Crête, *Letting the People Decide: Dynamics of a Canadian Election*, McGill–Queen's University Press, 1992.

Peter Hennessey, *The Prime Minister: The Office and its Holders since 1945*, Allen Lane, 2000.

Henry Milner (ed.), *Making Every Vote Count: Reassessing Canada's Electoral System*, Broadview Press, 1999.

Neil Nevitte, *The Decline of Deference: Canadian Value Changes in a Cross-National Perspective*, Broadview Press, 1996.

Neil Nevitte, André Blais, Elisabeth Gidengil, and Richard Nadeau, *Unsteady State: The 1997 Canadian Federal Election*, Oxford University Press, 2000.

Susan Pharr and Robert Putnam (eds.), *Disaffected Democracies: What's Troubling the Trilateral Countries?* Princeton University Press, 2000.

Robert Putnam, *Bowling Alone: The Collapse and Revival of American Community*, Simon and Schuster, 2000.

Donald Savoie, *Governing from the Centre: The Concentration of Power in Canadian Politics*, University of Toronto Press, 1999.

Donald Savoie, *The Politics of Public Spending in Canada*, University of Toronto Press, 1990.

Jeffrey Simpson, *Spoils of Power: The Politics of Patronage*, Collins, 1988.

Jeffrey Simpson, *Faultlines: Struggles for a Canadian Vision*, Collins, 1993.